Elizabeth Tickson

FEMINIST COLLAGE
Educating Women in the Visual Arts

D1446328

JUDY LOEB, Editor
Associate Professor of Art
Eastern Michigan University

TEACHERS COLLEGE PRESS

Teachers College, Columbia University
New York and London   1979

Library of Congress Cataloging in Publication Data
Main entry under title:

Feminist collage : educating women in the visual arts.

Includes index.
1. Feminism and art—Addresses, essays, lectures.
2. Women artists—Addresses, essays, lectures.
3. Art—Study and teaching—Addresses, essays,
lectures. I. Loeb, Judy.
N72.F45F45   701   79-15468
ISBN 0-8077-2561-7

Designed by Romeo M. Enriquez
8 7 6 5 4 3 2 1   79 80 81 82 83 84 85 86 87
Printed in the U.S.A.

Grateful acknowledgement is made to the following publishers and authors for permission to include the copyrighted articles listed below:

Allanheld & Schram for selections from *Women and Art: A History of Women Painters and Sculptors from the Renaissance to the 20th Century* by Elsa Honig Fine, © 1978 by Elsa Honig Fine.

American Artist for "Use is Beauty" from the Professional Page by Betty Chamberlain, March 1976, vol. 40, no. 404, © 1976 by Billboard Publications, Inc.

Anima for "Why Do We Speak of Feminine Intuition?" by Margaret Mead, Spring 1975, vol. 1, no. 2, by special permission. © 1975 by Conococheague Associates, Inc.

Art Education for "Society and Identity: A Personal Perspective" by June King McFee, November 1975, vol. 28, no. 7, © 1975 by June King McFee. Reprinted courtesy of the National Art Education Association.

Art in America for "Women's Art in the '70s" by Lawrence Alloway, May-June 1976. © 1976 by Art in America, Inc. Reprinted by permission of the author and *Art in America*.

Art Journal for " 'Of Men, Women, and Art': Some Historical Reflections" by Mary D. Garrard, Summer 1976, vol. 35, no. 4; "The Education of Women as Artists: Project Womanhouse," by Miriam Schapiro, Spring 1972; and "The Male Artist as a Stereotypical Female" by June Wayne, Summer 1973, vol. 32, no. 4, © 1973 by June Wayne; © 1972, 1976 by College Art Association of America, Inc.

Arts in Society for "Toward a Juster Vision: How Feminism Can Change Our Ways of Looking at Art History" by Linda Nochlin, Spring-Summer 1974, vol. 2, no. 1, © 1974 by the Regents of the University of Wisconsin System. Original title was "How Feminism in the Arts Can Implement Change."

Ellen Perry Berkeley for "Architecture: Towards a Feminist Critique" © 1979 by Ellen Perry Berkeley.

Feminist Art Journal for "Fancy Work: The Archaeology of Lives" by Rachel Maines, Winter 1974-75, vol. 3, no. 4; "Stereotypes and Women Artists" by Cindy Nemser, April 1972, vol. 1, no. 1; and "Women of Surrealism" by Gloria Feman Orenstein, Spring 1973, vol. 2, no. 12, © 1972, 1973, and 1974 by Feminist Art Journal, Inc.

Heresies for "Female Experiences in Art: The Impact of Women's Art in a Work Environment" by Ruth Iskin, January 1977, no. 1, © 1977 by Ruth Iskin and for "The Pink Glass Swan: Upward and Downward Mobility in the Art World" by Lucy R. Lippard, January 1977, no. 1, © 1977 by Lucy R. Lippard.

Studies in Art Education for material from "Conceptual Content and Spacial Characteristics of Girls and Boys Drawings" by Sylvia G. Feinburg, vol. 18, no. 2, 1977, © 1977 by Sylvia G. Feinburg. Reprinted courtesy of the National Art Education Association. "The Significance of What Boys and Girls Choose to Draw: Explorations of Fighting and Helping" © 1979 by Sylvia Gruber Feinburg.

Visual Dialog for selections from "Educating Women in the Visual Arts" by Judy Loeb, Spring 1977, vol. 2, no. 3, © 1977 by Judy Loeb.

Women's Caucus for Art for "Professionalism and the Woman Artist" by Dorothy Gillespie from *Women's Studies and the Arts*, © 1978 by Women's Caucus for Art; for selections from "The Growth of Women's Studies Programs" by Judy Loeb, from *Women's Studies and the Arts*, © 1978 by Judy Loeb; and "Excerpts from Joan Mondale Address," *The Women's Caucus for Art Newsletter*, April 1978, vol. 7, no. 2, © 1978 by Joan Mondale. "Introduction" © 1978 by Joan Mondale.

*This book is
dedicated with love
to my mother and my father.*

Contents

III. FEMINIST RESTRUCTURING OF ART EDUCATION

IV. FEMINIST MANDATES FOR INSTITUTIONAL CHANGE

Preface

The problem of being a woman artist has been posed by Linda Nochlin:

> The fault lies not in our stars, our hormones, our menstrual cycles, or our empty internal spaces, but in our institutions and our education— education understood to include everything that happens to us from the moment we enter, head first, into this world of meaningful symbols, signs, and signals.[1]

This book is a feminist collage of articles examining the changing world of visual arts education for women. Much of this collage also applies to women working in other arts.

In the late 1960s Martina Horner found that the symbols, signs, and signals our society present to women result in even the brightest most capable female students being handicapped by the fear of success. Her study, "The Motive to Avoid Success . . . ," showed that this fear was often an overwhelming factor in the lives of young college women. Horner concluded: "It is clear . . . despite recent emphasis on a new freedom for women, a psychological barrier continues to exist in otherwise achievement-motivated and able women to prevent them from exercising their potential, even if they are aware that it is happening and angry about it." She suggested that those women who are highly motivated to avoid success—an astounding 60 to 85 percent of individuals in the various college groups tested—performed significantly higher "in a strictly noncompetitive but achievement-oriented situation, in which the only competition involved was with the task and one's internal standards of excellence."[2]

An understanding of this need for a noncompetitive structure guided Miriam Schapiro and Judy Chicago in 1970 when they initiated Project Womanhouse, which Schapiro describes in this book. Working in an abandoned mansion in downtown Los Angeles, their goal was to provide "a nourishing environment for growth" for 21 women art students. Womanhouse was one of the first projects in which the techniques developed by consciousness-raising feminist groups were integrated into an art program.

The cooperative feminist studio school, especially when it is *both* noncompetitive *and* achievement oriented, may be the ideal learning situation for many women. After Womanhouse, other feminist studio classes were organized. Feminist art cooperative groups now exist in many areas of the country. (Some of these programs are described in this book.) However, for most women the traditional college art department, because of its proximity and its degree granting capacity, is still the reality.

In her chapter in this volume describing the Los Angeles-based Feminist Studio Workshop, Arlene Raven writes: "While the college and art institutions that have on occasion hosted our feminist programs have appeared to be congenial settings for those efforts, the programs have instead acted as foreign bodies in the organism of the university, and as any foreign body in an organism, have resulted in infection, fever, and ultimate rejection." I feel that Raven is overly pessimistic. Very real, unresolved problems do remain. However, there has been a proliferation of university-based women's studies programs in this country that parallel and far outnumber the feminist alternative schools established. Over 300 colleges now offer women's studies as a major or minor area of study.[3] Many of these programs include courses in visual arts areas.[4] These programs are striving to incorporate innovations developed by the alternative schools. This follows a long established pattern in American education of larger public institutions adopting and adapting the successful innovations of smaller private schools.

Pioneers who wished to teach in any area of women's studies had to begin by developing and researching their own texts. The omission of women from the history books has been a universal problem affecting each discipline. Throughout the '70s women wrote new art history books that surveyed the contributions of women artists.[5] What makes these books different from the previous survey books is that they deal not only with the reevaluation of the work of individual women artists, but also present a social history of women who were artists. It is the cross-disciplinary interest that characterizes women's studies. There has been not only the development of a history of women in art to parallel, for example, the history of American art, but also there has been a broadening of focus. There is a heightened interest in how social expectations, social roles, economics, and education affect women (and men) who become artists. Revisionist art history is concerned as much with new developments in psychology and anthropology as it is with searching through archives and museum storerooms for lost masterpieces. Women's studies in the visual arts examine art *and* society: in short, they study Nochlin's "world of meaningful symbols, signs, and signals."

Why are these broader questions being raised at this time? In the arts, it may be partially a reaction to the overconcentration on formalism that characterized the art criticism and teaching of art in the '50s and '60s. Colleges were overspecialized in many fields in the '60s. Women's studies are among the many interdisciplinary areas to develop in the '70s; they parallel the renewed vitality of the humanities. Increased interest in the variety of courses offered by women's studies programs may, in part, be due to the changing nature of college students themselves. Collier and Lovano-Kerr explain in their chapter that one-third of all undergraduate students in this country now are what are called "nontraditional students," i.e., returning students over the age of 25.

This is a radical departure from the past. The acceptance by colleges of nontraditional students offers great hope for increasing the creative, intellectual, and leadership contributions of women to society. The colleges are, at long last, accepting the humanistic philosophy of "education for life."

In the fall 1976 issue of *Psychology of Women*, Nancy G. Kutner and Donna Brogan analyzed the life-style of women in our society:

> We believe it is typical for many females in our society to reach a series of "career plateaus" at which they make decisions based on the options available to them *at that time*. Thus, as compared to males, females' plans for the future and related behavior are *less* likely to be characterized by

an essentially cumulative developmental pattern. When middle-class females near their senior year in high school, they consider college *if* there is no immediate prospect of their getting married. As they approach the senior year in college, they consider graduate school *if* there is no immediate prospect of their getting married (assuming availability of economic resources). After marriage, females plan to work *if* they do not have children, etc.[6]

Although females still follow Kutner and Brogan's pattern of career plateaus, they now seem more likely to consider these plateaus as postponements rather than lifetime decisions of *either* marriage *or* study towards a career.

June King McFee's chapter reviews the development of her career and the role of women in a society in which: "The stereotype is that there are many kinds of valued men, unique, different, but there is only one ideal woman." McFee points out that with the changes that are occurring in our society: "A woman no longer needs to feel she is abnormal in some degree because she has drives to be highly creative, independent, intellectual, or to take leadership. That is a heavy weight we are losing."

Women's studies programs in art and art history that examine the cultural, psychological, and economic factors that have affected women artists lead to a new understanding of the variety of roles that women have assumed in the art world. The present day woman art student will graduate knowing more about herself, more about her society, and more about the realities of the art world than was possible just a few short years ago. She will know the work and life-styles of a great many women artists from whom she may choose the role models that were denied her predecessors. The fears that women have that success will deny them the traditional roles of womanhood are being assuaged, even as those traditional roles offer more options and variations. We are creating new "symbols, signs and signals."

In the '70s three major changes in the art world were initiated by feminists. Each of the first three sections of this book examines one of the areas in which change has occurred: I, Feminist Reappraisals of Art and Art History; II, Feminist Reexaminations of Art, Artists, and Society; and III, Feminist Restructurings of Art Education. The book concludes with section IV, Feminist Mandates for Institutional Change.

I am deeply indebted to Dr. Bette Acuff for her sustaining interest and encouragement as well as for her unselfish giving of her time, energy, and professional advice every step along the way of this book's development. My sincere thanks goes to all those authors who contributed to this book. I especially want to thank those authors who by their early contributions of articles made the assembling of this anthology possible, those who developed material for this book (and then suffered through my many—excessive—requests for revisions—forgive), and those whose excellent work I could not include because it was repetitive of other material. I am extremely grateful to Carol Selby for supervising the compilation of the index. My thanks are due to Barry Avedon and Ruth Beatty for suggestions for the title, to the librarians of Eastern Michigan University for their assistance, and to all my friends who listened as I verbalized my problem solving processes. I wish to thank Mary L. Allison, Senior Editor of Teachers College Press, for her tender, loving care.

I am grateful to Dr. Henry Sauerwein and the Board of Directors of the Helene Wurlitzer Foundation of New Mexico as well as to the Board of the Montalvo Center for the Arts for residency grants in painting. Without those respites, intense periods of painting, I would not have been able to sustain the effort needed to complete this book. My thanks goes to the Regents of Eastern Michigan University for a sabbatical, which gave me time to work on the anthology. This book would not have been possible without the prior and continuing work of the Women's Caucus for Art, the National Art Education Association's Women's Caucus, and all the other feminist art groups across the country. It is my hope that this book reflects the whys, the hows, and the whats of their fine work.

JUDY LOEB

NOTES

1. Linda Nochlin, "Why Have There Been No Great Women Artists?" *Art News* 69 (January 1971): 22-39, 67-71.
2. Martina Horner, "The Motive to Avoid Success and Changing Aspirations of College Women," *Women On Campus* (Ann Arbor, Mich.: Center for the Continuing Education of Women, University of Michigan, 1970).

3. *Women's Studies Newsletter* (Old Westbury, N.Y.: The Feminist Press) publishes lists of self-supporting programs. This is the newsletter of the National Women's Studies Association.
4. *Women's Studies and the Arts,* eds. Fine, Gellman, and Loeb, contains descriptions of many courses now offered in various institutions in this country. It also contains specialized bibliographic material.
5. In order of publication: Eleanor Tufts, *Our Hidden Heritage: Five Centuries of Women Artists* (London and New York: Paddington Press, 1974); Cindy Nemser, *Art Talk: Conversations with Twelve Women Artists* (New York: Scribners, 1975); Karen Petersen and J.J. Wilson, *Women Artists: Recognition and Reappraisal From the Early Middle Ages to the Twentieth Century* (New York: Harper Colophon, 1976); Ann Sutherland Harris and Linda Nochlin, *Women Artists: 1550–1950* (New York: Knopf, 1976); Elsa Honig Fine, *Women and Art: A History of Women Painters from the Renaissance to the 20th Century* (Montclair, N.J.: Allanheld and Schram, 1978); Charlotte S. Rubinstein, *American Women Artists* (New York: Hart, 1979). This list does not include the numerous books published that reappraise the works of individual women artists.
6. Nancy G. Kutner and Donna Brogan, "Sources of Sex Discrimination in Educational Systems: A Conceptual Model," *Psychology of Women* (Fall 1976).

Introduction

JOAN MONDALE

In October 1977, I attended a reception with Midge Costanza, Special Assistant to President Carter, at the Brooklyn Museum. It was a marvelous afternoon. I had that rare privilege that an art lover like myself always longs for. I toured the special exhibition then on display with one of the curators responsible for the show, Ann Sutherland Harris, and for what seemed only the tiniest bit of time had the opportunity to learn from an expert.

And what a marvelous exhibition I saw! Women Artists: 1550–1950 was really an extraordinary experience. One saw not only splendid works of art but also tangible evidence that the art history books are wrong. No matter what Janson says or, more accurately and significantly, *doesn't say*, women artists were part of the entire evolution of Western painting.

It was an afternoon of revelations, not the least of which was Midge Costanza's announcement that she had just sent a letter to the heads of the three government agencies most closely involved with the arts—the National Endowment for the Arts, the Smithsonian Institution, and the General Services Administration. In her letter, Midge stated that representatives of various art groups had reported to her that these three agencies had not given significant recognition to women in the arts. She asked these organizations to look into this

---

Based on an address to the founding Convention of the Coalition of Women's Art Organizations in New York City, January 25, 1978.

matter and report to her the results of their own investigations. Midge is short, direct, and warm. In fact, the letter was very much like Midge herself: short, direct and warm. In its conclusion she offered her help and her thanks. The agencies themselves responded with promises to find out the facts; that process is still going on.

The process of examination is important in itself. It is a process of consciousness-raising on the part of these federal agencies. Consciousness-raising is awareness of the availability and eagerness of women to participate, in a professional capacity, in the arts.

But beyond the parameters of the federal government that three-paragraph letter generated lots of controversy. Because of that letter, the Carter administration was accused of politicizing the arts and sacrificing the artistic integrity of these three public agencies because of pressure from political interest groups. At least you know people are listening when they start complaining about you!

Inherent in this charge is the assumption that the Endowment, the Smithsonian, and the GSA must necessarily sacrifice quality in order to have more women on their panels and in executive positions on their staffs. These critics are saying—if not directly, then certainly by inference—that there are not enough qualified women in the arts to warrant their greater representation in these programs. Therefore, to have more women involved in the work of these agencies is to weaken them, all in the name of politics.

Since I read these charges, I've given them considerable thought. Finally, after much reflection, I have come to the conclusion that these critics are right: women are not qualified in the way these agencies have traditionally defined that term. Few women head major art institutions. Few women artists have been given one-person exhibitions in this country's great museums. Only a small percentage of the boards of American art organizations are composed of women. In this sense, the critics are right: women in the arts do not possess the requisite credentials for entrance into the highest levels of the art world.

But is this women's fault or is it that women do not qualify because they have not been given the opportunities to qualify? The modern American woman artist lacks neither talent nor training; she lacks only opportunity, and the time has come to give her *that* as well.

If 75 percent of the graduates who emerge from American art schools are women, what happens to them after graduation? If more than 50 percent of the Ph.Ds in art history are awarded to women, where are the women museum directors? If almost every arts organization you can name is staffed largely by women, where are the women at the policy-making level? If women dominate the field, why aren't there more of them at the top of their profession?

These are the hard questions that will have to be answered now and in the coming years—in Washington and around the nation.

Judith Brodsky gave testimony at hearings held in New York City on the proposed White House Conference for the Arts (see last chapter in this book, Ed.). I feel that her testimony—factual, lucid, strongly feminist but attuned to the needs of the art world as a whole—might serve as a model. Judith Brodsky was being heard in a forum that artists—women *and* men artists—have too long ignored, that of our nation's Congress. My hope is that you will spend time exhorting the legislatures and letting them hear the facts because the facts themselves are very sobering and need greater exposure.

It has always been my belief that an individual, an institution, or a movement defines itself through action. It is what you *do* that counts. It is the action that you are identified with that gives you an identity in the world; often, there is a split between the image we have of ourselves and the identity we have created in the eyes of the world through our actions. It seems to be one of the battles of life to lessen the gap between our own image of ourselves and the identity that the world thrusts upon us.

Marcel Duchamp spoke of the "arts coefficient"—the gap that exists between what the artist intends and what the viewer perceives. It is like the gap that exists now between what we, as women, know we are capable of and what the professional world allows us to be. It is up to us to close that gap through appropriate action.

Action and power are closely allied. Power is the ability to effect change. The amount of legislation and government programs affecting the lives of artists are steadily increasing. And yet, very few artists are aware of the *full impact* of the programs. Even fewer artists make their needs known to the legislators and administrators in the government.

There is a great need now for visual artists to make themselves heard. If the legislators have no information coming to them from visual artists, then laws will be passed and programs will be designed that touch the lives of artists but, quite possibly, in an ineffective and even detrimental way.

For example, the Tax Reform Acts of 1976 limited the deduction for home studios in a way that will severely hamper the income of artists who happen to make art where they live. Many artists knew about this amendment while it was being considered by Congress, but they did not understand *all* the implications of this law, nor did they know what to do about it. The artists were not fully informed; they were not mobilized to act. Not being mobilized, they were *powerless to effect change.* There is a vacuum here . . .

Let me give you another example: I had a meeting at my house. The topic was the arts component of the CETA program. I am sure you are all aware of the Labor Department's CETA program, which gives federal dollars to cities for what are termed "labor intensive" programs. About one and one-half percent of this money goes towards arts-related programs. This percentage amounted, in 1977, to about one hundred million dollars which funded over 10,000 artists and arts administrators working in museums, painting murals, conducting workshops, and so forth. At the luncheon, imagine my astonishment when the director of the CETA program stated that no one, *no one*, from the visual arts world ever came to him to offer suggestions, help, or advice on what CETA should be doing for artists.

Isn't this a call to action? The time is *right now* for women to play a leadership role in speaking for all artists. Remember your power cannot and should not be circumscribed by the problems of sexual discrimination. In order to be truly effective, you must reach out and play an active role in all aspects of the arts.

In seeking the right words to send you off as you begin a new phase of this historical struggle, I found myself searching for something not too sentimental, something not too trite. Then it came to me—that wonderful valedictory that the Romans used as they marched off to battle. I offer it to you today (adapted, of course, for this special audience): My sisters in the arts. Be well! Be strong!

I
FEMINIST REAPPRAISALS
OF ART AND ART HISTORY

1

Toward a Juster Vision
How Feminism Can Change Our Ways of Looking at Art History

LINDA NOCHLIN

The question I shall deal with is: "How can feminism in the arts implement cultural change, defining aims and developing a philosophy to deal with the outer and the inner realities of women? The goal is to resolve a conflict between ingrained attitudes and new possibilities and to develop a plan for translating philosophy and aims into practical reality in cultural institutions." This is a rather large order. The best way of approaching it is a way that I've learned from the woman's movement—that is, in terms of my own personal experience.

Since I am an art historian and since art history, and art, are cultural institutions, I should like to tell something about the way feminism has led me to question and reformulate my own position in relation to the arts and to history itself. Feminism has been an enormous intellectual, spiritual, and practical breakthrough in my life as a human being and as a scholar. Since, however, I don't distinguish between the self and society and don't see them as opposites—I see them, rather, as totally interconnected—in talking about myself, I'm talking about a social issue. I don't see a basic conflict between the individual and the social group. The self seems to me a piece of the social group that happens to be enclosed in a certain boundary of skin and bones and has incorporated a great many values and ideals of the larger society. Even the feelings that one thinks of as being

This chapter is based on a talk given at the National Conference on Women and the Arts, sponsored by the University of Wisconsin—Extension, Sept. 13–15, 1973.

most personal are ultimately gotten from somewhere. And what is that somewhere? I don't think it's nature in the raw. It's the particular historical, social, and cultural situations that one is born into. In turn, the individual or the self is constantly acting upon and modifying and changing the social group so that self and society of individuals and institutions are not hard and fast opposing entities but really a kind of process in a constant state of mediation and transaction.

Therefore, when I talk of my personal experience, I'm not opposing it to the nature of history or to the nature of an intellectual discipline. I see them as part of the same sort of structure and, therefore, I think any one individual's life and experience can be a paradigm for the whole and can stand as an example of the whole. It's not my little personal life as opposed to everyone out there or even to this country or to this historical moment that I'm really talking about.

How, in effect, does feminism have an influence on the way I look at art history? Or, to make the issue even clearer, how does the notion of feminism transform for me the institution of art, the nature of art, and the whole way I look at history? I'll give some examples because I think they are useful.

One of the primary notions that we have about art is the notion of genius. Art, great art, is created by great geniuses. And these geniuses are in some way mythical beings—different from you and me, more valuable than you and me—whose products are in some way inestimably richer and more important than anything that you or I could produce. And the genius who is looked up to by our society as the very apex of human achievement is seen, *par excellence*, as the individual, the one who is set apart from or rebels or is in some way elevated above the mass of ordinary human beings.

When I began to be interested in feminism and when I started looking into the actual, concrete historical situations in which art was created or could be created, I found some very interesting things. Far from being totally unpredictable or uncaused, great art was usually produced in fairly predictable situations. For example, very often great artists had had fathers or even grandfathers who happened to be artists; in other words, often it was a family endeavor. Naturally, someone who's interested in art is going to encourage progeny in that direction. I found many father-son or even grandfather-father-son art situations. Second, I found that if the talented child in question happened to be a woman, the chances of her going on to be what is considered a "genius," that is, an innovator in the field of art, were minimal, no matter what degree of early talent she showed. For example, going to the museum in Barcelona and looking at the early work of Picasso is really an eye-opener. He was a very, very talented little boy, and his early work is extraordinary—he was indeed a child prodigy. I might also point out that his father was an artist and a teacher of art. I asked myself: "What if Pablo had been Pablita? What if he had been a girl?" I went to the Brooklyn Museum class for talented children, and there were girls in that class who were also little *wunderkinders*—little child prodigies—who did work on the level of that of the 12-year-old Picasso. What happened to them? Why didn't their genius come to fruition in the way that Picasso's did? One tends to think that in any situation innate genius will come out no matter what the odds are against it. But it does not come out, no matter what the odds are against it. It comes out only in very special circumstances, and it fails to fulfill its potential in very definable circumstances too; one of those circumstances of almost guaranteed failure is if the child prodigy in question happens to be a female. There are no doubt many unsung Pablita Picassos who are washing dishes or being sales women simply because of the fact that they are females.

Now this, of course, forced me to raise other issues about art. Feminism not only asks questions about the position of women in society, it seems to me that it forces basic ideological questioning of many other assumptions we accept as normal in a given culture or a given society. In other words, if you ask why are there so few women who have pursued successful careers or are what we call geniuses in the fine arts, feminism forces us to be conscious of other questions about our so-called natural assumptions. That is one way in which feminism affects cultural institutions—it sets off a chain reaction. From feelings about injustice or feelings about wanting to push further into issues like that of genius, one can go on to question a great many other assumptions that govern the discipline as a whole. One can ask: "Why has art history focussed so exclusively on certain individuals and not others, why on individuals and not on groups, why on art works in the foreground and something called social conditions in the background rather than seeing them as mutually interactive?" In other words, you can question the entire paraphernalia and standards of the discipline or institution that you're working in.

In addition, my involvement in feminism has led me to question some of the standards and values by which we have judged art in the past. In the article I wrote, "Why Have There Been No Great Women Artists?"[1] I said that I thought that simply looking into women artists of the past would not really change our estimation of their value. Nevertheless, I went on to look into some women artists of the past, and I find that my estimations and values have, in fact, changed. That is another plus to feminism, which I think can make one more flexible, more open to abandoning or rejecting our own previous positions when we find that we're wrong. I think that's another thing that I've learned from the feminist movement—not to stick to a position because one's ego is involved in it but to let go of an old idea and see how a new one works. In any case, I have been looking into women artists of the past, and I find that in the process of examining them my whole notion of what art is all about is gradually changing.

For instance, one of the artists of the past whom I had always been taught to look down on as a horrid example of the salon *machine* manufacturer *par excellence* was Rosa Bonheur, a laughing stock, the prototypical academic painter. Now I've become very interested in Rosa Bonheur. First of all, it's interesting to know that she was the most popular painter in the United States. She was probably the only painter who was really known out in the Middle West or in the Far West, by means of prints and reproductions. She was practically the only painter that lots of people were acquainted with, and I still know older women who say they grew up in Kansas or upper New York State and the only art work they had was a print of *The Horse Fair* that hung in the kitchen. That was their contact with art—Rosa Bonheur. I asked myself: "Why has she been rejected?" It's not because she's a woman. I'm not naive enough to think that that is the reason—it's because the style of art that she created went out of fashion.

Being interested in realism and being interested in a kind of justice for art—rejected styles need some support and some help just as rejected people do!—I decided to look into the work of Rosa Bonheur, and I came up with intriguing results. The results were so interesting that I decided to look into other nineteenth century women artists as well and have done further work on Rosa Bonheur. It is certainly significant to Rosa Bonheur's development as an artist that her father had been an active member of the utopian Saint-Simonians who were firm believers in equality for women. They disapproved of marriage; they believed in equal educational opportunity; they advocated a similar trousered costume for both sexes; and they made strenuous efforts to find a woman messiah to share their leader's reign. All of this must have made an enormously strong impression on the young Rosa Bonheur whose father was an artist, although a struggling one, which supports the point that art tends to run in families. (Another interesting fact derived from research on Rosa Bonheur was that the Saint-Simonians were among the first to believe in total mutual dependency. Their garments all buttoned in the back, which meant that you had to get a fellow member of the community to button you—a very interesting symbolic idea.)

The notion of egalitarianism for women must have made a profound impression on the young Rosa Bonheur. "Why shouldn't I be proud to be a woman?" she once responded to an interviewer. "My father, that enthusiastic apostle of humanity, many times reiterated to me that woman's mission was to elevate the human race, that she was the messiah of future centuries. It is to his doctrines that I owe the great and noble ambition which I have conceived for the sex which I proudly affirm to be mine and whose independence I will support to my dying day." *The Horse Fair* is indeed a work of noble ambition. There is nothing stereotypically feminine, i.e., soft, delicate, or dainty, in this powerful, highly charged work. Its overpowering size itself constitutes a self-confident answer to the challenge of the young woman artist's abilities.

Adrienne Rich has commented on the stifling of women's energies and the resulting vague sorrow, melancholia, and despair characteristic of women's poetry in the nineteenth century. When we look at Bonheur's *The Horse Fair*, how refreshing it is to find an artistic statement in which a woman's energy, all her vigor and power, far from being stifled, find a direct equivalent in the grandeur and dynamism of the work itself. For the real subject of *The Horse Fair* is energy—physical freedom and power, energy as displayed by a woman and the pride and joy that both humans and animals take in the visible demonstration of energy. While many modern critics have disparaged Bonheur's masterpiece as a typical salon *machine* of its time, it is well to remember that present-day judgments of nineteenth century art are themselves in the process of reevaluation. Many of the works cast aside earlier in the twentieth century as salon *machines* or *Kitsch* are now being reconsidered in contexts less exclusively determined by formalism and the emphasis on "pure" pictorial qualities. Here, then, is an instance of how a feminist approach may bring about reevaluation, making us look again at pictures that have been cast aside and rethinking the implications of this rejection, making us ask what elements exist within the work of art that one might look at from a feminist viewpoint.

Still another area in art history that I have been examining is that of nineteenth century Britain. It surprised me to find out that approximately 3,000 names of women artists were listed in Grave's *Dictionary of Artists* who exhibited in London during the nineteenth century.[2] A lot of them, it's true, showed one flower painting in one minor show, but many of them showed consistently in the most prestigious showplace of all—The Royal Academy. How many people can call to mind a single nineteenth-century British woman painter? It is hard. These women, 3,000 strong, have been simply dropped from the rolls of history.

Since art history demands detective work and a desire to track down historical facts, I wanted to find out who these women were and what had happened to them. And I did find quite an interesting group of artists for Women Artists: 1550 to 1950, which opened at the Los Angeles County Museum of Art in 1977. This exhibition is itself an example of how feminism can affect our cultural institutions, because such a large scale show of women artists at a major museum would, I think, have been unthinkable ten years ago. This is an example of how feminist pressure, women's interest in the arts, and the work of feminist art groups, in Los Angeles particularly, have assured the fact that women are finally going to reappear in art history.

Some of the most interesting nineteenth-century British women painters are those who did narrative painting, painting that tells a story, which is generally realist in character and follows in the great British tradition established by Hogarth and carried on throughout the nineteenth century. Narrative painting has been singularly neglected and rejected for a variety of reasons (having nothing to do with the issue of women artists) by critics and art historians of today. Through my study of these nineteenth century women painters, my admiration for and my interest in the whole realm of narrative and genre painting has risen enormously. I began to ask myself: "Why is it that traditional art history has taught us to admire, respect, and devote our lives to the difficult and complex iconography of Van Eyck or Dürer or Michelangelo with its erudite religious references, its neoplatonic double meanings, its hidden references to contemporary events, and has simply cast aside or laughed at the equally rich, meaningful, and in many ways complex iconography of this narrative genre painting of the nineteenth century? Why is this content, often dealing with social issues in the lives of ordinary men and women and with the moral problems of the day, cast aside as trivial whereas what seems to me rather paltry and silly questions about neoplatonic doctrine in the sixteenth century is taken enormously seriously, suitable for a lifetime of scholarly work? Why is there this kind of value dichotomy governing our cultural institutions?" Here, again, feminism led me to ask questions that are not necessarily totally concerned with the issue of women. Feminism is like the key that unlocks many of the closed compartments in the mind, compartments created by one's "natural" expectations, which now have to be revised, cast aside, and sorted out again.

Still another issue raised by the examination of nineteenth-century women artists is that of the democratization of the very *creation* of art. I have been looking more seriously at decorative art since my involvement in the women's movement, for the decorative arts are one of the realms in which women were "permitted" to express themselves in the past. In the course of investigating the work of American women artists of the nineteenth century, especially those of the Peale family, I found out that there were a whole group of what are known as "theorem" painters—women painters who painted from patterns or stencils; these were the ancestors of our paint-by-dot kits. There were, in fact, rule books and stencils ("theorem" meant stencil) so that women could make their own works of art by using stencils, following directions about what colors to apply, using sample patterns, and so on. According to one authority in the field, nineteenth-century American women turned away from more elaborate types of embroidery, lacemaking, and stitchery because they simply did not have time to do it in the New World. They wanted an easier, quicker means of self-expression; theorem painting was one way.

In a certain sense, then, the democratization of artmaking took place in the United States in the hands of women. One may not think this is a good thing; the issues of "creativity" or "individual expression" raised by such activities are far from clear. Perhaps painting from stencils was a kind of conceptual art before its time. This raises all sorts of interesting issues as it is not so different from the intention behind what Seurat and the Neoimpressionists were to do later in France. Seurat and his friends, Signac, Cross, and the others, were ardent practising anarchists who really believed in the democratization of art. They believed in painting subjects from everyday life, in painting working-class suburbs. The *Island of La Grande Jatte* is concerned precisely with ordinary and upper-class people mixing in a working-class outing place. And Seurat and his friends also tried to invent a system whereby the making of art could be universally available to all. His friend, Charles Henry, invented something called the aesthetic protractor, which was a method of judging lines and colors suitable to the mood and subject one wanted to express. Seurat codified his system, saying that lines above the horizon created a gay mood, while lines below the horizon a sad mood. This was a way of making pictorial expression more generally available. He also boasted that he could work on *La Grande Jatte* by gaslight, for his "system" worked so perfectly that he knew exactly how many dots of which color he could apply to each area to produce a given effect, no matter what the lighting condition might be.

This does have democratizing implications. We may now object to Seurat's system as being a mechanization of art, a kind of dehumanization of it. But to Seurat and to many of the people around him, as well as to these women theorem painters, this was not the issue. The point was that more people could derive the satisfaction of creating something for themselves that they thought of as art, no matter what our particular present-day judgments of it are. We have to remember, too, that the whole notion of the standardized, the mechanical, and the repeatable did not necessarily have the negative implications at that time that is has now. Mechanization and standardization were seen as instruments of democracy, ways of making more and more available to more and more people, not as instruments of alienation or dehumanization. Here again my interest in the women's movement forced me to rethink certain issues and certain innovations in the field of nineteenth-century art that I hadn't really thought about before.

These, then, are some of the ways in which "we as individuals and members of social groups can effect change." That is, by doing, writing, publishing, spreading, and simply thinking about issues in our own fields. I don't believe one can separate thought and action—I think thought is action. I don't believe that going out and waving a muscle means that you're acting. I believe thinking is one of the most important forms of action because it's the form of action that leads you to the truth, and it is only through truth that you can arrive at what is really the whole point of the women's movement—the achievement of justice. If we don't know what is true, it seems to me we cannot achieve what is just, and for me, justice is the main goal of the women's movement, not all women loving each other, or women establishing a realm of special virtue (because I don't think that women are especially virtuous, nor need they be). But I think that our first priority is to implement justice.

By that I mean two different things: primary justice or the abolition of primary prejudice but even more important, the abolition and combating of secondary injustice or discrimination. Let me differentiate. By primary injustice I mean the very obvious fact that there are no women in the Supreme Court, that there are almost no women bank presidents, that there's never been a woman president of the United States, and that it is very hard, even in the realm of the arts, to mention a woman museum director. But in any case those are the obvious and visible manifestations of injustice. Women are simply openly deprived of visible opportunity. We can work on that with affirmative action or by making sure that faculties at colleges and universities are as coeducational as the student bodies. (Why is it that we call a college "coeducational" when it has a half male, half female student body, but not half men and half women faculty?) The area of overt discrimination—primary injustice—is our first fight, but it's not really the major fight.

The major fight is against secondary injustices. By secondary injustice I mean the whole way that women are dealt with from the moment they enter the world. I mean the fact that men very often show more attention to, are rougher with and more demanding with their male children than with their female children. I mean what a child entering a nursery school sees and experiences—all the teachers are women. In other words, immediately male and female children are indoctrinated with the notion that women are there to serve their needs, while men are off doing something else, presumably more important.

I would also question the notion that "boys will be boys"—in other words, permission and encouragement for roughness, brutality, violence, and ignoring the sensibilities of others granted to young people of one sex—male; reproval (and kids get the notion very quickly of what is approved and disapproved) either voiced or not of such behavior in women. I don't have to mention too many examples. Another example might just be the assumption that it is women's duty to arrange for child care and the management of the house, even is she does have a job, that she's the one who automatically is supposed to assume that burden. Would one dare ask a busy male executive to worry about the babysitters, the meal planning, and household trivia? But females who are the equivalent of busy executives or who work all day in supermarkets standing on their feet are constantly asked to assume these responsibilities, which in a just society would be taken care of in more positive ways by day care, by living arrangements in which some of these services are built in, or by actual sharing.

It seems to me that until this secondary discrimination is done away with, until truly we have created an androgynous society, a society where it doesn't matter what kind of sexual organs you have but you do what you are fitted for, dividing the burdens half and half or taking turns—until we have that, we still have injustice. I think that it is the business of the feminist movement in every field and on every level to combat both of these types of injustices, through action, through thought, through the pursuit of truth, and through the constant questioning and piercing through of our so-called "natural" assumptions. And it's only in this way that feminism can be a real weapon for justice for 51 percent of humanity, which is us.

NOTES

1. Linda Nochlin, "Why Have There Been No Great Women Artists?" *Art News* 69, 9 (January 1971): 22–39, 67–71.
2. Algernon Graves, *A Dictionary of Artists Who Have Exhibited in the Principal London Exhibitions from 1760–1893*. 3rd ed. with additions and corrections (London: H. Graves, 1901).

2

Past and Present
Inequities in Art Education

GORDON S. PLUMMER

The historical developments that led to art instruction in American schools paradoxically led also to the present less than exemplary status of women in the art professions. While critics of the feminist movement can fairly claim that women have often been deeply involved in the growth of art in America, the nature of that special involvement has been such that it has helped to bring about the very conditions that so irk women in the art professions.

The first factor was the concept of the "woman's role" in the American colonial or frontier society. Chroniclers of early American life and education have noted that many practical occupations were seen as "artistic" by early Americans. *Art's Masterpiece,* first published in London in 1768 and in America shortly thereafter, included such unlikely arts as dyeing cloth, spot and stain removal, elementary medical remedies, and "the art of perfuming and beautifying."[1] In the 1750s, Eleanor McIlvaine advertised the teaching of "painting on glass . . . and other works proper for young ladies." The "limners" or itinerant portraitists of Boston and New York also advertised "instruction" in occupations deemed to be "suitable" for young women.

Henrietta Johnston, who died in Charleston, South Carolina in 1728, the first woman painter in America, made several limner portraits. In many of these portraits, the figure of a governness also appears. This European import from the aristocracy remained a formative influence after the American Revolution as did also the "dame schools," so called because the principal instructor was considered to be a "lady" (cf. *The Society of Colonial Dames*, Charleston). Drawing, needlework, and painting on velvet were all topics of in-

14

struction in the dame schools. Women in early America were skilled in the handicrafts before they became drawn into the factory system. In the 1880s, Charles Leland's Decorative Arts Club in Philadelphia stated that this sometimes:

> had a truly awful effect upon certain fashionable women . . . pounding away at brass plaques . . . until they were red in their faces, endeavoring to create artistic designs. Society was stampeded by decorative art.[2]

Secondly, and coincidentally with the connection between women and decorative arts, was the deep-rooted idea that advanced work in the fine arts might be suspect and pernicious.

This kind of thinking came about as a result of the influence of American religious persuasion in matters of the arts, of women, and education. In 1792, there was a Young Ladies' Academy in Cherry Street, Philadelphia, and in 1795 Poor's Academy for Young Ladies followed. All the instructors were male, and many were ministers. The students were taught to work from stencilled designs known as "theorems." In the 1830s Frances Milton Trollope commented on:

> the influence of the ministers of the innumerable religious sects . . . on the females . . . It is from the clergy that the women of America receive . . . attention . . . I never saw, or heard, a country where religion had so strong a hold upon the women, or a slighter upon the men.[3]

She also mentions the "immaculate delicacy" of Cincinnati ladies as "not being very deep-seated."

Her experience at a gallery was recorded in detail. An open entrance was screened from view, and there was a very officious old woman in charge. With a secretive manner, she told Mrs. Trollope that her visitation time was especially suitable since "no one can see you—make haste." She further explained that, "The ladies like to go in that room by themselves, when there be no gentlemen watching them." Inside the room a written notice deplored the disgusting depravity that had resulted in the statues being indecently and shamelessly marked.

Trollope commented that this whole phenomenon was caused by the "coarse-minded" segregated visitation rules. Adding that she had never felt her delicacy shocked at such galleries as the Louvre, she declared herself "affronted" by the hint that in America a woman

might only "peep" hurriedly at what was deemed indecent material.
Frances Trollope concluded that the exhibition arrangement, "the
feelings which have led to them," and the resultant audience behaviors

> furnish as good a specimen of the kind of delicacy on which the Ameri-
> cans pride themselves, and of the peculiarities arising from it, as can be
> found anywhere.[4]

Calvin Ellis Stowe (1802–1886), considered one of the founders of
American art education, worked for most of his life in various
theological seminaries. At the Pennsylvania Academy of the Fine
Arts, Thomas Eakins was forced to work under the constraints of
sexually segregated classes. A letter of 1882 to the Academy President appealed to him "as a Christian gentleman," to consider the
effect upon the daughter of the writer when "entering a class where
both male and female figures stood . . . in their horrid nakedness."
The writer added "the stifling heat of the room adds to the excitement."[5] Thomas Eakins was esteemed by his students, who paraded
in protest at his dismissal from the Pennsylvania Academy because of
the furor aroused by his studies of the human anatomy.
The art professoriat took a paternalistic attitude on the education
of women. In 1898, Charles Dana, President of the Academy Fellowship and also a professor at the Philadelphia Art School wrote on
the "Paris Girl Question:"

> to prevent . . . so far as possible . . . the exodus of young and unprepared
> girls to study Art in Paris . . . our schools are so far superior to the studios
> for women in Paris . . . girls . . . have no conception of the life they will
> be forced to lead; the obnoxious companionships, the disease-breeding
> sanitary arrangements, the scanty food . . . dirt, dishonesty, etc., while we
> would be wanting in respect . . . to suspect for a moment their ability to
> resist the temptations to which they are sure to be subjected, our object
> . . . is to do away . . . with the necessity for exposing them to such.[6]

Even as late as 1924, when a great outcry was raised in protest at
the University of Pennsylvania's recognition of courses at the Barnes
Foundation, the Dean of the School of Design for Women, Harriet
Sartain, described herself as "aghast" and added:

I cannot appreciate a course with such art as source material. It is a bad thing to put any such ideas before susceptible minds.[7]

The collection included many nudes by Renoir, Matisse, and other French masters.

The third negative contributory factor in the treatment of women in art developed from our society's ambiguous feelings towards the education of women and public education, especially at the elementary level. Benjamin Franklin's *Proposals Relating to the Education of Youth in Pennsylvania*, published in 1749, are full of references concerning what is needed for the education of boys and gentlemen but no references to females.[8] Over one-hundred years later, in 1863, at the First California State Teachers Institute, John Swett, the California Superintendent, reflecting on "common sense in teaching," was still asking:

Girls will, most of them, become the wives of farmers, mechanics and laborers . . . they are of average mental capacity . . . What shall be done with them?[9]

In Chicago, following the establishment of manual training for girls in elementary schools in 1892, a tremendous attack by public and press was made on "unnecessary fads and frills." The *Chicago Tribune* in 1893 referred to "mud pie making."[10]

While the sentiment toward the education of women was for long ambiguous in this country, the view of society towards public education was epitomized in the public administrative reports:

no elementary teachers should be so ambitious . . . nor even liberally paid. Common education should be low in price, and the places occupied by patient, unambitious men, well content with small things.[11]

The reports for 1861 mention:

growing appreciation of the Female Agency, the favorable numbers employed, and the salary. This is as it should be . . . there will ever be a greater compensation to males than females, owing to the fact that a larger number of the former will be employed as principals.[12]

and the Report summed up with the comment, "The great draft upon our male teachers has rendered it necessary to call into the field other laborers, in order to supply the places of those fighting."

During the Civil War in 1865, the Annual Report indicated that:

> The State (of Pennsylvania) has nobly sustained her educational system, even amidst this devastating war . . . the decrease in the number of male teachers from last year is 367, and the increase of females, 593, (from 7,172 to 7,765).[13]

By the time the Western Drawing Teachers Association in 1893 and the Eastern Art Teachers Association in 1899 were organized, the officers and leaders were women. For many years women were highly influential in both the Eastern and Western Drawing Associations. However, in the period during and after World War I, the gradual effect of "manual training" and "industrial art education" brought more and more men into positions of influence.

These lines of stratification continued to develop, especially during and after the Second World War. In 1944, President of the Massachusetts School of Art Palmstrom declared the "duty" of those in charge of the school was to keep it in its original state as a "matter of trust" for the "boys in the service."[14] There was no mention of the many service women or women in wartime occupational specialties. A universal post-war climate of opportunity for male veterans combined with increasing professionalism in art education to further define women in the field as second class citizens. The G.I. Bill, for the most part, gave assistance to the education of men, but few ex-service women received it.

It may therefore be postulated that the present iniquitous status of women in the profession began with the peculiarly American frontier concept of women as practitioners of decorative arts. It has been caused, also, by the deep-seated conviction that advanced work in the fine arts is pernicious, especially to mixed classes of men and women. The early influence of religion and its ministers cultivated prudery in America and also to a considerable extent directed the development of early education. To this day public education continues to be perceived as a relatively simple process, easily and cheaply effected by persons of low aspiration, i.e., women and men content with small things. The art professoriat retains parental attitudes toward women students. Graduate or professional level studies continued to be a male-dominated area until the last few years.

The rise of women in teaching was rapid. In 1870, the ratio of women to men was three to one in Michigan and New York, five to one in Maine, and seven to one in Massachusetts. Yet in the National Teachers Association of 1857, the Constitution restricted membership to "gentlemen." The effects of wars, especially two major world confrontations, created universal acceptance of women in many occupations within Western nations. Yet, paradoxically, at the conclusion of hostilities, programs for resettlement, re-education and re-employment all combined once again to relegate women to lower, or second-class status, especially in the secondary and tertiary levels of art teaching employment.

Truly, prejudicial treatment of women in American art education comes from a well spring of popular sentiment that is deep, strong, and polluted.

NOTES

1. *Arts Masterpiece: or, A Companion for the Ingenious of Either Sex,* 7th ed. by C. K. (London: I. Jackson, 1768), and in U.S. Library of Congress, Rare Books Division, 1975.
2. Edward M. Robins, "Random Recollections of Hans Breitman," *Pennsylvania Magazine of History and Biography* 49 (1926): 145–47.
3. Frances Milton Trollope, *Domestic Manners of The Americans* (London: Whitaker, Treacher, 1832), p. 75.
4. Ibid., p. 269.
5. Letter, signed R. S., to President James Claghorn (Philadelphia: Archives of the Pennsylvania Museum of The Fine Arts, filed April 26, 1882).
6. Charles E. Dana, "The Paris Girl Question," *First Annual Report of The Fellowship of the Pennsylvania Academy of the Fine Arts* (Philadelphia, 1898).
7. Theodore M. Dillaway, "Art Circles Flay Barnes Foundation," *North American* (May 20, 1924): 3.
8. Benjamin Franklin, "Proposals Relating to the Education of Youth in

Pennsylvania," *American Journal of Education* 27, (April 1877): 442–473.

9. John Swett, "Concerning Common Sense in Teaching," *Address to First California State Teachers Institute* (San Francisco: Records of the Superintendent of Public Instruction, 1863).

10. Mary J. Herrick, *The Chicago Schools: A Social and Political History* (Beverly Hills, Calif.: Sage Publications, 1971), p. 73.

11. John F. Watson, *Annals of Pennsylvania in the Olden Time* (Philadelphia: Edwin S. Stuart, 1887), pp. 286–297.

12. *Report of the Superintendent of the Common Schools of Pennsylvania* (Harrisburg, Penn.: Singerly and Myers, State Printers, 1864), p. 13.

13. Ibid., p. 25.

14. Arthur J. Philpott, "The Week in Art World," *Boston Globe* (July 29, 1944): 21.

3

Women Artists and the Twentieth Century Art Movements

From Cubism to Abstract Expressionism

ELSA HONIG FINE

From all over Europe and America women flocked to Paris to study art in the beginning of the twentieth century. They came from the cities and provincial areas of Italy, France, England, Germany, Russia, and the United States to absorb the excitement of the Parisian art scene. Some merely continued in the academic tradition within which they were trained; others, more adventurous, shed both their academic background and their Victorian upbringing to join the radical art movements and bohemian life-style in Paris, which they took back to their native lands when they eventually returned.

Although Paris (Fauvism, Cubism) was the center of the art world at the beginning of the twentieth century, revolutionary ideas were also fomenting in Italy (Futurism), Germany (Expressionism), Russia (Rayonism, Constructivism, Suprematism) and America (the Ash Can School). Artists traveled from one center to another, exchanging new ideas and carrying with them the sense of vitality engendered by such visits. Thus, art prior to World War I was international rather than provincial. To be sure, unique national sensibilities were evident; essentially, however, the various movements of the pre-World War I avant garde were all seeking to come to terms with the formal elements of art in an increasingly industrialized and dehumanized society in which the need for art was being questioned. This was a time of experimentation, challenge, and optimism. The questions explored by the revolutionary artists in the first decade of the century are those still being explored.

There were no women associated with the original Fauves and Futurists. While Apollinaire labeled Marie Laurencin (1885–1956) a "scientific cubist," she was more muse than colleague to the group that surrounded Braque and Picasso. Rodin labeled her a "fauvette: she knows what grace is; she is serpentine." Indeed, Laurencin's work has always drawn praise for its essentially "feminine" quality, and Apollinaire, at another time, declared that she had brought "feminine art to a major status."[1] When Laurencin first met Apollinaire, she was earning her living as a porcelain painter. Enchanted by her naivete, the poet introduced her to his circle of friends who frequented the Bateau-Lavoir, the cafe in Montmartre where the radical artists and poets could be found at almost any time of the day debating the merits of Cubism and other affairs of taste. Although she rarely participated in these theoretical exchanges, Laurencin— unlike the women Impressionists—was actually there to witness the excitement. When Gertrude Stein purchased Laurencin's group portrait of artists Apollinaire, Picasso, Fernande Olivier, and Picasso's dog, Frika, she began to be taken seriously as an artist. Organized around the central figure of Apollinaire, the painting is composed of the sweeping arabesques and flat patterning that suggest the contemporary vogue for orientalism. The only suggestion of Cubism is in the geometric structuring of Olivier's face.

Working in collaboration, Sonia Terk-Delaunay (b.1885) and her husband Robert developed the theory of simultaneity, a system that incorporated the structural elements of Cubism with the expressive color of the Fauves. Robert became the public theorist and exhibitor, his reputation secure. Sonia, who rarely spoke of her art and avoided the restrictions of the dealer-artist relationship, allowed herself to become known as an artist only after the death of her husband in 1941. They were supportive rather than competitive, were each other's best critics, and were able to build two separate *oeuvres* based on mutual dependency, mutual respect, and shared theories. Although she deliberately limited her search to a narrow area, her influence has been universal. Through her fabric and poster designs, costume and fashion creations, book illustrations, playing cards, stained glass windows, and automobile interiors, she surreptitiously introduced modern art to an unsuspecting public. Ironically, the birth of the Delaunay's son, Charles, in 1911, was the occasion of Sonia's first experiment with complete abstraction. She described the project created for the baby thus:

> I had the idea of making . . . a blanket composed of bits of fabrics like those I had seen in the homes of Russian peasants. When it was finished, the arrangements of the pieces of material seemed to me to evoke Cubist conceptions, and we tried then to apply the same process to other objects and painting.[2]

Although born in Lisbon (1908), Maria Elena Vieira da Silva has been traditionally identified with the School of Paris, the loosely linked group of abstract painters who worked in Paris between the wars. Vieira da Silva arrived in Paris in 1928 to study sculpture with Bourdelle and Despiau. When she decided to concentrate on painting, she entered the studios of the Fauvist Othon Friesz and later the Cubist Leger. Her inspiration came from cities: from electric railways, steel scaffolding, bridges, and rocky landscapes. "The space of her cities and the architecture of her landscapes are translated in terms of a natural spontaneous geometry. Form is neither compressed nor silhouetted, and there are no flat elements in her constructions."[3] Indeed, her cityscapes are a strange combination of perspective and lack of it, a fusion of Renaissance space and Cubist grid.

There were no women associated with Die Brücke, the Dresden-based German Expressionist group founded by three architectural students in 1905, and those who exhibited in Munich with Der Blaue Reiter—Gabriele Münter, Marianne von Werefkin, Elisabeth Epstein, Erma Barrera-Bossi, and Maria Franck-Marc—had personal involvements with the men. Nevertheless, at least two of the women, Münter (1877–1962) and von Werefkin (1870–1938) each produced a significant body of work independent of their mentors.[4]

Gabriele Münter first met Wassily Kandinsky at the Phalanx School in Munich where he was her teacher. He was the first to treat her seriously as an artist: he "explained things in depth and looked at me as if I was a human being, consciously striving, a being capable of setting tasks and goals."[5] (Münter had previously taken some drawing lessons, "as many girls did in those days," and had studied briefly at the Women's Art School in Düsseldorf. But she found that neither she nor any of the female students were taken seriously.) Both Münter and Kandinsky were deeply moved by a Gauguin retrospective they had seen in Paris and by an exhibit of the Fauves. The influence of Matisse can be seen in Münter's 1909 portrait of von Werefkin. At Murnau, where the young German avant-garde began summering in 1908, the landscapes of Kandinsky and Münter were quite similar, but by the following year, Kandinsky's were bursting with the emotional violence that led him increasingly toward abstraction. In *Cottage in the Snow*, 1908–9, Münter applied her color with slablike strokes outlined in darker colors to create gridlike forms and a scintillating surface. Her use of flat areas of bright color surrounded by dark heavy outlines was learned from the Bavarian *hinterglasmalerei* (behind-the-glass paintings), the centuries-old folk art of religious purity and extreme simplification, which she collected.

Born in Russia of aristocratic parents, Marianne von Werefkin followed her companion, Alexie von Jawlensky, from Repin's studio to Munich in 1896. For the first several years in Munich von Werefkin painted very little; most of her energies were devoted to nurturing and supporting Jawlensky's talent. Because of their admiration for Gauguin and Van Gogh and for the French Fauves, Jawlensky and von Werefkin spent more time in Paris than in Munich and became involved in the politics of modern art. Von Werefkin worked briefly in what began to be called the "Murnau style." More a Symbolist than an Expressionist, she produced works of a "genuine, visionary power." A painting such as *The Country Road*, 1909, has the haunting quality of a work by Edvard Munch. The flat, anonymous, isolated figures in the foreground are dwarfed by the swirling lines, intense colors, and broad brush strokes of the background. According to Juliane Roh, the history of Der Blaue Reiter cannot be completely written until von Werefkin's diaries are published. As early as 1900, she wrote of "literally being obsessed by abstraction," which she understood as a "distance from reality, that which is wonderful and dreamlike." (These ideas she shared with Kandinsky. Roh believes that Kandinsky's rejection of the concrete world in his paintings was related to the mystical speculations of von Werefkin.)[6]

Many of the artists in Russia's pre-World War I avant-garde were women. They organized exhibitions, issued manifestoes, influenced life-styles, and with the coming of the Revolution, took an active part in bringing art to the service of the new regime. Because of the vastness of the country, there were many art centers; the proliferation of art societies and exhibitions was astounding, and women played significant roles in all of them.

Stemming from a new found pride in traditional folk art, a Neoprimitive movement took hold in Russia between 1909 and 1912, with Natalya Goncharova (1881–1962) and her companion for the next fifty years, Michel Larinov, as the leaders. In fact, this interest in naive art led to the advocacy of a Russian national art distinct from Western art and values, and by 1910 there was an extreme reaction against European domination of Russian art. The Italian Futurists, however, had a profound effect in Russia, especially on Goncharova. Rayonism became the Russian counterpart of the Italian movement; like their Italian counterparts, the Rayonists were concerned with the reality of urbanization and mechanization and the forces of speed and dynamism. Rayonism was also concerned with "spatial forms that can arise from the intersection of the reflected rays of different objects."[7] Goncharova's Rayonist paintings date from about 1911 to 1914 (when she left Russia to work with Diaghilev's Ballet Russes in Paris, an association that lasted until the master's death in 1920). *The Laundry*, 1912, shows the artist in transition from the broad flat areas of color, inverted perspectives, and flattened forms of the Neoprimitivists to the more abstract Rayonism. The dynamics of Futurism and the machine aesthetic are revealed, even though most of the tools— iron, washboard, wringer—are meant to be used by women.

The Russian Constructivists' desire to create a public art was most effectively implemented in their works for the theater, a vital aspect of Russian culture. One of the most successful artists in creating this synthesis was Alexandra Exter (1882–1949), a native of Kiev, who, through her tireless teaching in Kiev, Odessa, and Moscow, saw her ideas spread to all areas of Russian theater before she was forced into exile in 1924. (Her bold and revolutionary conceptions met with hostility when the Kremlin took a hard line on the arts.) After six years studying and exhibiting with the Cubists in Paris and the Futurists in Milan, Exter came to Moscow in 1914 and began her association with Alexander Tairov, founder of the Moscow Karmeny Theater. Since the audiences were composed largely of students and intellectuals, Exter was free to experiment with Cubist and Futurist ideas, and with Tairov developed a system of "synthetic theater" in which "set, costume, actor, and gesture were to be integrated to form a dynamic whole."[8] In Paris, Exter lived modestly with her second husband, George Nekrasov, an actor and son of wealthy tea merchants. He managed the household, delivered her work to exhibitions, and in deference to his more famous wife, frequently introduced himself as "George Exter."

A devotee of nonobjective art, Olga Rozanova (1886–1918) wrote in "The Bases of the New Creation and the Reason Why It is Misunderstood" (1913): "We propose to liberate painting from its subservience to the ready-made forms of reality and to make it first and foremost a creative, not a reproductive, art."[9] The year before her death she created a painting with a dark green stripe placed slightly off-center on a scrubbed canvas of a much lighter green—a painting that predates American minimalist conceptions by more than thirty years. After the Russian Revolution, as head of the Industrial Art Faculty of IZO Art College, Rozanova began a restructuring of the country's industrial arts education programs. Her attempts to merge art and industry were later realized by the Constructivists.

When Goncharova and Larinov left for exile in Paris, the leadership of the Russian avant-garde fell to Tatlin, Malevich, and Liubov Popova (1889–1924). After study in Moscow, Popova spent several years studying and traveling in Italy and France and, with her fellow exiles, returned home in 1914 when war began. She soon developed a personal style of abstraction. In *Architectonic Painting*, 1917, the jutting angular shapes are conceived as layers of planes; the movement is swift and the colors brilliant. Like the other Constructivists, Popova abandoned easel painting for production art and, in addition to designing revolutionary posters and theater pieces, worked for a time in a textile factory.

During and immediately following World War I, there came together in neutral Zurich a band of exiled artists recoiling from and reacting to what they felt to be the madness of society and the arbitrariness of human experience. At once anarchic, negative and destructive, they created an art of the absurd throughout which, however, ran a seriousness of purpose—the reexmination of the traditional functions of art and the basic foundations of society. Known initially as the Dada movement and later as Surrealism, it produced many styles, most of which were more or less concerned with the illustration of dreams, intuition, and the subconscious as interpreted by Freudian psychology. The Surrealists had a dual and conflicting view of woman. She was either the "woman-child," the incarnation of innocence, purity, and naivete, more intuitive and spontaneous than the mature and intellectually developed man, and therefore closer to her unconscious, (which was prized), or she was a sorcerer, seer, or divine.[10] It was within these ideological confines that the women artists of Surrealism sought to define their roles. Among them were Sophie Taeuber-Arp, Merit Oppenheim, Lenora Carrington, Dorothea Tanning, and Kay Sage; all were closely associated with the men of Dada and Surrealism.

When Sophie Taeuber (1889–1943) met Jean Arp in 1915, she was teaching weaving and textile design at the Zurich School of Arts and Crafts. The couple did not marry until 1921, but their artistic collaboration began almost immediately. Of their first work together, Jean wrote: "[We worked with] the simplest forms, using painting, embroidery, and pasted paper. They were probably the first manifestations of their kind, pictures that were their own reality, without meaning or cerebral intentions."[11] Both were active in the Dada movement; some of Sophie's most inventive pieces include a series of mechanical puppets and a Dada head (1920) a painted wood sculpture made from a hat stand decorated with geometric forms and including the letters DADA and the numbers 1920. Taeuber-Arp is also among the pioneers of geometric abstraction. A duo-collage of 1918 constructed of rectangular-shaped luminous colors attached vertically and horizontally like so many bricks is credited to her initial invention. A continual exchange of ideas took place between the two artists throughout their lives. At times their work is quite similar, but there remains an essential difference; Sophie's work always retained a "certain craftlike quality" and was "delicate but precise." While her ideal was always "clarity," Jean was more concerned with the unconscious and the "law of chance."

Although born in Albany, New York, Kay Sage (1898–1963) spent most of her early life in Italy and France, returning to the United States briefly during World War I. With the onset of the Second World War, she returned home again, settling in Connecticut with her husband, the Surrealist painter Yves Tanguy. Their country home became a mecca for many of the artists displaced by the war. Sage was an early abstract artist—at her first exhibit in Milan in 1936, she showed mostly abstractions—but after becoming acquainted with de Chirico's metaphysical paintings and meeting the Surrealists in

Paris the following year, she changed her approach to painting. An early work in the Surrealist mode, *Danger, Construction Ahead* (1940) is closer to Tanguy than her later architectural vistas. At their joint retrospective at the Wadsworth Atheneum in 1954, the couple's separate styles became apparent. Whereas Tanguy's paintings were concerned with organic, enigmatic forms in "moonscapes," Sage created an architecture of "poetic shelters." (Gloria Feman Orenstein writes of Lenora Carrington, Merit Oppenheim, Dorothea Tanning, and others in her article, "Women of Surrealism," in chapter 4 of this book. Ed.)

In the years prior to World War I, most American artists were still entrenched in a nineteenth century aesthetic. The renegades who organized "The Eight" in 1908 were radical only in their choice of subject matter—the poor, the urban environment. (There were no women associated with "The Eight.") A few artists who had studied abroad, among them Marguerite Thompson Zorach (1887–1968), were aware of the turmoil that was occurring in European art circles and introduced the styles to a hostile public. Zorach's Fauvist interpretations of the Sierra mountains, such as *Man Among the Redwoods* (1912), are statements of that aesthetic drawn from an American landscape. Most of what is known about Marguerite Thompson Zorach comes from the loving memoir written by her husband of fifty-four years, the sculptor William Zorach. Like the Delaunays and Arps, the Zorachs had a supportive, noncompetitive relationship. Each was the other's most enthusiastic advocate and most respected critic. New ideas were explored simultaneously; the couple exhibited together, often collaborated on the same project, and shared in the management of the household and in the raising of the children. Until 1920, when William decided to concentrate on sculpture and Marguerite on tapestries, there was also a similarity in the work they produced. In the years between 1912 and 1920, they were considered artists of equal merit, but after she adopted the more "feminine" medium (with which she was commercially successful), his reputation soared while hers diminished. It was only while engaged in research for a *catalogue raisonné* on William Zorach in the early 1970s that Roberta K. Tarbell discovered the cache of paintings that Marguerite had rolled up for storage sixty years earlier.[12]

The international section of the 1913 New York Armory Show created an uproar; the innovations challenged the complacency of many American artists and changed the direction of their work. However, during the 1920s and 1930s many became disenchanted with European art styles and went back to their roots to create an art that glorified the best of an American past that was slowly disappearing. This movement, known as Regionalism, along with the politically motivated Social Protest or Social Realist art, dominated the American art scene during the Depression years.

Isabel Bishop (b.1902), along with Kenneth Hayes Miller, her former teacher, and Reginald Marsh, first achieved celebrity in the 1930s as a kind of Urban Regionalist. She was also linked to the Social Realists, but her art protests nothing. She does not appeal to the viewer's sympathy—her derelicts and working people are neither picturesque nor depressed figures. Even the most downtrodden are often protrayed in a small amount of triumph—a man meeting a girl, a bum getting a free drink on a hot day, a derelict discovering a cigarette butt, two shop girls sharing a snapshot, gossip, or food. Although she admits that the "female nude is an unlikely subject for a female artist," the nude female has formed a major part of Bishop's *oeuvre*. According to the artist, it can "have the summing up possibility of a metaphor."[13] Although Bishop does not consciously attempt to create a "feminine" vision, she believes that her work must be feminine since it is the product of a female sensibility.

Artists were included in the various New Deal programs implemented to find work for the unemployed during the Depression. The programs reflected the fiercely egalitarian spirit of the Roosevelt years, and of the artists receiving aid, 41 percent were women. Among the several who can be identified as Social Realists were Marion Greenwood (1909–1970), Elizabeth Olds (b.1919), Minna Citron (b.1896), Doris Lee (b.1901), Concetta Scaravaglione (1900–1975), and Lucienne Bloch (b.1909). Greenwood was a muralist who had previously worked with José Orozco and Diego Rivera in Mexico. During World War II she was the only woman appointed an official artist-correspondent. Olds, the first woman to be awarded a Guggenheim Fellowship (1926–27), worked in the graphics division developing serigraphy as a fine art. Concerned with social issues, she sought a way to create fine prints for mass production. Citron first taught painting and then worked as a muralist in the Tennessee Valley. Lee, a creator of charming scenes of domestic rural life, was active in the Artists Congress. Scaravaglione's massive sculptures can still be seen in various federal buildings around the country. Lucienne Bloch's frescoes describing the *Cycle of a Woman's Life* for the House of Detention for Women, New York, have been destroyed.[14]

From the confluence of innovative European artists displaced by World War II and the younger, well-trained American painters already sophisticated in the history of modern art emerged a new school of painting. Abstract Expressionism was part of the existential movement that swept Europe after the holocaust of war. The disaffection with public institutions and public solutions to world problems caused a general turning inward to personal expressions in art and other media. The women of the first generation of Abstract Expressionism, Lee Krasner and Elaine Fried de Kooning, were the wives of its leaders, Jackson Pollock and Willem de Kooning, and existed for many years in their shadows. The women of the "second generation," Helen Frankenthaler, Joan Mitchell, and Grace Hartigan, achieved fame independently. Although it has been labeled a "macho" movement, Abstract Expressionism introduced to the American public the first group of female "superstars" in the visual arts. (However, since they were all photogenic, more attention was given to their elegant looks and life-styles than to their paintings.)

Lee Krasner (b.1908) had already won accolades from Mondrian and Hofmann and was an active exhibitor with the American Abstract Artists, the group organized to introduce abstract art to the American public, when she met Jackson Pollock. Surprised that there was an American painter unknown to her who could paint with such power (they were both among the exhibitors at a 1942 show of American and French painting), Krasner immediately visited his studio. When she looked at Pollock's work, she later wrote, she "almost died." When he saw her paintings, he too was generous with praise. They became each other's best critics and supporters until Pollock's death 14 years later. Krasner introduced Pollock to the critics and collectors who began to promote his work. Ironically, Krasner existed in Pollock's shadow for years and only recently has the extent of her talent been recognized. According to B. F. Friedman, Pollock's biographer, although she "had confidence in the quality of her own work, she never thought of it in the same terms as those in which she thought of Jackson's." When Friedman first visited Lee and Jackson, he did not know that "Mrs. Pollock" was a painter. She was known as "the great man's wife."[15] Krasner rejects this image of herself. When queried as to why she did not promote her work along with Jackson's, the artist responded bluntly: "I couldn't run out and do a one-woman job on the sexist aspects of the art world, continue my painting, and stay in the role I was in as Mrs. Pollock. . . . What I considered important was that I was able to work and other things would have to take their turn."[16] Krasner's earliest paintings show the influence of Picasso and Matisse. In the 1940s she began developing her "little images" or hieroglyphic paintings, composed of small, self-contained geometric forms, each with a different linear pattern that turns in on itself. It is only in the first paintings that Krasner did after the death of her husband—mural-sized works such as *The Seasons* and *The Eye is the First Circle*—that his influence is evident.

Elaine Fried (b.1920) was a student of Willem de Kooning's. At the time of their meeting (1938) Willem was beginning his series of paintings of women that became an important part of his *oeuvre*. Before exploring the automatism of the Abstract Expressionists, she was recognized as an expert draftswoman. After a year of teaching at the University of New Mexico, she began in 1959 what may be considered her most important body of work—the "Arena" series. *Bull*, from this series, is a 13-foot battleground of reds and oranges. A restless artist, Elaine de Kooning works on several paintings, both portraits and abstractions, at the same time. In portraits, she seeks a characteristic resemblance rather than a photographic likeness. Indeed, one of her most effective portraits has no features, yet the six-foot high likeness of the late poet and art critic Frank O'Hara is instantly recognizable because the artist has captured his peculiar posture, the set of his head, and his languid stance. Elaine de Kooning objects to being classified as a woman artist: "To be put in any category not defined by one's work is to be falsified."[17]

In her first one-woman show in 1951, Grace Hartigan (b.1922) paid homage to two of her heroines, George Sand and George Eliot, by signing her name "George" Hartigan. Because of this, the artist has been accused of using a male name to hide her female identity. After her third one-woman exhibit in 1953, from which the Museum of Modern Art purchased *Persian Jacket*, her reputation was secured. For a brief period she worked in a completely nonobjective manner, but the image persisted on reappearing. Landscape is her *métier*; in the 1950s it was the urban, man-made landscape, the billboards and clashing traffic of the highways, or the sights and sounds of the urban marketplace. The paintings of the 1970s, such as *Summer to Fall*, pay homage to birds, leaves, and flowers and may reflect the artist's change of environment. She has left New York (as has Joan Mitchell) and now lives in the Baltimore suburbs.

Although Joan Mitchell (b.1926) is traditionally classified as a second generation Abstract Expressionist, she rejects the category, claiming her work is not "autobiographical or emotionally self-expressive. It comes from and is about landscape, not about me."[18] When Mitchell arrived in New York in 1950, the art world was in ferment. After settling in a Greenwich Village studio, she became part of the local scene, attending lectures at The Club and frequenting the Cedars Tavern. Invited to exhibit in 1951 in the now historic Ninth Street Show, where Abstract Expressionism was introduced in force to the art world, Mitchell has been exhibiting at respectable intervals ever since; her first one-woman show was also held in 1951. The artist is convinced that her self-deprecation about being a woman during a decidedly masculine phase of American art ultimately served her well. Although at first it was difficult to find a gallery, "I had it easier because I never even thought that I could be in the major competition, being female."[19] The gestures of Mitchell's early New York paintings are built up with the dense horizontals and verticals of the city. In contrast, those painted from remembered vistas of her travels to Mexico or the Midwest, or from her visits to Long Island, are more open and expansive. Since 1969 the artist has lived in Vétheuil, a suburb of Paris, on a compound that adjoins that in which Monet once lived and worked. The paintings inspired by the fields and gardens that surround her home, such as the huge triptych of 1973, *Clearing*, are filled with the light, color, and exuberance of the late Monets.

On the occasion of Helen Frankenthaler's (b.1928) one-woman exhibit at the Whitney Museum of American Art in 1969, Eugene Goossen, in his catalog essay, paid her an extraordinary tribute: "The recent history of American painting would have been notably different without her presence, and the absence of her work would deprive us of any number of major paintings upon which the premises of contemporary art rely."[20] When Frankenthaler completed her art studies at Bennington College, Pollock and de Kooning were the reigning forces in American art, and when her mentor, the art critic Clement Greenberg, brought her to Pollock's studio, she succumbed to the power of Pollock—"With de Kooning you could assimilate and copy; (but) Pollock instead opened up what one's own inventiveness could take off from." From the work of Pollock and the analysis of Greenberg, Frankenthaler began to develop her own sense of technique and imagery. She began working on the floor, pouring and staining great fields of unsized canvas, creating a unity of image and surface. Colors, shapes, and lines that appear to be in deep space are actually resting next to each other: "Her goal . . . has been the definition of space through a parity of color, line, and area."[21] Frankenthaler's first successful painting in the stained technique, *Mountain and Sea* (1952), is remarkable in that it showed both her sources and subsequent searchings. In it can be seen Gorky's and de Kooning's biomorphism as well as the playfulness and lyricism of Kandinsky's improvisations. It evokes the spirit of landscape, as do many of her subsequent paintings.

Mountain and Sea had a profound effect on the Washington artists Morris Louis and Kenneth Noland. As Greenberg explained, when Louis saw the painting, he "change[d] his direction abruptly."[22] Frankenthaler continues to work and grow, exploring certain themes until a new one emerges, continually challenging herself within the technique she has made her personal signature. After the Whitney show, her public expanded, and Frankenthaler became the "mother" to a generation of lyrical abstractionists rebelling against the hard-edged geometry of the Minimalist aesthetic then dominating the New York art world.

Women artists have continued to respond to the challenge and ferment within the art world. As innovators as well as followers, they have participated in all the important movements of the later twentieth century.

NOTES

1. From her obituary, *Arts Magazine* (January 1956): 34.
2. Arthur A. Cohen, *Sonia Delaunay* (New York: Harry N. Abrams, 1975), p. 45.

3. Alexander Watt, "Visages d'Artistes: Vieira da Silva," *Studio* (May 1961): 172.

4. Although Käthe Kollwitz has frequently been pigeonholed by art historians within the German Expressionist category, she dismissed their work as "pure studio art" and completely irrelevant to the needs of the people to whom she devoted her life.

5. Lisolette Erlanger Glozer, "Gabriele Münter: A Lesser Life?" *Feminist Art Journal* (Winter 1974–75): 11.

6. Juliane Roh, "Marianne von Werefkin," *Kunst und Das Schoene Heim* (December 1959): 425–455.

7. John Bowlt, ed., *Russian Art of the Avant Garde: Theory and Criticism* (New York: Viking, 1976), p. 93.

8. Camilla Gray, *The Great Experiment: Russian Art 1863–1922* (New York: Harry Abrams, 1962), pp. 69–70.

9. Bowlt, *Russian Art of the Avant Garde,* p. 148.

10. Gloria Feman Orenstein, "Women of Surrealism," reprinted in chapter 4 in this book.

11. Herbert Read, *The Art of Jean Arp* (New York: Harry N. Abrams, 1968), p. 34. (As with many married women artists, the researcher has to refer to biographies of the husband to find material on the wife.)

12. See William Zorach, *Art is My Life* (New York: World, 1967)' and Roberta K. Tarbell, *Marguerite Zorach: The Early Years, 1908–1920* (Washington, D.C.: Smithsonian Institution, December 7, 1973–February 3, 1974).

13. Karl Lunde, *Isabel Bishop* (New York: Harry N. Abrams, 1925), p. 60.

14. Most of this material was culled from 7 *American Women: The Depression Decade* (Vassar College Art Gallery, January 19–March 5, 1976).

15. B. H. Friedman, *Jackson Pollock* (New York: McGraw Hill, 1972), pp. 220–221, 87.

16. Quoted in Cindy Nemser, "The Indomitable Lee Krasner," *Feminist Art Journal* (Spring 1975): 7.

17. Elaine de Kooning and Rosalyn Drexler, *Art and Sexual Politics,* eds. Thomas Hess and Elizabeth Baker (New York: Collier, 1973), p. 57.

18. Quoted in Marcia Tucker, *Joan Mitchell* (New York: Whitney Museum of American Art, March 26–May 5, 1974), pp. 7–8.

19. Ibid., p. 7.

20. Eugene C. Goossen, *Helen Frankenthaler* (New York: Whitney Museum of American Art, 1969), p. 8.

21. Ibid., p. 13.

22. Ibid., p. 9.

4

Women of Surrealism

GLORIA FEMAN ORENSTEIN

The history of the Surrealist movement in art and literature has been frequently analyzed, repeatedly documented, but only partially told. We are all now familiar with the radically innovative ideas introduced by André Breton in his *Surrealist Manifestos* of 1924 and 1929 and the individual works of such writers as Aragon, Eluard, Artaud, Desnos, and Péret and of painters such as Ernst, Dali, Tanguy, Miro, Lam, Magritte, Matta, and countless others whose genius and vision contributed to opening a new chapter in twentieth century art history. Yet this history remains incomplete until the individual works of such women artists as Léonor Fini, Leonora Carrington, Meret Oppenheim, Toyen, Remedios Varo, Elena Garro, Joyce Mansour, Jane Graverol, Dorothea Tanning, and many others become accessible on an international scale through exhibitions, monographic studies, and translations and until their own interpretations of the spirit, themes, and techniques of Surrealism are given their rightful place alongside the canons of thought that until now have been the only official version we have had of the meaning and importance of Surrealism.

The Surrealists' quest was for total knowledge. It was an endeavor to unify all areas of human experience and to bring to light the discoveries made in the vast domain of human consciousness that logic and abstract thought do not even begin to encompass. Through exploration of the dream, trance states, simulated states of insanity, and through the techniques of games, automatic writing, and painting, as well as an investigation of many branches of the occult such as alchemy, magic, and telepathy, the Surrealists sought to bring to this world a vision of a vaster reality in which the subjective and objective aspects of human experience would no longer be dissociated.

Breton defined his ultimate goal most precisely in his *Second Manifesto of Surrealism* when he stated that: "There is every reason to believe that there exists a certain point in the mind at which life and death, real and imaginary, past and future, communicable and incommunicable, high and low, cease to be perceived in terms of contradiction. Surrealist activity would be searched in vain for a motive other than the hope to determine this point."[1]

Surrealism can be credited with having made the strongest case for releasing art from all constraints and for recognizing the validity of utilizing the powers of the imagination and intuition as instruments of knowledge and in the search to expand the sources of human experience and to enrich the vocabulary of the communicable. Yet, despite all this, Surrealism would be inadequately described if the love relationship between man and woman were omitted from our definition. For, above and beyond the ideal of total revolution both in art and in life, the Surrealists were committed to *love* as a means of creation, as a form of artistic expression, and as a path towards revelation. "The true Revolution for the Surrealists," writes Maurice Nadeau in his *History of Surrealism*, "is the victory of desire."[2] In the *Second Manifesto of Surrealism* Breton states: "The problem of woman is all that is marvelous and troubling in the world. And it is so to the very degree to which a noncorrupted man must be able to put his faith not only in Revolution, *but even more so in love*. . . . Yes, I believe, and have always believed that renouncing love, whether authorized or not on any ideological pretext is one of the rare inexpiable crimes that a man gifted with any intelligence can commit in his lifetime."[3] Further on, in his *Prologmena to a 3rd Manifesto,* he continues: "The problem of the relationship between man and woman must be totally revised without a trace of hypocrisy . . ."[4] Finally, in *Arcane 17,* Breton makes his powerful plea for a total reevaluation of the role of women when he says: "The time should have come to make the ideas of woman prevail at the expense of those of men . . . to declare oneself in art unequivocally against man and for woman. . . . The woman-child. Art should be systematically preparing for her accession to the whole empire of perceptible things."[5]

The role of woman in Surrealism is equivocal, ambiguous, and fraught with contradictions. It is worthwhile to consider some of the conflicting aspects of the role of woman in the movement as defined by the men in order to understand the kinds of obstacles that were encountered by the Surrealist women, both artists and writers, who ultimately forged their own autonomous identities above and beyond the restricting confines of any of these definitions. Without negating the high esteem in which the men held woman, and without denying the authenticity and sincerity of their exaltation of her, it is still necessary to take a closer look at the exact nature of the woman they admired in order to understand the degree to which each of the women we will discuss managed to transcend the limitations of the role imposed upon her, while, at the same time, preserving the qualities with which she was uniquely endowed. Breton, in *Arcane 17* exalts the *Femme-Enfant,* the Woman-Child, precisely because she incarnates a purity, a naivete, and innocence which, he feels, puts her in closer contact with her unconscious. She is spontaneous, uncorrupted by logic or reason, and therefore closer to the dream and to intuitive knowledge. According to Benjamin Péret, the totally virile man would be naturally attracted to the *Femme-Enfant* because she would complement his nature trait for trait. She bears within her the seed of Sublime Love, but it is only man who can reveal this love to her and make it blossom. The ambiguity of this position relates to the fact that while it calls for the ideas of woman to prevail over those of men, it elevates the triumph of a kind of woman who is, in fact, totally dependent upon man for the full realization of her own identity. Not only does this definition deprive woman of the right to growth and development by imprisoning her in a world of childhood, but it also implies that maturity would mean abandoning the unique powers with which she is gifted and intimates that a mature woman is not capable of making a valid contribution to creative art because her uniqueness is linked to her immaturity. The women artists of the Surrealist movement had to succeed not only in outgrowing the stereotypes of the *Femme-Enfant,* but also in proving that the masculine system of values was not the necessary concomitant of autonomy. They had to maintain their independent identity and create their own artistic worlds without sacrificing their ability to penetrate the realm of the imagination or to capture the magical imagery of the dream.

The ideal of the restitution of the Primordial Androgyne was also espoused by the Surrealists, for it represented the desire to return to a primitive unity or harmony of opposites, which was not only an essential element of their search for totality, but also the basis for their definition of Sublime Love. In this androgynous union, ideally, the man would realize his feminine counterpart in woman and the woman would seek her masculine double in man, so that in each other they would experience totality. Although the position might be defended theoretically, in practice it was deformed in favor of the male. Robert Benayoun, in his book *Erotique du Surréalisme*, maintains that while the Surrealists exalated *la femme*, they did not equally revere *les femmes*. He also explains that this androgynous state of totality to which they aspired was, in reality, a relation of inequality. He cites another contemporary Surrealist, Gérard Legrand, to corroborate his interpretation. Legrand writes: "One would be tempted to say that alongside of the androgynous state of complementary partners there is outlined the androgynous state of supplementary partners in the geometrical sense of the term. Here the woman would play the role, from the man's point of view, of that 'drop of being' poured into an already saturated solution that would transform it into crystal."[6] Man is thus defined as that almost totally perfect being who lacks only one small drop of essence to complete his perfection. Woman is merely the subordinate supplement to man's nature, rather than his equal and complementary counterpart. Not only does this definition render woman inferior to man, but even if it did grant her equal status, the concept of the androgynous union works against autonomy for both partners, because it makes them totally dependent upon each other for self-realization. In proving that Sublime Love was not necessarily in contradiction with independence, the Surrealist woman had to prove that the ideal of the androgyne could also mean the unification of the masculine and feminine principles within a single individual.

Benjamin Péret felt that man might also achieve Sublime Love through union with *La Femme Fatale*, for she was a revolutionary muse, one who inspired subversion, antisocial action, violence, despair, and revolt against order. However, since *La Femme Fatale* had so often driven poets and artists to the brink of suicide, she was viewed more as a potential threat and danger. Ultimately, it was only *La Femme-Enfant* who could save man, according to Péret. The Surrealist woman as artist had to show that individual autonomy was as necessary for creativity as was Love and that the two were not mutually exclusive.

From what we have seen thus far, it is obvious that the role of woman in Surrealism was clearly molded by the men who led the movement and who bestowed an identity on woman that suited the particular needs of their own artistic inspiration.

Simone de Beauvoir in *The Second Sex* makes a critique of Breton's ideal of Reciprocal Love because it does not bring up the question of woman's private destiny apart from that of man. She makes the observation that for the Surrealists woman did not represent the conventional "sex object," but rather the more unconventional "Surrealist Object." In writing about the Surrealist woman as defined by Breton, she says: "This unique woman, at once carnal and artificial, natural and human, casts the same spell as the equivocal objects dear to the Surrealists: she is the spoon-shoe, the table-wolf, the marble-sugar that the poet finds at the flea market or invents in a dream; she shares in the secret of familiar objects suddenly revealed in their true nature, and in the secret of plants and stones. She is all things."[7]

This discussion brings us to a consideration of the very first *drame surréaliste*, a pre-Surrealist play *The Breasts of Tiresias* by Apollinaire, for it is here that the basic ambivalence about the role of woman in Surrealism is first encountered. It is quite ironic that Appollinaire's heroine, Thérèse, turns out to be a clairvoyante just when she is released from the traditional demands of the conventional feminine role, because the play was really meant to be a satire on feminism. In Apollinaire's play, for which the term *Surréaliste* was initially coined, Thérèse, after renouncing the role of childbearer and housewife, is magically transformed into Tiresias, the Seer. It is her husband who then takes on the task of child-rearing in her place. Oddly enough, although she is supposed to be ridiculous, her words resound with total familiarity today, for they could be the very words of the feminists of the 1970s for whom little has changed since Thérèse protested:

> No Mister husband
> You won't make me do what you want
> I'm a feminist, and I do not recognize the authority of men
> Besides, I want to do as I please
> Men have been doing what they want long enough
>
> ———————
>
> No Mister husband, you won't give me orders
> Because you made love to me in Connecticut
> Doesn't mean I have to cook for you in Zanzibar[8]

The play, written from a man's point of view, shows the concept of women's liberation to be preposterous. Yet the most interesting aspect of the play is that by giving up the conventional woman's role and by demanding power and autonomy, Thérèse is metamorphosed into an androgynous being and acquires the psychic powers of a clairvoyante. The Surrealists have always associated the role of woman with that of sorceress, diviner, and seer, but never has it been so evident that these powers are directly linked to her emancipation from a subservient position. It is obvious that Apollinaire has inadvertently proved that woman is as capable of being the creative source of magical transformations of reality as man, once she becomes autonomous, and that she is traditionally rendered ineffectual by the restrictions placed upon her by her role. He has also proved that liberation and independence do not imply the sacrifice of these unique psychic powers or of contact with the unconscious, but that, on the contrary, they foster the unfolding, the discovery, and the development of them.

It is against this background that we can now appreciate more readily why the subject matter of the paintings and writings of the women of Surrealism is largely dominated by the theme of Woman as Subject, rather than as Object. Surrealist women have long been involved in a search for their own definition of their role and have been probing the symbolism related to the Feminine Archetype in order to postulate the attributes of this emerging identity: woman as Goddess, as The Great Mother, as the Alchemist, as the Spinner and Weaver of the destinies of men, and above all as Creator, Spiritual Guide, and Visionary. She is ultimately the *Magna Mater* not the *Femme-Enfant*.

Léonor Fini is one of the artists who was always supremely conscious of the problems involved in woman's sacrifice of her creative autonomy. Although a close friend of all the Surrealists, she never attended group meetings, because she insisted on maintaining her independence. However, she has always participated in their group shows. She arrived in Paris from Italy in 1935 and exhibited with the Surrealists at their International Exposition in London in 1936. Her first New York show was held at the Julian Levy Gallery in 1938. Her works were presented by de Chirico and Paul Eluard. Since then she has had exhibitions in Paris, New York, Rome, and Switzerland, has done the decors for plays by Pirandello, Dumas Fils, Gracq,

Racine, and Oscar Wilde, and has illustrated the tales of Edgar Allan Poe and the texts of Audiberti, Béalu, Cocteau, André Pieyre de Mandiargues, Lise de Harme, and Francis Ponge.

I had the privilege of meeting Léonor Fini and discussing the nature of her imagery with her. She told me that she works directly from the unconscious, but that her intuition leads her to the discovery of archetypal symbols that are alchemically correct. In the series of paintings "The Guardian of the Phoenixes" and "The Guardian with the Red Egg," her imagery, which had been intuited, turned out to have precise alchemical significance. The Egg is the name of the alchemical vessel of transformation of the alchemist's oven. It is the vessel in which spiritual transformation transpires, and as the symbol of the female, it indicates that woman is also the universal vessel of creative, spiritual rebirth. The conclusion of the alchemical process is the production of the philosopher's stone, which is red and represents the unification of opposites and the integration of the conscious with the unconscious. It is a symbol of totality. When linked with the phoenix (who is reborn from his own ashes) as it is in her paintings, it suggests a parallel between alchemical transmutation and spiritual creation. Léonor Fini presents the Alchemist as woman and identifies the womb as the alchemistic retort in *La Dame Ovale*, whose title is inspired by Leonora Carrington's book of short stories. *The Spinners* and *The Seamstress* also depict the archetypal feminine principle of the Great Mother, who weaves the web of new life as she creates the fabric of the child within her body. Her feminine sphinxes such as *Sphinx Amalburgia, Sphinx Philagria* and *Pettit Sphinx Gardien* posit woman as the embodiment of the total life enigma and of the universal mystery. Marcel Brion in his study *Léonor Fini et Son Oeuvre* elucidates the meaning of the images of skulls and skeletons in her paintings.[9] According to Brion, they represent the most durable and interior part of the body—its mineral essence. In this sense they are the objective correlatives of the psychic interior, or the spiritual essense, which is the theme of most of her work. When this theme is associated with that of the sphinx, it conveys the durable permanence and mystery of the psychic world, which is ultimately our only eternal essence.

Léonor Fini's world is a matriarchy. Her love of cats in both her paintings and her life is partially related to worship of The Goddess, for in Egypt the cat was linked with the moon and sacred to the

Goddesses Isis and Bast. Bast was, in fact, a cat-headed Goddess. The cat also evokes the world of sorcery and witchcraft.

Yet, Léonor Fini's women are often unexpectedly bald, for she leans towards the ideal of the Androgyne. She is in favor of a world that does not worship virility. She has said about her painting *Le Fait Accompli*, where "in a cafe full of girls the outline of a man is drawn on the ground in chalk in the same way that police mark out the position of a dead body,"[10] that: "It is in this outline that the witch rebels against all the social opacity of men. . . . I am in favour of a world where there is little or no sex distinction."[11] This theme is echoed in *Capital Punishment*, which is a symbolic castration. In *Morgenstunde* the masculine presence is intrusive and threatening. Her universe depicts love of humanity in its most ideal and, at the same time, in its most sensual aspects. This does not exclude the physical love of women for each other. *Phaebus Asleep, The Conversation, Along the Way,* and many other paintings of recent date explore frankly and openly the theme of lesbianism with lyricism and sensuality. Léonor Fini was a precursor of the women's movement in her conscious and intelligent exploration of themes relating to woman's identity in her art and in her life. By delving into the female psyche to unlock the symbols that the unconscious reveals, she has shown that individual autonomy enhances woman's intuitive contact with her inner being, that, in fact, the ideal of the *Femme-Enfant* would have been detrimental to the discovery of a certain kind of knowledge that only experience and maturity can interpret and communicate in art.

Léonor Fini's painting *La Chambre Noire* (1939) includes a full portrait of Leonora Carrington (standing), a dear friend of hers, and another Surrealist artist who has extended her interest in the theme of woman in her art to a commitment to women in life by becoming one of the originators and leaders of the feminist movement in Mexico.

Leonora Carrington's art is born of a deep inner necessity to refine our perception of that point referred to by Breton at which contradictions cease to exist, by putting us in contact with the multiple realms and levels of our experience through a visionary process. In order for us to evolve, we must become seers of the unknown. Carrington's art thus probes and delves into the unexplored and unchartered vistas of the imagination, searching for the new horizons that we discover when we are in touch with our psychic powers and with a fuller knowledge of our interior and the beings both mythical and archetypal that inhabit it.

She was born in Lancashire, England, in 1917, and studied art in England, Italy, and France. Rebelling against her family, who considered it anathema for a woman to become an artist, Carrington left home at 18 and went to Paris to live and paint in freedom. There she was a student of Amédée Ozenfant and was soon introduced to the Surrealist artists and writers with whom she has worked closely ever since her first participation in the International Surrealist Exhibition of 1938 in Paris.

Her name became associated with that of Max Ernst with whom she lived in France for several years until he was taken prisoner in 1940. Her book of short stories, *La Dame Ovale*, was illustrated by Ernst and published in Paris in 1939. Its Spanish translation was published in Mexico in 1965.

During the war she fled to seek refuge in Spain, where she suffered a mental breakdown and was interned in a psychiatric hospital in Santander. The torment and anguish of this experience as well as the incredibly rich universe of oneiric, mythic, and visionary imagery that emerged from this psychic voyage inward were recaptured in her narrative *Down Below*, which was first published in the Surrealist review, *VVV*, in February 1944.[12] Intuitive knowledge of the need for woman to be given her rightful place in our religious and human systems was revealed to her within the context of this experience. In *Down Below* she relates:

> I felt that through the agency of the Sun I was an androgyne, the Moon, the Holy Ghost, a gypsy, an acrobat, Leonora Carrington, and a woman. I was also destined to be, later, Elizabeth of England. I was she who revealed religions and bore on her shoulders the freedom and the sins of the earth changed into knowledge, the union of Man and Woman with God and the Cosmos, all equal between them. . . . The son was the Sun and I the Moon, an essential element of the Trinity, with the microscopic knowledge of the earth, its plants and creatures. I knew that Christ was dead and done for and that I had to take His place, because the Trinity minus a woman and microscopic knowledge, had become dry and incomplete. Christ was replaced by the Sun. I was Christ on earth in the person of the Holy Ghost.[13]

Carrington's vision is both psychologically and alchemically precise. The symbolism of the Holy Ghost, according to Erich
Neumann's study *The Great Mother*, represents alchemically the supreme spiritual principle and psychologically the archetype of the
Great Mother. The experience thus symbolically signifies the need
to recognize and reintegrate the supreme value of the spiritual wisdom inherent in the feminine principle as a prerequisite for individual growth, for personal transformation, and for human evolution.

In the early 1940s she made her way to the United States and
there joined the other self-exiled Surrealist artists; she participated
in their exhibitions and contributed to the Surrealist reviews, *View*
and *VVV*, which originated in New York. In 1942 she moved to
Mexico and has lived there ever since. She is married and the mother
of two grown sons.

Carrington's fantastic mural *El Mundo Mágico de los Mayas*[14] can be
seen in the Chiapas exhibit of the Museo Nacional de Antropologia
in Mexico City. It is based upon her observations made during several extended visits to Chiapas, where she gained an intimate
knowledge of the people who are today the descendants of the
Mayas. Her mural is also a visual interpretation of the imagery of the
Popol Vuh, which is the Mayan Bible. It combines an imaginative
depiction of the magical beliefs of Chiapas culture with the legen-
dary, mythical, and marvelous elements of Mayan civilization in a
poetic evocation, which brings out the affinity between the magical
beliefs of the Mayas and those of the Surrealists. According to Mayan
tradition, man has two souls—one immortal, which survives him
after death and passes on to the other world; the other mortal, which
takes the form of an animal and lives in the mountains. Knowledge of
one's mortal soul (or souls, for some men had several) was revealed
during sleep through the dream. Thus, for both the Mayans and the
Surrealists, the oneiric element that provides the link between our
sleeping and waking lives is the key to discovery of knowledge about
that point at which our subjective and objective experiences are unified in a vaster totality.

Carrington's most important personal exhibitions, apart from the
International Surrealist Exhibitions from 1938 to the present, in-
clude her first American show at the Pierre Matisse Gallery in New
York in 1948, various shows in Mexico City, a retrospective at the
Museo Nacional de Arte Moderno in Mexico in 1960, and a retro-

spective at the Instituto Anglo-Mexicano de Cultura in June 1965. She also had an important exhibition at the IX Bienal de Sao Paulo in Brazil in 1967.

Her paintings attest to her deep involvement in the study of alchemy, magic, Tibetan Tantrism, Zen, the Kabbalah, and other domains of the occult. She has spent many years in a Gurdjieff group, has studied with Suzuki and other Zen masters, and has lived with the Tibetans in Canada studying the Tantra. She is also greatly influenced by the themes and imagery of fairy tales, nursery rhymes, and mythology.

In his *Second Manifesto of Surrealism*, André Breton observed that Surrealist research and alchemical research had analogous goals. For the alchemist, the process of transforming base metals into gold was concomitant with another transformation—that of the alchemist himself, towards the enoblement of his soul in his quest for spiritual enlightenment. In this sense, all of Carrington's paintings are an alchemical process in which visionary knowledge is revealed and through which psychic evolution can transpire.

A watercolor *The Godmother* is directly inspired by the nursery rhyme "Goosey Gossey Gander, Whither dost thou wander?" The query immediately opens the door to speculation about the nature of the worlds we inhabit. Suddenly the invisible becomes manifest. The central being with the invisible face shows no differentiation between the five senses, and it also contains the seventh. It is blue for the earth, (the blue planet), for the sky; it is Baraka, the life essence, and Prana. Anti-being is contrasted with Being in the image of the beasts chasing each other in the endless karmic circle around the Being whose black monkey face is the Black Sun. It is said that in order to reach true illumination, one must see through the Black Sun. This symbolism parallels the alchemical imagery of transforming black primal matter into gold.

In *The Lepidopterus* and *The Butterfly People Eating a Meal* the Black Swans are suggested by the refrain of the bards' song, "I am the Black Swan, Queen of them all." Their food is red, for the Britons of the Stone Age painted the food for the dead red. A meditation on the meaning of the song releases all the latent imagery revealing the deeper significance of the words. For the Black Swan is also the secret sign of The Goddess of the Old Religion to which all women belong. The Swan is being fed food for the dead because the Old

Religion has been buried, but by eating this food, it is being revived
and the power of The Goddess is being resurrected. The Black Swan
is also equivalent to the Black Sun through which enlightenment is
attained. The egg of the Black Swan is the philosopher's stone.

Who Art Thou Pale Face? represents a chimera or fantastic being
who has just laid an egg. The Being's black sun face is located in its
solar plexus, which represents the essential self. It is invisible. The
egg signifies mythological procreation, a new birth, the piercing
through to a new dimension, and the philosopher's stone.

Her Women's Liberation poster specifically rejects the traditional
Biblical interpretation of Eve because woman's procreative powers
are negated. By describing Eve as born of Adam, the Bible relegates
woman to a position that is both inferior and subservient to that of
man. Carrington's poster depicts the rising of the new woman or the
goddess resurrected. She is identified with the power of the serpent
or the concept of Kundalini. Through Yoga, this power or energy
rises up through the chakras of the body until it reaches the third eye
corresponding to illumination. The new woman (on the right), who
through this psychic evolution attains higher knowledge, returns the
apple to Eve (on the left) and thus refuses to accept the false role that
the Bible conferred upon her. The rise of the new woman is also
concomitant with the reflourishing of Planet Earth through birth
control, which would restrict the size of the human population
so that all species might have a chance to survive. Since the
process of psychic evolution is a kind of interior alchemy, the green
of the poster reminds us of the emerald tablets of Hermes
Trismetistus.

These touchstones to the interpretation of Carrington's paintings,
by pointing out the depth and multidimensionality of her symbolism,
show why her art, which is felt to be so mysterious, is also experienced as being somehow deeply familiar. For she paints the exact
portrait of an archetypal essential and universal self, one that we
encounter in our dreams, our visions, our myths, our legends, and in
our plunges into the territory of the human psyche. Her art is a kind
of magic that while making the invisible visible, also fulfills the Surrealists' desire to make the imaginary real.

Her other written works include the plays *Pénélope*[15] *Une Chemise
de Nuit de Flanelle*[16] and *L'Invention du Môle*[17] and the short stories
"White Rabbits,"[18] "The Sisters,"[19] "La Debutante,"[20] "L'Homme

Neutre,"[21] "Waiting,"[22] "The Seventh Horse,"[23] and "Et In Bellicus Medicalis Lunarum."[24] Her unpublished works include a recent novel and short stories for children.

As stage designer she has done the sets and costumes for the Mexican productions of Ionesco's *Exit The King*, Shakespeare's *The Tempest*, Octavio Paz's *Rapaccini's Daughter*, and her own play *Pénélope*, which was directed by Alexandro Jodorowsky. She has also collaborated with Jodorowsky on a play *The Blue Prince*. Jodorowsky is familiar to film audiences as the director of *El Topo*.

The female symbol of the egg is prevalent in both her paintings and her plays. However, as the egg is also the name of the alchemist's oven, in her work this symbol has a double meaning. For, when the symbol of woman is identified with that of alchemical transformation, it suggests that in woman lies the hope for the creation of a new race of humankind.

In a recent unpublished play "Opus Siniestrus," the egg is used in this way. The play, which is a Surrealist opera-fable for our planet, is a total-theatre spectacle expressing a radical protest against the destructive aspects of contemporary civilization and a plea for the redirection of our psychic energies towards more humanitarian goals. Carrington's belief in the need for women to undertake the task of interior evolution and psychic liberation extends the original formulation of the goals of the Surrealist movement, which were "to transform the world, change life, and remake from scratch human understanding," and gives them renewed value within the context of a more complete commitment to the total transformation of humankind.

No discussion of Leonora Carrington's work would be complete if it failed to mention her sense of humor. She would never have written about herself as I have done. In fact, when asked to present an autobiographical sketch for one of her expositions, this is how she depicted her birth:

> In the early part of the latter nineties I was born under curious circumstances, in a Eneahexagram, mathematically. The only person present at my birth was our dear and faithful old fox terrior Boozy, and an X-ray apparatus for sterilizing cows. My mother was away at the time snaring crayfish which then plagued the upper Andes and wrought misery and devastation among the natives, etc."[25]

The charm of Carrington's humor is that while mocking every conceivable human institution and seeing the absurd and the ridiculous in all forms of social and political pomposity, she criticizes everything with a pervading sense of humility and is always the first to find humor in herself, as well. She is one of the few women whose works are included in André Breton's *Anthologie De L'Humour Noir*. Carrington's comic humility comes from the fact that she sees mankind as just one species among many that inhabit our earth. She feels that in a deeper sense we are really sisters and brothers of the plants and animals with whom we share our terrestrial abode, and that we are intimately related to the sun, the moon, and the planets whose celestial courses affect our lives. She firmly believes that we must learn to revere nature in order to permit all forms of life to flourish, not only on our planet but in the entire universe. From this cosmic point of view, our vain pretentions to power over other beings and over all forms of organic and inorganic life are an insane form of suicidal hysteria. Her humor is caustic, satirical, or sardonic because she criticizes the petty gods we worship. But her paintings remind us that true devotion should be reserved for the realm of the human spirit, which has only begun its evolution, and that in terms of what we have yet to learn about human consciousness and our place in the universe, we are like Pithecanthropus or Cro-Magnon Man. We are only beginning to be awakened. Carrington's personality and art express her total commitment and devotion to the development of human faculties to their highest potential. Here is a most inspiring example set for us by an artist whose concerns are truly planetary and universal.

Meret Oppenheim's *Fur-Lined Teacup and Saucer*, originally entitled *Le Déjeuner en Fourrure* is probably the surrealist object that is most familiar to the American public. Born in 1913 in Berlin, Oppenheim spent her childhood in Switzerland and studied at the Ecoles des Arts at Métiers in Bâle. In 1932 she left for Paris to enroll in the Académie de La Grande Chaumiere. In the same year Arp and Giacometti visited her studio and were so impressed with her work that they spoke about her to André Breton. She soon began to exhibit her work with the Surrealists Ernst, Dali, Magritte, Tanguy, Man Ray, and Miro at the Salon des Surindépendents in Paris. In contrast to Léonor Fini, Meret Oppenheim regularly frequented the meetings of Breton's group and identified closely with the Surrealists in her life as well as in her art. She feels very fortunate to have met the Surrealists so early in her career, for they always encouraged her and accepted the kind of work that she was doing. If she didn't frequent them during the last few years before Breton's death, it was merely because their increasingly dogmatic opinions began to bore her. In 1936 she modeled for Man Ray, created the *Fur-Lined Teacup* and her her first personal exposition in Bâle. The catalog of the exhibition was prefaced by Max Ernst. In 1937 she returned to Bâle and experimented in the creation of fantastic furniture, shoes, belts and gloves.

Between 1944 and 1956, approximately, Oppenheim's artistic productivity declined, for she went through a troubling period of questioning and self-doubt that is so familiar to many women artists. Little by little, through a careful Jungian analysis of her dreams, her self-confidence returned, and in 1958 she began to paint, sculpt, and exhibit her works again. In December 1959 she created the inaugural feast at the International Exposition of Surrealism in Paris. The image of a woman served up as a sumptuous meal, an object of beauty to be consumed, combines black humor with a sense of the unexpected in a critique of conventional society and its treatment of women. In 1960 she had an exhibition at the Galerie Schwarz in Milan; in 1965 she took part in the Surrealist Exposition in Brazil, and between 1966 and 1968 had expositions in Paris, Belgrade, New York, Rome, Turin, Cologne, Brussels, and Israel.

When I met her in 1972, she had just opened a studio in Paris. Oppenheim's story is exemplary for women, because it renews our faith in the ability of the creative spirit to reemerge triumphant after a period of self-doubt. As I wrote these words, I received in the mail an announcement of Meret Oppenheim's exhibition at the Galerie Suzanne Visat in Paris. A presentation of her work by Alain Jouffroy praises her renewed ability to provoke and shock us into the discovery of astounding new images by her refusal to conform at any moment to any esthetic formula, moral code, or philosophical system. Oppenheim's sculptures are *objets porteurs d'idée* (objects bearing an idea). Every idea comes to mind dressed in its own form—this is what art is about. Since each new idea presents itself in an entirely new form, it takes a certain amount of time for it to be understood by the contemporary public. The concept of the "multiple" according to Oppenheim, defeats the purpose of the *objet porteur d'idée*. The only

time that the multiple would be justified, would be if the concept of
mass reproduction of the object were inherent in the artist's original
conception. This would be the cause for the design of statuettes of
gods, goddesses, and saints. Oppenheim's newest objects remind us
that the Surrealist spirit of invention is never exhausted.

Remedios Varo was a dear friend of Leonora Carrington and one
Surrealist artist I regret not having been able to meet. She died quite
suddenly and unexpectedly in October 1963. Remedios was born in
1913 in Cataluña, Spain, and came to Paris to flee the Civil War.
There she joined Breton, Ernst and Leonora Carrington and married
the Surrealist poet Benjamin Péret. They settled in Mexico, and
although she separated from him and remarried, she remained permanently in Mexico. After her death the Palacio de Bellas Artes in
Mexico gave her a complete retrospective exhibition in 1964 and
published an important book of her works in 1966.

Intellectually and spiritually Varo seems to resemble Leonora Carrington; both women were engaged in a search for revelations that
would enable them to decipher the occult significance of the great
mysteries. Yet her pictorial universe is almost a scientific explanation
of the marvelous, whereas that of Carrington is a revelation of the
mystery without any attempt at explanation. For Varo, too, woman is
the alchemist. But in *Planta Insumisa*, we see the female scientist
herself rather than her alchemical symbol. In letters to her brother,
Varo has given her own explanation of the imagery in her paintings.
In *Armonia*, for example she explains that the woman is trying to
uncover the invisible thread that unites all things. When all the objects are in their correct places on the metal staff, a harmonious
music will be produced. The figure on the wall represents *le hasard
objectif* or objective chance that intervenes in all discoveries. *The
Flautist* shows her interest in esoteric theories, for the musician is
constructing an octagonal tower of tones that are levitated by the
vibrations produced by the music. The octagonal tower symbolizes
the esoteric theory of octaves. The other half of the tower is
sketched in, because although it is not yet built, it already pre-exists
in the imagination of the creator and is potentially real. The tower
symbolizes ascent in the spiritual sense.

Varo's imagery makes the impossible appear plausible; she reveals
the secret connections between spirit and matter, between the tangible and the intangible, the abstract and concrete. The voyage of

exploration is aided by a fantastic array of vehicles adapted to suit the needs of the voyager, depending on whether it is inner or outer reality that is being explored. In *Vagabundo* the outfit of the vagabond can be hermetically sealed at night. It can even be locked with a key. It comes fully equipped with its own propellers and wheels and is furnished with a library, a living room, and a kitchen, all integral parts of the outfit of this astronaut of psychic spaces. Varo's sense of humor and mystery combined are visible in *Papilla Estelar* and *Encuentro*. She depicts woman as alchemist, voyager, inventor, scientist, explorer, and cartographer of a world that intersects with our own in imperceptible ways. She is searching for the lost key to explain the ties between the worlds that penetrate our own and those worlds we have yet to discover.

Another Surrealist woman of Mexico is the playwright Elena Garro. She was born in Pueblo, Mexico, in 1920 and studied theater at the university. An early marriage to the Surrealist poet Octavio Paz ended in divorce, and she turned to writing for the theater. The female protagonist of most of Garro's plays is in search of *le merveilleux*. Her quest is often thwarted by the male protagonists, whom she must initiate to the sources of the Surreal. Her triumph is seen in *El Encanto Tendájon Mixto*. Here woman represents pure magic and is a guide who initiates men to respond to mystery and enchantment. She leads three men away from *el camino real* to an encounter with a vaster, multidimensional reality. Her little shop reflects the golden rays of the light of the alchemists, for she is the poetess-alchemist, who opens the world of the imagination to men so that they may embark on a voyage towards illumination and inner vision. This new female Surrealist protagonist of Garro's theater revolts against conventional interpretations of banal reality and becomes a seer as a result of claiming her autonomy and independence. Her most important plays on this theme are found in the collection *Un Hogar Sólido*.[26]

Another artist whose work is of capital importance in the history of the Surrealist movement is Toyen (Maria Cernisova). She was born in Prague in 1902 and participated in revolutionary and avantgarde activities in Czechoslovakia. She belonged to the *Devetsil* group and had her first exhibition with them in 1923. From abstract art she evolved to Surrealism and in 1933 was one of the main founders of the Czech Surrealist group whose other artists were Jindrich Styrsky (her husband) and Karel Teige. The group received

Breton and Eluard enthusiastically when they attended the International Surrealist Exhibit in Prague in 1935. In 1938 Toyen had her largest personal exhibition in Prague. During the war her works were banned and in 1947 she left for Paris and eventually renounced her Czech citizenship after the coup d'état in 1948. She is one of the few women artists to whom Breton devoted a chapter in his book *Surrealism and Painting*, which has been published in English.

Toyen's imagery, particularly in her drawings of the '30s and '40s describes the remains of an exterior universe that has been devastated by war and an interior landscape haunted by fear. Opposed to these images of terror are her images of love. Later, themes that are closer to the inspiration of the other Surrealist women, such as *The Clairvoyante* (1958) begin to reappear. Since Toyen comes from Prague, the magical city of the alchemists, it is natural that her titles, such as *At the Golden Wheel*, evoke resonances of the alchemists and their search for illumination.

Bona de Mandiargues has written to me that she recently spoke out against the myth of the *Femme-Enfant* on a program about Surrealism on French radio. She wrote: "It seems to me that every self-respecting artist is born a child—and dies a child; but that the 'woman-child' is merely a doll, a pin-up, or a strip tease artist." De Mandiargues is the niece of the Italian artist Filipo de Pisis. She was born in 1926 in Italy and owes her origins and Surrealist roots to Ferrare, "the metaphysical city" where the esoteric movement was born. When her father died in 1946, de Mandiargues went to live permanently with her uncle, de Pisis. In 1950 she married the Surrealist writer André Pieyre de Mandiargues and began to participate in the meetings of the Surrealist group in Paris. She writes that Surrealism incarnated for her the love that she sought. It was the living symbol of freedom, yet at times denied her personal freedom until she had passed through the trials of initiation that permitted her to freely enter their world. Then she discovered the pleasure of writing dreams, of reading all the writers whom the Surrealists loved, of talking for hours in the cafes with Aragon, Elsa, Eliza, and André Breton, and of loving all the art that the Surrealists loved, particularly the Italian Renaissance; she owes to Surrealism the fact that it permitted her to discover *la clé des champs*.

Writing about the situation of women artists in Europe, her husband, André Pieyre de Mandiargues, has remarked, "in France and

Italy the situation of women in the art world, like in marriage, is still under the domination of a sort of Napoleonic Code." He adds that society "imbued with the principle of masculine superiority treats women in a manner similar to the way witches were formerly treated by the Church. They don't burn women artists," he admits, "they don't torture them either—not in their carnal body at least—but their activity is relegated to a shadowy zone, and they are oppressed with a sort of malediction or more precisely excommunication that separates them from the vaster public which deprives them of the warm approbation that they need as much as all other artists."[27] He is alarmed and terrified by the vast number of women artists who have ended in psychiatric hospitals because their work has been totally ignored.

de Mandiargues' technique evolved from the influence of de Chirico to a use of the technique of *Décalcomanie* created by Ernst and Dominguez. Later, after trips to Egypt and Mexico, she began to explore assemblages, collages, and sewn tableaux, which use bits and pieces of materials and textures to evoke images drawn from the subconscious in a style resembling Art Brut. de Mandiargues' works are done when she feels possessed by a certain frenzy or when she is in a state of intense inspiration. These works seem to emanate vibrations to which certain people respond in mysterious ways. Some of the people who have purchased her paintings have confessed to being drawn to a certain corner of a huge exhibit by her work. They responded to some unknown force within them and were totally unfamiliar with the artist and unable to explain the nature of the power these works exerted over them.

Dorothea Tanning is an American artist from Illinois, whose career became closely linked with that of Max Ernst whom she married after meeting him in New York in the early forties. Her first personal exhibition was held at the Julian Levy Gallery in New York in 1944. Since then her career has blossomed, and her works have evolved from imagery of the dream world depicting solitude, unfulfilled wishes, frustrations of a puritanical childhood and maternity, to abstractionism. Despite the understandingly overwhelming influence of Max Ernst on her early work, she has nevertheless succeeded in creating a personal style and in speaking for women in her art by depicting their desires and anxieties within the Surrealist esthetic. Her paintings *Maternity I* and *Maternity II* show the dehumanization of woman overwhelmed by the consequences of unquestioning acceptance of the dictum that "biology is destiny." Although she is an American artist, the only study I have found of her work is by Alain Bosquet, in French.

Jane Graverol was born in Brussels. Her father was an illustrator (Pre-Raphaelite) and frequented Verlaine and other artists and writers of his time. She attended the Beaux Arts Academy in Brussels and had her first exhibition at 18. In 1948 she wrote to Magritte and in 1949 met the Belgian Surrealists Magritte and Scutenaire. In 1952 she met Paul Nougé, who has written "Portrait d'Après Nature" about her work. She founded a group called *Temps Mêlés* in collaboration with André Blavier, and since 1952 they have been publishing the review *Temps Mêlés*. Her main influences have been those of Magritte, Nougé, and Marcel Marien. She combines a fine sense of humor with a kind of melancholic nostalgia within the Surrealistic vein of the *insolite*. She painted the famous tableau *La Goutte d'Eau*, which is at the Musée de Beaux Arts in Liege and is a group portrait of the principal Belgian Surrealist writers and artists. Her most important personal exhibitions have been in Holland ('57), Leopoldville ('57), Buenos Aires ('58), Geneva ('61), Nassau ('63), Washington ('63), and throughout Belgium.

Her pictorial images are often related to her titles in a humorous way, disclosing hidden *jeux de mots* (double entendres). *The Memorial of St. Helena* illustrates her wit and tongue-in-cheek asides to the viewer. It depicts the dream of the apotheosis of the dinosaur, as he would dream if he were the Napoleon of dinosaurs. The analogy between the dinosaur and man is not without relevance, but it makes its statement through a subtle wit rather than through violent overstatement.

Joyce Mansour, of Egyptian origin, was born in England in 1928. She collaborated on the review *Le Surréalisme Même,* on the catalog of the Surrealist Exposition of 1950–1960, and on many other publications and events. As a poet, novelist, and playwright, she is the author of *Cris, Déchirures, Jules César, Les Gisants Satisfaits, La Pointe, Rapaces, Carré Blanc and Ça.* Her play *Le Bleu Des Fonds* explores the problem of woman as the dream object in man's creative fantasy. Her works express eroticism and sensuality through an evocative style that culls imagery from the sources of the dream, the nightmare, and the vast landscape of inner vision. Although most of her published works are in French, she also writes in English. She studies and collects dreams. By way of introduction to American readers, I thought it would be appropriate to quote one of her poems in English.

Wild Glee from Nowhere

For Reinhoud

Hard calloused dreams
Burst palefully
Through the seams of tasteless
Yesterday
Don't whine for help
Lie bleeding
Life is a perpetual sneeze
Listen to the screech of iron in the rocky
Vacuum
Of an eyeless
Socket
To the mouthless prayer of ambiguous men
Stretched out in anguish and surgical green
Listen
Sharpen your tongue on the soft white womb
Nestling in formol
Then ALL shouting done
Watch brittle sperm rain down like cheese
Collect the bubbles
Hustle sour winds up the sidewalk
Suck the fresh flesh of the ruby
Leave it screaming
No matter
Strange shallow dreams eat at random
And shrink not with age
Soundless laughter like the midnight sea
Will toil back to slumber
And there will the bodiless breaker unroll its metal
Dip thunder and vanish
In a thousand grim echoes
Far beyond the bloody swelling of a mother's breast
"Pardon me" said she dressed in small town bereavement
And Humpty-Dumpty closed a huge savage eye[28]

Joyce Mansour

This presentation of the women of Surrealism was intended as background material that will foster the further investigation of a subject that could provide rich and varied documentation in the fields of art, literature, and women's studies. Naturally, it has been impossible to include all the women who have played an important role in the Surrealist movement within the limits of a short article. Some of the women whom I have left for future studies are: Lise de Harme (writer, organizer of a salon for Surrealists in Paris), Giséle Prassinos (writer, Greek), Jacqueline Lamba (painter, second wife of Breton), Valentine Hugo, Dora Maar, Rachel Baes (painter, Paalen's wife, Mexico), Kay Sage (painter, American, wife of Tanguy), Annie Le Brun (poet), and finally Gala (Dali's wife) and Eliza Breton.

All the artists discussed are presently living in France, except for Leonora Carrington and Elena Garro who reside in Mexico. Only Remedios Varo is deceased. Most of these women know each other or have met at some time. Many of them participate in group showings, periodicals, and catalogs of Surrealist exhibitions throughout the world, and all are today actively involved in their own creative work.

The translation, publication, dissemination, exhibition, and serious study of the works of these women artists and writers is imperative at this time. If, in addition, major group and personal shows of their works could be held in the States, it would help to fill a large gap in our knowledge of Surrealism and would enable us to study the ongoing history of one of the most important artistic movements of the twentieth century whose full impact continues to be felt today. 1974 marked the fiftieth anniversary of the publication of the *Surrealist Manifestos*. It is the ideal time for a complete retrospective of the work of the women of Surrealism.[29]

NOTES

1. Patrick Waldberg, *Surrealism* (New York: McGraw-Hill, 1966), p. 76.
2. Maurice Nadeau, *Histoire Du Surréalisme* (Paris: Le Seuil, 1964), p. 187.
3. André Breton, *Manifestes du Surréalisme* (Paris: Jean-Jacques Pauvert, 1963), p. 141.

4. Ibid., p. 165.
5. André Breton, *Arcane 17* (Paris: Jean-Jacques Pauvert, 1965), p. 62.
6. Robert Benayoun, *Erotique Du Surréalisme* (Paris: Jean-Jacques Pauvert, 1965), p. 185.
7. Simone de Beauvoir, *The Second Sex* (New York: Bantam, 1961), p. 219.
8. Guillaume Apollinaire, "The Breasts of Tiresias" in *Modern French Theatre,* eds. Michael Benedikt and George E. Wellworth (New York: Dutton, 1966), p. 68.
9. Marcel Brion, *Léonor Fini et Son Oeuvre* (Paris: Jean-Jacques Pauvert, 1955).
10. Constantin Jelenski, *Léonor Fini* (New York: Olympia Press, 1968), p. 14, 15.
11. Ibid.
12. Leonora Carrington, *Down Below* (Chicago: Black Swan Press, 1972).
13. Ibid.
14. The color reproductions of the mural as well as the preliminary sketches for it are reproduced in Andrés Medina and Laurette Séjourné, *El Mundo Màgico de los Mayas* (Mexico City: Instituto Nacional de Antropologia et Historia, 1964).
15. Leonora Carrington, "Pénélope," *Cahiers Renaud-Barrault,* no. 70 (Paris: Gallimard, 1971).
16. Leonora Carrington, *Une Chemise de Nuit de Flanelle* (Paris: Collection L'Age d'Or, 1951).
17. Leonora Carrington, "Invention du Môlé," in *Poètes Singuliers du Surréalisme et Autres Lieux,* eds. Alain-Valéry Aelberts and Jean-Jacques Auquier (Paris: Christian Bourgeois, 1971).
18, 19. Leonora Carrington, "White Rabbins" and "The Sisters," *View,* (Feb-March 1942).
20. Leonora Carrington, "La Débutante" in *L'Anthologie de L'Humour Noir,* ed. André Breton (Paris: Jean-Jacques Pauvert, 1966).
21. Leonora Carrington, "L'Homme Neutre," *Le Surréalisme Même,* no. 1.
22. Leonora Carrington, "Waiting," *VVV* (June 1942).
23. Leonora Carrington, "The Seventh Horse," *VVV* (March 1943).
24. Leonora Carrington, "Et In Bellicus Medicalis Lunarum," *Opus International,* no. 30, (1970).
25. Leonora Carrington, "Jezzamathatics or Introduction to the Wonderful Process of Painting," *Catalogue for Exposition in Sao Paolo,* June 1965.
26. Elena Garro, *Un Hogar Sólido,* (Xalapa: Editorial Veracruzana, 1958).
27. André Pieyre de Mandiargues, *Bona, L'Amour Et La Peinture* (Geneva: Skira, 1971), p. 378.

28. Joyce Mansour, *Phallus Et Momies* (La Louviére, Belgique: Daily-Bul, 1969).

29. Additional references consulted: Xaviére Gauthier, *Surréalisme et Sexualité* (Paris: Gallimard, 1971); Octavio Paz and Roger Caillois, *Remedios Varo* (Mexico City: Ediciones ERA, S.A., 1966); and Alain Bosquet, *Dorothea Tanning* (Paris: Jean-Jacques Pauvert, 1966).

5

Women's Art in the '70s

LAWRENCE ALLOWAY

Women's art as a movement emerged in the 1970s in a form unlike that taken by earlier art movements. However, women artists developed faster than either art critics or dealers were able to handle. This gap between the production and the consumption of art reflects both the originality of women's art and the inertia of present opinion. I want to draw attention here to what seem to me to be discrepancies between work and theory. To do this, it is necessary to give a general picture of the rapid development of women's art in the past few years. The chronology here is not meant to be comprehensive but rather a preliminary arrangement of representative events.

From the '50s on, there has been an increase in the number of women artists who have achieved public careers soon after early one-artist shows. The reputations of Chryssa, Helen Frankenthaler, Grace Hartigan, Marisol, and Joan Mitchell, for example, began with little delay after their entrances. The situation was generally accepted at the time, and no particular significance was attached to it. It was an intensification of the process in which twentieth-century art had always made room for women such as Sonia Delaunay, Hannah Höch, Gabrielle Münter, Sophie Taeuber-Arp, and Georgia O'Keefe.

In the past ten years women artists have appeared in the United States on other terms, however. They are no longer fringe contributors to a succession of movements that they have not shaped; they have become a constituency, growing in number and consciousness. A diminishing sense of peripherality is expressed as self-awareness takes various forms, from the intimation of personal identity to group affiliation. So far as artists are concerned, the National Organization for Women (founded in 1966) is not the model of action. On the contrary, artists have acted in small coalitions that are informally structured. In fact, the low prestige of organizational skill has led such groups to rate efficient timetables below the web of person-oriented attitudes. Reciprocity has counted for more than good management in these groups. Nonetheless, the cumulative effect has been the conversion of women's demands into cultural issues.

It is necessary to see the women's movement in art in relation to the movement at large. It belongs in a nexus of women's caucuses and committees studying federal employment rules and consumers' rights, faculty hiring patterns at universities, and sports programs in high schools. In this context, attempts to accept women's art without acknowledging its ideological content are seen to be mischievous. An example of this kind of transitional argument is Athena Tacha Spear's text on Joan Jonas, Ann McCoy, Mary Miss, Ree Morton, and Jackie Winsor (along with two male artists), written in 1973, in which she proposed that their work, like, "the whole history of twentieth-century art could be described in terms of reduction."[1] The theory rests on Clement Greenberg's notion of "expendable conventions" and Lucy R. Lippard's "rejective-art" theory, which Lippard herself, under the pressure of women's art, had already dispensed with. This kind of acceptance of women artists into existing esthetic systems could be paralleled by examples from other writers who, like myself at the time, did not recognize the cultural importance of women's art.

Important to my thinking on this matter was a meeting on December 12, 1971, at the Brooklyn Museum. Discussions between woman-artist representatives of various groups with the museum's director concerning a projected exhibition broke down, but the women forced him to make the auditorium available for a discussion on "Are Museums Relevant to Women?" A panel of women addressed a large audience on the inequity of the art system as symbolized by museums at large.[2] It was the first conspicuous gesture of feminist dissent in the art world that was based on the assumption that the political and cultural oppression of women was a constituent factor in contemporary art.

Like every new term (not to mention every old one), feminism means this and that, according to who is using it. I will define a feminist here as a woman who is willing to work with other women to reduce inequality in the long run or to achieve a specific short-term reform. Without the aspect of collaboration, whether it is to found a cooperative gallery, infiltrate an art school, or expose the prejudices of art dealers, a woman artist is not a feminist. Individual stands and victories are an important part of the general despecialization of the sexes but are not explicitly political in function. To claim your own life or some aspect of it for art can certainly be part of the presenta- tion of women's lives as subject matter, but it is an individual, not a shared, enterprise. When Audrey Flack paints her dressing table, the subject is feminine but not feminist. Feminist coalitions are informal and local, but the acquiring of a shared experiential base is the point, not personal and untransmittable skills and insights; open access to other women is essential. Elaine de Kooning and Rosalyn Drexler are both on record in defense of personal accomplishment—as if a feminist sacrificed some authentic part of her being by her sense of community. De Kooning said: "To be put in any category not de- fined by one's work is to be falsified. We're artists who happen to be women and men among other things we happen to be;" Drexler: "No one thinks collectively unless they are involved with propaganda."[3]

EXHIBITIONS

At the end of the 1960s there was in New York a convergence of various factors that decisively separated pro-feminist art groups from the commercial, established art-delivery system. The Art Workers Coalition (AWC) was formed in 1969 to protest "establishment" policies, especially (but not only) at the Museum of Modern Art. Out of it developed in the same year a group called Women Artists in Revolution (WAR) and in 1970 the Women's Ad Hoc Committee was formed, which included some former AWC members. An early demand of both groups, vigorously expressed by demonstrations, was for equal representation of women artists in the Whitney Annu- als (now Biennials).

Women also started organizing their own exhibitions. X[12] at Museum, a downtown loft, may have been first; it was organized by members of WAR. Then followed Women Artists Exhibit, organized by WAR as part of the SoHo Festival in May 1970, along with Mod Donn Art, 11 Women Artists at the Public Theater. The artists were Alida Walsh, Ann Wilson, Faith Ringgold, Inverna, Iris Crump, Juliette Gordon, Kate Millet, May Stevens, Muriel Castanis, Nancy

Spero, and Sara Saporta. In December there was a brief show of
women artists at International House in New York, which included,
among 45 or so artists, Marjorie Kramer, Pat Mainardi, Irene Peslikis, Janet Sawyer, and Lucia Vernarelli of the Redstocking Artists
group.

In 1971 two new organizations of artists were founded: Women in
the Arts (WIA) and the Women's Interart Center. In May the
cooperative Prince Street Gallery presented an invitational show of
women, and in December at Museum there was the first open show
of women's art. It had a rough downtown look, which seemed to
discourage critics, and the show was noticed only by *The Daily News*;
it was important, however, for affirming the principle of complete
artist control, a factor that is still crucial in the loosely structured,
anti-authoritarian women's movement. It should be noted that all
these shows were put on outside the existing gallery and museum
circuit; dealers and curators were not interested, so the artists themselves improvised.

An exhibition of singular importance was also staged in 1971, 26
Contemporary Women Artists, at the Aldrich Museum, Ridgefield,
Connecticut, selected by Lucy Lippard (active in the Ad Hoc Committee). (The same year Lippard curated her first exhibition predicated on artists' sex, she published her book, *Changing: Essays in Art
Criticism*. There are no articles on women artists *as* women artists in
Changing, so we can take 1971 as the year in which feminism was
added to a Minimalist esthetic by Lippard.) She wrote in the catalog
of 26 Artists: "I have no clear picture of what, if anything, constitutes
'women's art,' although I am convinced that there is a latent difference in sensibility."[4] She proceeds tentatively: "I have heard suggestions that the common factor is a vague 'earthiness,' 'organic images,'
'curved lines,' and, most convincingly, a centralized focus (Judy
Chicago's idea)."[5] With this text, public speculation about specific
characteristics in women's art began.

In 1970 students at the State University College at Potsdam, New
York, requested an exhibition of work by women artists; it occurred
in 1972 under the title Women In Art.[6] Organized by Harriet
FeBland, the show included Mary Bauermeister, Marisol, Eleanore
Mikus, and Beverly Pepper, among others. That is to say, the show
was selected from established galleries (Bonino, Janis, O.K. Harris,
Marlborough). The selection is a reminder that women had been

entering the commercial system in moderate but increasing numbers since the second generation of Abstract Expressionists. However, as most of the art was fairly well adapted to prevailing taste, it did not raise the question of female sensibility so much as it acknowledged female adaptiveness.

The development of the women's movement was away from the kind of commercial gallery-based alignment shown at Potsdam and in the direction indicated by 26 Women at Ridgefield. In March 1972, 13 Women Artists staged a once-only cooperative exhibition in rented premises at 117–119 Prince Street in New York City. Three of Lippards's 26 were among the 13 (Audrey Hemenway, Mary Miss, Paula Tavins), and two of the 13 (Loretta Dunkelman, Patsy Norvell) became founding members of the cooperative gallery A.I.R. when it opened the next fall, with two more of the 13 joining later (Kazuko and Pat Lasch). Group exhibitions, as a form of temporary coalition, gave women artists the opportunity of personal contact, not dissimilar to the experience of consciousness-raising groups.

In the summer of 1972 an exhibition of 34 artists drawn from the Women in the Arts membership was held at the C. W. Post Auditorium, juried by Helen Soreff, Joyce Rosa (curator of the Post collection), Joyce Kozloff, June Blum, and Carolyn Mazzello. This was followed in the fall of 1972 by two more group shows, one curated by June Blum, Unmanly Art, the other by Joan Vita Miller, Ten Artists (Who Also Happen to Be Women).[7] (Neither of these two shows was seen in New York City: Blum's was at the Suffolk Museum, Stony Brook, New York, and Miller's at two State University of New York campuses.) Lippard wrote the catalog for the latter, pointing out that "in a few years, shows like this one will hopefully be unnecessary" but stressing, correctly, their current usefulness. They were needed to raise the level of public information concerning a new group and to facilitate contacts among the participating artists. It must be recorded that art critics, in the course of their regular reviewing, made no use of the opportunity to write about women's art. In the absence of critical response, therefore, the shows rested on the feedback of the artists among themselves, stressing their interrelationship rather than outside contact. The exhibitions contributed to the artists' self-recognition in a way that seems similar to the collaborative undertaking of the Feminist Art Program in Los Angeles in 1972, Womanhouse. A series of significant one-woman exhibitions began in 1971 at Douglass College, New Brunswick, New Jersey, not, it is relevant to note, in the gallery run by the art department, but in the Mabel Smith Douglass Library.

The effect of shows like these, and of the founding of women's co-ops in 1972 (A.I.R., New York), 1973 (SoHo 20, New York, and Artemisia and ARC, Chicago), and 1974 (Hera, Providence, Rhode Island) should not be underestimated. Most people, including women artists, had not seen much art by women grouped together before. It was widely known that there were many women artists, but they usually appeared, disadvantaged by a male-favoring selection system, as part of shows with other purposes. A substantial sample of the women's art that we had known to exist but had not seen started to become available. In the '70s, for the first time, women's art began to be accessible in quantity. This has had two effects. One is that women artists could begin to work knowingly in relation to the work of other women; the other is that the traditional question—are men's and women's art different?—could be discussed again, but with adequate samples of women's art for the first time.

Between 1971 and 1973 there was, as we have seen, a rapid cycle of women's shows. Both participating and nonparticipating artists saw that they had company, and they were given the opportunity to compare themselves with others. The culminating show was Women Choose Women at the New York Cultural Center in 1973. The show was originated and executed by artists from Women in the Arts—a reversal of the usual practice in which the institution takes the initiative. The jury consisted of painters Pat Pasloff, Ce Roser and Syliva Sleigh (WIA), with guest jurors Laura Adler and Mario Amaya (both of the New York Cultural Center) plus Elizabeth C. Baker (then of *Art News*) for sculpture and Linda Nochlin (art historian, Vassar College) for painting.

Without this run of exhibitions, from 1971 on, the definition of women's art might have stayed restricted to the politics of resentment that characterized the WAR-like dissenting propaganda. However, though the exhibiting of women's art had begun, there was no adequate critical response. In the '60s, new artists' debuts were associated largely with one-person exhibitions. Not since the Museum of Modern Art's mixed shows (15 Americans, 1952, 12 Americans 1956, and so on) had group exhibition been as essential a medium of communication, revealing an extraordinary wealth of new work.

During this period when so many new women artists were emerging, what was the position of male artists? My impression is that newly appearing male artists were not the equals either in number or intensity of the women. The reason for this may lie in what is called in economics "the retarding lead effect." This is a rule that holds that highly developed economies may have greater difficulty adapting to change in a period of transition than underdeveloped countries. Having less to lose, an underdeveloped country may adapt faster; for the highly developed country, early success may retard later adaptation.

The expectation of many male artists was certainly that the art world would continue in the shape that crystallized in the '60s, a time of high consumption. This did not happen, and at the same time exhibition schedules increasingly included women artists. If I am right, the development of male artists could have been retarded by their anticipation of public success based on attitudes of the preceding decade. (The faltering developments of many artists born in the '20s may also have provided younger male artists with a confusing set of models to emulate.) Women artists, on the other hand, had no inheritance to disappoint them by its attenuation. In addition, women benefited from energizing effect of self-discovery and the early formulation of shared goals. This, as much as individual effort, gave them an early advantage over newly entering male artists.

The rapid arrival of women artists as a group was facilitated by the general discontent (different from individual cases of neglect and disappointment) of the late '60s and early '70s. However, this convergence of causes was accidental and is not likely to recur in ways that will strengthen the women's movement. On the contrary, as protest becomes more precisely formulated, the differences, indeed the antagonism, of different interest groups is likely to become evident. The process of differentiation has begun, as was evident at the first United Nations World Conference of Women in 1975. The women of the third world emerged as a dominant subject for concern. Their destiny, to be "underfed, ill, uneducated, and pregnant from the day of their first menstruation until menopause,"[8] was stressed. If one compares the lives of these women at the very edge of survival with the demands of North American women for a greater role in the definition of culture, the disparity is absolute. Those women for whom homemaking is no longer a full-time occupation, owing in part to improved goods and services, and who thus have time to produce art, appeared suddenly, in a jolting perspective, as the concubines of imperialism.

It is a fact that the various demands for legitimate reform cannot be coordinated with one another, except occasionally for special purposes. There is no common cause of dissent, and each group determines its own priorities; no general front of reform has emerged from the victories of separate groups. One should not expect an all-purpose relevance in each attempt to correct inequality; the demands of different groups are bound to be competitive with one another. Today in the United States, for example, white and black women artists have shown no instinct or talent for sustained cooperation.

CRITICISM

There are no manifestos of women's art that set up the future course of work to be done, like the Futurist and Surrealist declarations of policy. Propaganda and reassurance have been prominent, and texts are scattered in catalogs, parochial newsletters, and magazines. The first big year for writing on the subject was 1971.[9] In January *Art News* published a special issue on "Women's Liberation, Women Artists and Art History," with statements by artists and several articles. The famous text here is Linda Nochlin's "Why Have There Been No Great Women Artists?" but there is also Elizabeth C. Baker's "Sexual Art Politics," an early and precise survey of the problems of women in art.

In May 1971, WAR's *A Documentary Herstory of Women Artists in Revolution* appeared, reprinting leaflets, correspondence, and press clippings dealing with the group's antagonistic separation from the Art Workers Coalition and its subsequent harrassment of institutions. The texts are vivid and authentic. In the winter the first number of what was to have been a quarterly was published, *Women and Art.* In newspaper format, like the underground papers *East Village Other* and *New York Element,* and in a manner reminiscent of WAR, it presented reports and documents dealing with institutional iniquity, including Cindy Nemser's "Critics and Women's Art." Nemser reported the results of a questionnaire that revealed the impatience or indifference of most of her male respondents. Also notable was Christine Smith's "Rosa Bonheur," a revisionary art-historical piece, expanding on a neglected woman artist whom Nochlin had discussed in *Art News*.

As I see it, the discussion of women's art has developed in two ways, typified by these two articles in *Women and Art*. One is the polemical-documentary approach, which recounts male critics' failings, women artists' humiliations, and all the misunderstandings at the interface of women's groups and the institutionalized art world. These reports possess the urgency of a good cause and the appeal of gossip. The other direction is toward revisionist art history. A later example of this is Carol Duncan's "Virility and Domination in Early 20th-Century Vanguard Painting," a skeptical account of Expressionist Bohemia.[10] Nochlin is the leader of this approach, and Smith, Duncan, and others have picked up on aspects of her exceptional drive. Thus the accusatory and analytical functions of art writing have been separated.

It is between these poles of protest and analysis that the *Feminist Art Journal* (FAJ, 1972–1977) was stretched. It recorded cases of museum exploitation, university discrimination, and gallery callousness, and published various art-historical articles, notably Gloria Orenstein's "Women of Surrealism."[11] In an early issue, reporting on a panel at the College Art Association in 1973, Pat Mainardi's objection to the growing identification of female form-making with central imagery as just another "stereotype" was recorded.[12] And in the same issue, Miriam Brumer published a piece based on her College Art Association paper on the same topic. Her criticism of the theory is that the central image is generally organic but not specifically female.[13] And that was it: a dispute about one of the few general ideas that has emerged about women's art was signaled, then dropped.

This was typical of the way in which the only journal of women's art failed to develop or discuss ideas germane to its constituency. One function of art criticism, when it is done by writers who are close to artists, is to bring into public use early formulations of the ideas and words orginated by artists about their own work. Lucy Lippard in her early essays on Minimal art performed this function admirably. However, the *FAJ* was never sensitive to the special articulateness of innovative artists. As a result, the artists who were its

subjects were made to seem (and perhaps to feel) mute. In this
journal, too, the early phase of resentment continued as an inertial
weight against speculation and new ideas.

What is the situation if one consults writers more ambitious to
elucidate women's art by investigation of its problems? Nochlin
seems not only to have grasped the fundamental situation when she
wrote her remarkable first paper, but to have seen what is needed to
carry the ideas further. She began as an art historian of the
nineteenth century but has extended her work from Courbet and
nineteenth century Realism to today's wide-spread revival of realism
as a continuing esthetic in opposition to abstract art, and specifically
to women realists.[14] What this sequence indicates is an approach to
realism and to women's art that is intellectually consistent and developable. It is precisely the lack of developable ideas that has handicapped most of the critical discussion of women's art.

Two years after her 26 Artists text, Lippard listed the following
possible female characteristics in art: "A uniform density, an overall
texture, often sensuously tactile and often repetitive to the point of
obsession; the preponderance of circular forms and central focus
(sometimes contradicting the first aspect); a ubiquitous linear 'bag' or
parabolic form that turns in on itself; layers, or strata; an indefinable
looseness or flexibility of handling; a new fondness for the pinks and
pastels and the ephemeral cloud-colors, that used to be taboo."[15]
That was in 1973; in 1975 she suggested that the following forms
were more frequent in women's than in men's art: "A central focus
(often 'empty,' often circular or oval), parabolic bag-like forms, obsessive line and detail, veiled strata, tactile or sensuous surface and
forms, associative fragmentation, autobiographical emphasis."[16]
There are differences in emphasis between the two lists: post-
Minimalist pattern has been slightly reduced and centralism advanced somewhat, and the autobiographical mode of Conceptual art
has been added. It is clear that Lippard is responsive to the changing
output of women artists, but the two lists remain at the same level of
tentativeness. Lippard has not followed her initial conviction of a
female sensibility in art by any definition of what it might be.

The leading candidate for a general theory of women's art at present remains central imagery. Miriam Schapiro has described (referring to her 1968 painting OX, which has an O in the center of an X)
the interior of the O as "painted in tender shades of pink." She

records that "Judy Chicago and I began a dialogue in 1970" concerning, among other matters, such imagery. "We called it the 'cunt' image and looked for it in other women's works. We found it in Georgia O'Keeffe, Barbara Hepworth, Lee Bontecou, all sorts of people." [17] Schapiro and Chicago together wrote an article, "Female Imagery," in which they cite O'Keeffe's *Black Iris* (1926), as an antecedent of *OX*: "She painted a haunting mysterious passage through the black portal of an iris, making the first recognized step inside the darkness of female identity. . . . There is now evidence that many women artists have defined a central orifice whose formal organization is often a metaphor for a woman's body." [18] Arlene Raven, an art historian in contact with Schapiro and Chicago, wrote about the latter's *Pasadena Lifesavers* in these terms: "Dissolution of form is a metaphor for the dissolution of self that a woman feels at the moment of orgasm." [19] Thus centralist imagery is interpreted in terms of female somatic experience and more specifically as female sexual metaphor.

Schapiro and Chicago assume that women artists' "femaleness shapes both the form and content of their work." [20] They claim the central image as an inherent quality, derived from the body image, and consequently different from men's imagery. They relate it to the discovery of female sexuality. But what is the difference between Chicago's *Lifesavers* and Kenneth Noland's circles, especially his earlier ones where the edges melt and tremble? Chicago has anticipated the question and answered it by saying: "The difference between *Pasadena Lifesavers* and a Noland target is the fact that there is a body identification between me and those forms, and not between Noland and the target." [21] According to the artist, the four shapes in *Lifesavers* can be further related to her "discovery that I was multiorgasmic." [22] This, however, is not apparent until we have been told so; without the instructions for interpretations, we might just as easily relate *Lifesavers* to, say, the centralism in Billy Al Bengston's paintings.

As I see it, the careers of Schapiro and Chicago, both articulate and dogmatic artists, do nothing to weaken my reading of the central image as a somewhat strenuously imposed ideological program. No reason has been advanced to prove that central configurations are inherently female. Their use is inter-sexual: as many male as female artists have used concave, centered, and compartmented forms; the difference is that women's use of it has become topical and political.

What I think has happened is that a consciously formed, deliberately identified image is being presented as if it were a biological absolute. The central image is evocative as an established sexual symbol and as such has worked admirably. It is an image with a set of meanings attached to it that are known, with varying degrees of sophistication, by its users: it spans a gamut from deep womb symbolism, as in Louise Bourgeois, to clitoral agitation,[23] as in Juanita McNeeley.

Cindy Nemser organized a show in 1974 called In Her Own Image,[24] which is the main statement for the rational viewpoint that women's social experiences will affect their art (the equivalent of the "environmental" rather than the "hereditary" theory in psychology). She collected a group of artists whose subject matter is the visualization and presentation of themselves or other women. It was clear from the show that there has been a marked iconographical expansion in the depiction of women. Subjects ranged from images of manic solitude, like McNeeley's, to composed self-reflection, like Jillian Denby's. Supplementing this self-imagery is the work of artists who have reinterpreted the painting of male nudes in terms of a feminine viewpoint and sensibility. The paintings of Martha Edelheit and Sylvia Sleigh, in their different ways, reveal a scrutiny of male anatomy very unlike the attention formerly given to male models. And Joan Semmel adopts a literally first-person perceptual viewpoint, in which the space of the picture is seen as through the eyes of a painted participant—presumably herself.

Another way that women artists have minted a specifically feminine iconography has been elaborated by Rosemary Mayer, who in 1973 showed (at A.I.R.) three sculptures titled *Hroswitha, Galla Placidia* and *The Catherines*. Her purpose was to build a pantheon of heroines: the first woman was a German Latin poet of the tenth century, the second an empress of the late Roman Empire, and the third a conflation of Catherines, including Catherine Sforza, Catherine de'Medici, Catherine of Aragon, Catherine Cornaro, Catherine the Great and Catherine of Siena.[25] Mayer offered this information in written form at the gallery; also included was information about the composition of underskirts and overskirts from a book on historic costume. The sculptures were multi-leveled soft constructions of satin, rayon, nylon, cheesecloth, netting, and ribbon; drapery itself connoted femaleness here. A comparable interest in historicizing sexuality was expressed in Chicago's *Great Ladies* series, which started in 1972: here, centralist abstractions were named after past heroines such as Christine of Sweden, Marie Antoinette, and Queen Victoria.

Craft techniques, such as sewing, weaving, and knotting fibers, comprise another important subcategory within the broad effort to isolate female form-characteristics. Such techniques are in broad use among men *and* women at present but can be programmatically associated with women because of their traditional domestic application. Many women working with these means do construe a kinship with their female ancestors or with third-world women—that is, with women in whose lives these operations really are (or were) fundamental. Pat Lasch's sewn paintings declare this by her linking of symmetrical display and kinship pattern. If today there is a female penchant for crafts, it would seem to be on this conscious basis, as an iconography in which process acts significatively, not because there is an instinctual female urge to craft. In fact, craft techniques, as practiced by today's artists, signify primitivism more than utility. There is a strong pastoral, anticonsumer undercurrent to craft in those forms in which it interpenetrates with sculpture or painting. There are allusions to a *Whole Earth Catalog* kind of iconography that does not lend itself to sexual characterization at all. As the esthetics of art and the operations of craft have overlapped, so a common base of work, accessible to men or women, is apparent. A recent plethora of soft sculpture, fetishes, and simulated shelters is generationally rather than sexually attributable. Such work is largely produced by young artists motivated by an optimistic belief in a nonspecialized technology and a primitivist ideal that we can live on our personal resources.

A recurrent problem in art since the nineteenth century, the definition of decoration, belongs with the themes of craft and primitivism. It still separates high art from craft devotees and form- from content-oriented critics: Is decoration compatible with thought and feeling, or is it their antithesis? I shall assume that art and decoration are compatible and that the opposition between them is specious. But the problem here is different: we want to know if decorativeness is more likely to show up in women (because of canons of domesticity) and if there are any predispositions toward it that can be identified sexually.

The form of decorative art that applies here is essentially architectural, whether in the transfer of symmetrical and repetitive patterns to painting (Joyce Kozloff, Mary Grigoriadis) or of sequential forms to sculpture (Jackie Ferrara, Athena Tachà). But the works of these sculptors are so clearly allied to precedents in Minimal art that no sexual reading seems called for. The architectural schemata and allusive color of Kozloff and Grigoriadis also seem to pertain to art in general rather than to sexual characteristics in particular. Agnes Martin used both American Indian textiles and Gothic architecture as image sources in her early (pre-grid) paintings and drawings. But there is no reason to assume from this that either the tribal or medieval reference is specifically female. Both seem rather to be part of an intersexual interest of artists concerned to keep their pictures flat while incorporating evocative image-traces. Martin would be as close to Adolf Gottlieb's *Pictographs* as to any built-in female taste for patterning, craft, or shelter.

The centralist theory is a form of mythologizing in which the function of allusion is to universalize personal experience. In this respect it is similar to primitivistic theories of women's art, such as Mary Beth Edelson's. Edelson posits a matriarchy that preceded male-oriented classical mythology. Her myth claims a more primal content than later mythologies, but I see her work as a consciously adopted program rather than authentic revelation. Both centralism and primitivism aim to provide women's art with ancient, even archetypal justification.

The search for sexual specifics in women's art has led to the neglect of intersexual comparisons, however. In this case, for instance, the play with myth is similar to that of the New York School mythmakers of the 1940s. The mythologies of Gottlieb and Mark Rothko were a patchwork of ideas from Frazer, Freud, Jung, and Nietzsche. Portentousness lurked behind the poetic symbols of these artists because their access to myth rested on the idea of the artist as seer, gifted beyond other people. What has feminism to gain from the revival of these affected attitudes? Surely women artists do not want to enhance their sex at the expense of their individuality. To compare the improvised myths of the '70s with the male equivalents of the '40s shows that the mother-goddess is an intellectually disreputable as the hero-king.

AVANT-GARDE

Earlier avant-garde groups were numerically small; the women's movement is very extensive. Nevertheless, the women's movement in art can be considered as an avant-garde because its members are united by a desire to change the existing social forms of the art world. It may be that women will avoid the trap that snared those past avant-gardes who proclaimed social change as a part of their program but who settled for a change of style within the history of art. Many of the claims of privileged status made by an avant-garde for its products depend on empty assertions of social relevance. New art is *supposed* to presage a new set of social values. By its broad base the women's movement in art presents something genuinely new—it is already bound to real social change, which is an index of a basic shift in values.

Innovative avant-garde ideas used to be distributed comparatively slowly to a small public. This has not been the case with women artists; they are numerous and their audience is large, because of both the improved level of women's education and women's increased expectations. Thus, though the ratio of innovating artists to the public may not exceed by much that of earlier avant-gardes to their select publics, the numbers involved now are enormously greater. Today we have the possibility of an avant-garde that is actually inducing change beyond the revision of formal matters. (Because of its inclusivity, the movement can expect to be criticized for its lack of professionalism, for in the United States professionalism of style and career building have become set forms for those who want to be counted as advanced artists.)

If common imagistic, technical, and stylistic factors do not define most women's art, what is the basis for looking at it in a unified way and for calling it avant-garde? The innovative factor is precisely the attribute of *nonstylistic* homogeneity—the factor that makes some women abstract artists feel closer to women representational artists than to male abstract artists. The pattern of cross-stylistic contacts among today's women is unusual in the history of active artists' groups in the twentieth century. Obviously, stylistic kinship will be a factor among others. If we take a co-op like SoHo 20, we can see the resembled one another stylistically, for instance); but this is one factor among others. If we take a co-op like SoHo 20, we can see the principle of nonstylistic homogeneity in action: members are as diverse as Barbara Coleman, with her granulated monochrome surfaces, and Lucy Sallick, with her loose-linked chains of still life objects; but the members are compatible for social and political purposes, and these take priority. The capacity to suspend esthetic criteria under pressure produces an enhancement of the power of artists to collaborate with each other.

One limitation of centralism and primitivism is that they have not been validated in any respect, and their authors seem disinclined to attempt it. A detailed comparison of central imagery as used by men and women, for instance, would seem the minimum next step, but if this has been undertaken, the result is unpublished. (See chapter 17, "Female Art Characteristics: Do They Really Exist?" Ed.) Another limitation is their exclusiveness: neither Lippard nor Schapiro-Chicago pay any attention to representational artists. Instead of nominating one tendency as the essential form of feminist art, it would be both more rational methodologically and more in keeping with the movement's desire for diversity/equality if critics were to avoid exclusionist tactics of this sort. The insight that is to be gained by others (both men and women) from looking at women's art will not be restricted by stylistic criteria derived ultimately from formalist models. We need a concept elastic enough to account for such work as Nancy Spero's *Codex Artaud*, in which a woman artist appropriates a man's writing so that the visual encroaches on the verbal as well as female on male. Artaud's rejection of "humanity" is ambiguously paralleled by Spero's embrace of Artlaud in an extrapolation of her own dehumanizing experiences as a woman. Such extraordinary enlargements of our consciousness as Spero's cannot be restricted in favor of partial arguments. It is time for a general theory of women's art.

Group shows and cooperative galleries have established the first public phase of women's art. One-artist shows are necessary now, and the demand for them exceeds the system's capacity to supply them. The co-ops could be crucial inasmuch as they are the only independent organizations devoted to one-artist shows. A co-op member normally expects to show once in an 18-month or two-year cycle, but this limits membership. Co-ops have proved themselves highly successful in introducing new artists, but they have not yet demonstrated that they can develop careers in terms of reviews, collections, out-of-town galleries, and museums. However, the next requirement (after recognition) is distribution, in terms of both information and marketing. One possibility is that if co-ops continue to increase in number, they may be able to achieve more on the basis of collaboration with one another than they could do singly. They could form a basis for the alternative gallery system that is so often wished for. It is a measure of the radical social base of women's art that it should require changes in the distribution system in a way never needed by Minimal art, Pop art, Op art, or even Conceptual art, which all flourished happily within the given commercial structure.

NOTES

1. Athena T. Spear, "Some Thoughts on Contemporary Art," *Allen Memorial Art Bulletin* (Oberlin College, Spring 1973): 90. However, she subsequently compiled *Women's Studies in Art and Art History* (New York: College Art Association, Jan. 1974), a useful report on the burgeoning of women's studies across the country.
2. For details of the abortive Brooklyn Museum project, see "$50,000 for a Women's Show?," *Women and Art* (Winter 1971): 1, 15. For reports with quotations from speakers at the meeting see "Women Speak Out at Brooklyn Museum" *Elements* (Feb.-March 1972): 2, 3, 14; and "Open Hearing at the Brooklyn Museum," *Feminist Art Journal* (April 1972): 6, 26, 27.
3. Elaine de Kooning with Rosalyn Drexler "Dialogue," in *Art and Sexual Politics*, eds. Thomas B. Hess and Elizabeth C. Baker (New York: Collier Books, 1973), p. 57 (reprint of *Art News* special issue on women's art, Jan. 1971).
4. Lucy R. Lippard, introduction to *Twenty-Six Contemporary Women Artists* (Ridgefield, Conn: Aldrich Museum of Contemporary Art, 1971).
5. Ibid.
6. Benedict Goldsmith, introduction to *Women in Art* (Potsdam, N.Y.: Art Gallery, SUNY College, 1972).
7. June Blum, *Unmanly Art* (Suffolk Museum, Stony Brook, Oct.-Nov.,

1972); Joan Vita Miller, *Ten Artists (Who Also Happen to Be Women)* (Lockport, Kenan Center, Nov. 17, 1972 to January 14, 1973); and (Fredonia, Michael D. Rockefeller Arts Center Gallery, Jan. 19– Feb. 18, 1973).

8. A United Nations report quoted in *The New York Times*, June 24, 1975.

9. *Art News,* Jan. 1971; *A Documentary Herstory of Women Artists in Revolution,* eds. Jacqueline Skiles and Janet McDevitt (1971); *Women and Art,* eds. Marjorie Kramer, Pat Mainardi, and Irene Peslikis (Winter 1971).

10. Carol Duncan, "Virility and Domination in Early 20th-Century Vanguard Painting," *Artforum* (Dec. 1973): 30–39.

11. Gloria Feman Orenstein, "Women of Surrealism," reprinted in chapter 4 in this book.

12. Judy Seigel. "Women's Panels at the CAA," *Feminist Art Journal* (Spring 1973): 14.

13. Miriam Brumer, "Organic Image: Woman's Image," *Feminist Art Journal* (Spring 1973): 12–13.

14. Linda Nochlin, *Realism* (New York: Penguin Books, 1971); "The Art of Philip Pearlstein," *Philip Pearlstein* (Georgia Museum of Art, 1970); "The Realist Criminal and the Abstract Law," *Art in America* (Sept.-Oct. 1973): 54–61; "Some Women Realists; Painters of the Figure," *Arts*, no. 8 (1974): 29–33.

15. Lucy R. Lippard, "A Note on the Politics and Aesthetics of a Woman's Show," *Women Choose Women* (New York Cultural Center, 1973).

16. Lucy R. Lippard, "The Women Artists Movement—What Next?" (Paris Biennale Catalogue, 1975). I am grateful to the author for letting me read this in typescript; it appears in her *From the Center* (New York: E. P. Dutton, 1976).

17. "Interview with Miriam Schapiro by Moira Roth," *Miriam Schapiro* (La Jolla: Mandeville Art Gallery, University of California of San Diego, 1975), pp. 12–13.

18. Miriam Schapiro and Judy Chicago, "Female Imagery," *Womanspace Journal* (Summer 1973): 11 (A note dates the article as having been written in 1972).

19. Arlene Raven, "Women's Art: The Development of a Theoretical Perspective," *Womanspace Journal* (Feb.-Mar. 1973): 18.

20. Schapiro and Chicago, "Female Imagery," p. 13.

21. "Judy Chicago Talking to Lucy R. Lippard," *Artforum* (Sept., 1974): p. 64.

22. Ibid., p. 60.

23. For the latter, see Betty Dodson, *Liberating Masturbation* (New York, Body Sex Designs, 1974).

24. Cindy Nemser, "In Her Own Image—Exhibition Catalogue," *The Feminist Art Journal,* (Spring 1974): 11–18.
25. Rosemary Mayer, typescript distributed at A.I.R. Gallery in 1973; extended in the article "Two Years, March 1973 to January 1975" by Mayer in *Lives*, ed. Alan Sondheim (E. P. Dutton, 1977).

6

Fancy Work
The Archaeology of Lives

RACHEL MAINES

The widely recognized need for a feminist approach to art history has generated considerable discussion about whether the progress of women's aesthetic thought can be reconstructed at all. The history of art, like the history of events, is dependent on the survival of artifacts, including written documents, from which historians derive, and occasionally invent, information.

The artifacts of women's lives have been systematically lost, destroyed, or reconstructed beyond recognition, leaving the feminist scholar more or less high and dry. Particularly frustrating is the realization that while the history of male culture consists largely of recorded destruction, warfare, and conquest, female culture is documented almost exclusively in creative forms, especially art, because of the historical exclusion of females from male activities. Thus the value of feminist history lies not only in what it can tell us about half the world's population in terms of pure social chronology, but in its significance for humanism generally. Historiography as a way of viewing the future and as a focus on historical creativity rather than violence can radically alter our progress into the next millenium. Feminist art history, therefore, should not only be a subdivision of art research, but the central medium through which we interpret the history of society and events.

Since we lack even the most basic resources on the lives of women, especially women artists, we must look for new methodologies and broaden our definition of what constitutes historical documentation. What data we have on female painters, writers, sculptors, architects, and even dancers and actresses is discontinuous, scattered, and heavily influenced both by the male cultural definition of what art is and should be and by the contemporary status of women. What is needed is an aesthetic and social history that fulfills a number of requirements: first, it must be continuous, that is, it should be traceable from one generation to the next, century by century, within a reasonable degree of accuracy; second, it should reflect the experiences of "mainstream" women. In the past, women who have become well known in the male-dominated arts have been those with resources and the inclination to take on a male role and separate themselves from the structure of female culture. A history of exceptional women may be valuable for its own sake, but it tells us very little about the aesthetic thought of the "silent majority." A third factor, heavily dependent on the second, is the reflection of honesty in art history: the artist must be free to express her own experience without fear of reprisal, ridicule, or censure from the men who monitor her conformity to her social role.

A resource does exist that fulfills all these requirements, and more, one that is so fully integrated into the traditional female role that we seldom regard it as an art form—needlework. Textile evidence for the lives of women extends back some 60 centuries continuously; previous to about 4000 BC the evidence begins to be less coherent. No known culture has ever excluded women from the needle arts; some, like the Inuit of North America, have reserved textiles as the exclusive province of women. Their traditional association with the female role, especially in Western society, guarantees their innocuous facade to the male community. Furthermore, they are so ubiquitous in both primitive and advanced societies, that men tend to filter them out at a very low level of consciousness. Since men are not now and seldom have been educated in the complex language of needlework symbology, any message transmitted in a textile medium was almost complete safe from the danger of falling into the wrong hands.

We therefore find stunningly honest and forthright statements in needlework, delivered to us across time, space, and cultural barriers, on every subject from politics to sex. The decodification of this enormous body of precious documentation has barely begun; needlework has very few secondary sources and even fewer scholars.

Many art historians still do not believe that textiles can provide the kind of social, psychological, political, and sexual information that is needed for a structured history of women's aesthetic thought.

Although a thorough introduction to needlework aesthetics and interpretation is a subject for a rather lengthy book, a brief example can illustrate the historical methods by which needlework scholarship operates within the framework of feminist art history.

Essentially, the historian relies on five sources: (1) extant textile work; (2) printed needlework literature and ephemera; (3) written documents such as letters; (4) photographic documents; and (5) oral history, especially readings of needlework evidence by living artists. From these sources, a historian can reconstruct not only the aesthetic history of various technical and regional needlework dialects, but also the actual life events and social identities of the artists whose work she studies. Often there is not enough background data to permit a complete evaluation of a particular work or group of works, or even make an attribution possible.

I have put forward these and similar theses on a number of occasions and been criticized on many points, both by the predominantly male aesthetic establishment and by feminists. The first observation generally made about needlework is that it is decorative, it is a craft, the product of which is applied to some useful purpose, such as clothing or home decoration. Here, as always, the distinction between "craft" and "fine art" is used for the purpose of denigrating some group of artists not currently in vogue, e.g., an unknown craftsperson "whittles" wood, a known artist "sculpts" it.

Further, the charge that art should serve no practical purpose is seldom leveled against architecture. If form did not transcend function, we would not make an aesthetic distinction between paintings and wallpaper. The fact that doilies are supposed to "protect" tables from dust and scratches should not disqualify them from consideration as art. If doilies are to be regarded as table coverings, then paintings should be regarded as wall coverings. Because of the pressure on women to be constantly productive and practical, it is hardly surprising that the hundreds of hours devoted to their art form are rationalized as the creation of useful goods. There are far easier ways of constructing table coverings and clothing.

A more complex criticism of the needle arts is the frequent use of patterns, an issue often discussed in the needlework subculture itself. Needlework designs sometimes fall into traditional categories, and many needle artists may be perceived as producing work in the same genre. There are two responses to this aspect of textile art: first, that it ignores the vast body of evidence relating to designs of known authorship[1] and secondly, that needlework is in some contexts an art of interpretation. Great needle artists, of whom several hundred names are known historically in the United States alone, generate work that is interpreted by the needle artist at the grassroots level, much as the work of a composer is interpreted by a musician's performance. Even in textile arts that have achieved some degree of recognition, such as quilts,[2] we still fail to research adequately and to attribute designs to such well known artists as Rose Kretsinger and Scioto Danner. In art forms such as the doily and the knitted garment, our stubborn ignorance of aesthetic authorship is even more exclusive.

To a great extent, this cultural blindness is traceable to our deep-seated prejudice against textiles as a woman-dominated area of society. When men are involved in textile art, a strong and noticeable semantic effort is made to alter our perceptions of how their work differs from that of the needlewoman. The work of male textile artists, for example, is generally referred to as "soft sculpture," to lessen the negative impact of textile associations.[3] These artists will frequently and emphatically deny their debt to the needlewoman. They want no part of an art form that expresses itself almost exclusively in the home. The same attitude is evident in museum curators and art historians—textiles are a dangerously "inferior" form and grassroots needlework is especially frightening in its implications for a broadening of artistic definitions to include mainstream women.

It will be many years before traditional American needlework, especially doilies and other household articles, begin to appear in male-dominated museums. I am putting together several gallery shows of this kind of work and will be teaching needlework history at the University of Pittsburgh. These are beginnings, but it is incumbent upon all of us to reexamine, both in an aesthetic and an historic light, the needlework that has for so many centuries formed the cultural background of our lives in history.

NOTES

1. Particularly notable among dozens of artists in textile fields are Anne Orr's designs, 1910–1945, Sophie La Croix (fl. c 1920), and Elizabeth Hiddleson, prolific doily artist now working on her twenty-eighth volume of designs.
2. Samplers, too, have been accorded some historical status, as in Ethel Stanwood Bolton and Eva Johnston Coe, *American Samplers* (Boston: The Massachusetts Society of the Colonial Dames of America, 1921).
3. Mary T. Ventre, *Crochet* (Boston: Little, Brown, 1974) contains some instances of this; Del Pitt Feldman, *Crochet* (Garden City, N.Y.: Doubleday, 1972) takes a more feminist position.

7

A "How To" for Feminist Art Research

J. J. WILSON
and
KAREN PETERSEN

The only places we have not found women artists are places we have not yet looked; women artists have worked everywhere, in all cultures, in all ages, and in all media. Do not be discouraged if you do not find evidence of them in the usual textbook sources or in schools' collections of reproductions. You cannot expect simply to look up women artists in a library subject index. We tried this in 1971 when we began our own research on women artists and found only some rather pious, dated compendiums such as Mrs. Ellet's *Women Artists in All Ages and Countries* (1859), Clara Clement's *Women in the Fine Arts* (1904), and Walter Sparrow's *Women Painters of the World* (1905).[1]

Now, thanks to the women's movement and women's studies, publishing on such "quaint" topics as women artists is relatively thriving. Artists and art educators joining together in the Women's Caucus for Art (meeting with but independent from the College Art Association), have taken leadership in developing this hitherto neglected area. While the general texts still do not include a representative selection of artists, there are some surveys devoted specifically to women artists. Eleanor Tuft's *Our Hidden Heritage* (Paddington Press, Ltd. 1974), though focused on 22 individual artists, includes considerable data on other women. The fine catalog from the Los Angeles County Museum's *Women Artists: 1550–1950* exhibition curated by Ann Sutherland Harris and Linda Nochlin has been published by Knopf (1976). Our own paperback, *Women Artists: Recogni-*

tion and Reappraisal (Harper & Row, 1976) is simpler in format and in content. It works well even for students who are not art history majors. (It also contains an excellent example of student research in Lorri Hagman's appendix on Chinese women artists.) Elsa Honig Fine's *Women and Art* (Allanheld and Schram, 1978) is now published.

The increasing number of monographs, *catalogues raisonnés,* and articles provide positive examples of what unbiased scholarship can do to reestablish the reputation of women artists; for example: Marianne Roland-Michel writing on Anne Vallayer-Coster, Anne-Marie Passez on Mme. Labille Guiard, and Ward Bissell on Artemisia Gentileschi.[2] Specialists, being genuinely interested in their topics, usually do justice to women artists. Charles Sterling's books on still life painting include truly representative samplings of women artists in that genre, as does Peter Mitchell's book on flower painting. Wilenski is careful to mention women artists' roles in the history of painting whenever he can.[3] You will develop a feel for fair-minded art historians who are not just keeping score on the century's top ten (men).

Exhibition catalogs form a valuable resource for the study of women artists. Over the last decade an increasing number of museums have mounted exhibits of work by women in their collections. These catalogs are well documented and often well illustrated. The *World Wide Art Catalogue Bulletin* (available in most large libraries) even gives a special bibliography of selected women's shows over the last 20 years.[4]

In a talk at the 1977 College Art Association convention, Professor Josephine Withers (University of Maryland) warned against limiting reading to secondary sources on women artists. One must not rely only on these accounts, which are often by condescending or even hostile authors.[5] Professor Withers went on to recommend that one concentrate on primary, first person materials whenever they are available. Look for interviews, diaries, letters, wills, memoirs, and documents such as guild and marriage laws; minutes of meetings, contracts, and the like can be surprisingly helpful. This kind of activity may not seem as glamorous as reading lavishly illustrated, well written art books, but it is the necessary prelude to producing such books, this time about women.

Fortunately, the Archives of American Art collects these primary materials on many American artists. The main archive is at the National Collection of Fine Arts in Washington, D.C., with regional repositories (mainly on microfilm) in New York, Detroit, Boston, and San Francisco. To quote from the foreword to its *Checklist:*

> The Archives' collection consists of over five million manuscripts, letters, notebooks, sketchbooks, clippings, exhibition catalogs, and rare and out-of-print publications. These are the papers of artists, craftsmen (sic), collectors, dealers, critics, historians, museums, societies, institutions. There are, in addition, 70,000 photographs and 1,200 tape-recorded interviews.[6]

To give some specific samples in our interest area, they have some of Mary Cassatt's letters, Kay Sage's journals, and a taped interview with Anais Nin; this invaluable material is available to any serious student.

The Archives joined with the Smithsonian staff to do an inventory of art works executed by American artists before 1914. Their computerized listings enable us to locate the many paintings by women artists owned privately. An index of works by women artists in public collections is being compiled by S. DeRenne Coerr, working with volunteers across the nation.[7]

The Frick Art Reference Library in New York and the Fogg Art Museum Library in Cambridge are storehouses of photographs of works of art.[8] Local museums and historical societies also often have reference libraries semi-open to the public; be persistent. Sister Judith Stoughton of St. Catherine's College in Minneapolis recommends the slide repositories at St. John's University in Minnesota and at St. Louis University in Missouri. We have had good luck turning up material on women artists in rare book collections in various universities.

Women's colleges often have special archives of materials on women, such as the Sophia Smith Collection at Smith in Northampton and Radcliffe's in Cambridge, Massachusetts. The Women's History Sources Survey, a project funded by the National Endowment for the Humanities and the University of Minnesota, has conducted a nation-wide search for women's archival and manuscript sources, for which catalogs are now becoming available.[9] At the

Women's Building in Los Angeles, Ruth Iskin, Arlene Raven, and others in their collective hold classes at The Center for Feminist Art Historical Studies.

Further material can be obtained from the ever-increasing number of women's studies journals, such as *Heresies, Signs, Chrysalis, Women's Studies,* and *Feminist Studies.* Of course, articles from different disciplines provide new ideas, approaches, interpretations, and methodologies, helping integrate discoveries within the full social and cultural context. Research on women artists (and on male artists too) benefits from a broadly interdisciplinary approach. You will find yourself wanting to know more about such apparently nonaesthetic concerns as guild and union rules, birth control, and property rights. Suddenly the lives and careers of women composers, the position of women writers in the Renaissance, or sex roles in Samoa assume importance. Natalie Z. Davis, now a professor at Princeton University, has compiled a thoroughly annotated bibliography of useful primary and secondary historical sources for such research on women.[10]

The more traditional sources such as art dictionaries like Thieme-Becker and Benezit can be quite rewarding too, even if one does not read German or French. They include lists of books and locations of works at the end of each biography. An entry that looks interesting should be photocopied and translated. *Art Index,* though it only goes back to 1929, provides leads to articles and illustrations. Especially useful are the entries listing location of hard-to-find color reproductions. And do not ignore art auction catalogs.

One can write to museums for black and white photographs or slides, if available, from their collections. Costs are not high, as no reproduction rights (fees) are charged for photographs being used only in educational study files. A good secondary effect is that the museum's attention is thus drawn to works they own by women artists, often basement-stored and ignored. Researchers might want to develop a letter that propagandizes a little along with the request, i.e.: "In my attempts to compensate for the omissions in my art history texts, I am writing to ask if you have photographs or slides available of the following works by women artists. . . ."

Those wishing to establish contact with living artists should write to them directly or through their galleries. Addresses are sometimes hard to find; the numerous who's who type books on artists, which purport to include "everyone who is anyone," often overlook important women artists. Gallery representation is usually listed in *Who's Who in American Art* (Bowker) or in the advertisements in art journals. Be as specific as possible in all queries and enclose a self-addressed, stamped envelope. Allow plenty of time for the artist or the gallery to respond, as few of them have secretarial help and all have busy schedules.

For researchers with no reading knowledge of foreign languages, the first area to investigate is American, Australian, Canadian, or English artists. Some will wish to work in the rich and neglected area of minority ethnic artists within this country.[11] Others may concentrate on a certain genre—women sculptors are a sizable and important group, active in the nineteenth century as well as at present—or on a certain period in history—say, WPA artists. The more specific the focus, the better.

For those who have a focus already on some period or genre, the research is fairly straightforward. Find the best books on the subject; read them for general background and for any traces of women artists. Sometimes, however, the best discoveries will be surprises—a beautiful color reproduction in some "coffee table" book organized around a theme such as "The Letter in Art," "Musical Instruments in Great Paintings," or, of course, "Mothers and Children." A scholar in quest of a certain image cannot afford a selection bias against women. (We finally found a color print of one of Artemisia Gentileschi's more graphic portrayals of Judith beheading Holofernes in a book on erotic art!) Another trick is to look in biographies of famous male artists for what we call the *uxor ejus* trace (Latin for "his wife"), i.e., information about a wife/sister/mother who was also an artist.[12]

Despite Virginia Woolf's theory that all poems listed as by Anon. were probably written by women, women artists rarely choose anonymity. It is forced upon them by absorption into the family name, by mislistings (for example: Giovann*a* Garzoni was miswritten as Giovann*i* for several centuries), or by being dropped from encyclopedias because the editor could not decide which name to use (as seems to have happened to Adelaide Labille Guiard Vincent, who married twice—a not infrequent occurrence, after all). Sometimes respectability imposes reticence, as was well described by an early sister-searcher, Eola Willis:

The quest for the history of the first woman painter in America (Henrietta Johnston) has been beset with as many difficulties as stalking the yale, or locating the lair of the unicorn, and the results are not quite so satisfactory, for while the yale has been found in the tombs of Luxor . . . and the unicorn's unique horn was held as a verity as late as 1862 in the pages of the London Athenaeum, the only verified history of this colonial limner is the notice of her funeral. . . . in this was carried out the unwritten law of the Carolina code—"A lady's Name should never appear in public print but twice: first to announce her marriage, and again to announce her death." As she died a maid, her history is simply "the shadow of a name."[13]

Fortunately, more information has since been discovered about Henrietta Johnston. Research on women artists has progressed since Eola Willis's day, but her problems should serve to remind us never to be overwhelmed by the difficulties in researching women artists!

Some further warnings: do not get bogged down in "images of women in art." It is tempting to do so, as there is so much more readily accessible material here—for example, Kenneth Clark's *The Nude*. Ultimately, such studies are still of male artists. The analysis of images can be consciousness (and blood pressure) raising, but if you do only that you will not be learning about the images women themselves make. Do not assume that paintings identified only as School of _____ are necessarily by males. Even works that seem securely labeled can be misattributed, especially if the art dealer felt that a male artist's name would fetch more money on the market; reattributions are being made constantly.[14]

The so-called naive artists are too often dismissed by traditionally trained art professionals, as are the anonymous folk or plantation arts such as crewel work, quilting, crocheting, silversmithing, dough sculpture, china painting, dollmaking, dressmaking, lacemaking, bookbinding, and so forth. There are several chapters in this present volume that deal with the spurious and injurious distinctions drawn between the arts and the crafts. We are coming again to appreciate the art done in those areas where women knew their tradition, had the materials, tools, and training, and felt confident of their skills and of society's support.

Also do not ignore the many women in all the art-related categories—the patrons, donors, collectors, gallery owners, art teachers, and historians. They make fascinating areas of study, from

Catherine de Medici to Betty Parsons. And who actually was Madame Tussaud?

We recommend, however, to our students that they start with their own family histories, checking back as many generations as possible. We suggest they be alert for any accounts of spinsters, widows, breadwinners, teachers, invalids, expatriates, or crazies— often these descriptions are clues pointing to a creative woman in an unsympathetic setting. They may find a diary or some letters saved, or even artifacts, up in their attics.

Then we expand the search to include regional women artists.[15] Those especially interested in the past will benefit from materials lovingly collected by local historical societies and libraries, art academies, grand houses, and small regional museums. Take field trips. Give some attention to the public statuary in your area; often these taken-for-granted pieces are by women and have quite a story behind them.[16] If you are more geared to contemporary art, begin by paying attention to the often unrecognized women artists working in your communities. Find them, take slides of their work, tape interviews, make up a central slide registry, and invite them to come present their work to classes. This kind of person-to-person research can have the effect of encouraging new work as well as uncovering what is being done.

Those who are themselves artists should be encouraged to write about their own art and that of their friends and thus combat first hand the later distortions of critics and historians. Think how grateful we are for the first-person accounts in the letters and diaries of Paula Modersohn-Becker, of Berthe Morisot, and of Käthe Kollwitz, which give us the sound of their voices. More recent examples, such as Barbara Hepworth's *Pictorial Autobiography* (Praeger, 1970) or Judy Chicago's *Through the Flower: My Struggles as a Woman Artist* (Doubleday, 1975), should inspire everyone of us to give our side of the story. Women really need to know more about the lives of women artists from the women artists' points of view.

Valuable material that is not yet available in printed form is often presented at panels or symposia of artists.[17] A panel organized at Sonoma State College in California by Wopo Holup and Susan Moulton, entitled Is There Life After Art School for the Woman Artist? was a painful, comic, truthful, and memorable occasion for participants and for the audience. Transcriptions of tapes from such events might well be publishable, as indeed is much of the material uncovered by feminist art research. Do not waste time doing rehashes of earlier published material with so much important original work to be done. And good luck!

NOTES

1. For a critique of these books, see Therese Schwartz, "They Built Women a Bad Art History," *The Feminist Art Journal* (Fall 1973). For a recapitulation of much of the material from them, see Hugo Munsterberg's recent *A History of Women Artists* (New York: Clarkson N. Potter, 1975).
2. We are here making no attempt to provide a bibliography of works on women artists, of course, but rather mentioning certain representative samples. Aside from the references listed in this volume and from those in the surveys mentioned, the Women's Caucus for Art includes announcements of new and in-progress research in its newsletter. S. De-Renne Coerr, 479 34th Ave., San Francisco, Calif. 94121, will send you what she has called *Art by Women: A Happy Hunting Bibliography*, at 50¢ a copy.
3. Charles Sterling, *Still Life Painting from Antiquity to the Present Time* (New York: Universe Books, 1959); Peter Mitchell, *Great Flower Painters* (New York: Overlook Press, 1973); and R. H. Wilenski, *Dutch Painting* (New York: Beechhurst Press, 1955).
4. The selected bibliography can be ordered from Worldwide Books, Inc., 37–39 Antwerp St., Boston, Mass. 02135, for $1.
5. Sarah Phillips has done a bibliography of the criticism on the fine artist, Loren MacIver, which just by the annotations demonstrates the effects of patronizing attitudes of certain male critics; it can be ordered from her at 12 Bass St. #7, Wollaston, Mass. 02170.
6. "A Checklist of the Collection," *Archives of American Art* (Washington, D.C.: Smithsonian, Spring 1975). Offices of the Archives are: 41 East 65 St., New York, N.Y. 10021; 5200 Woodward Ave., Detroit, Mich. 48202; 87 Mount Vernon St., Boston, Mass. 02108; c/o M. H. de Young Memorial Museum, Golden Gate Park, San Francisco, Calif. 94118; and, of course, the home office at the National Collection of Fine Arts, 8th and F. St., N.W., Washington, D. C. 20560.

7. This Inventory is available from all the addresses in note 6, but its intricacies make it difficult for the nonspecialist to use. If you or your students would like to assist in the project of indexing works in public collections by checking with your local museums, please write (including a self-addressed stamped envelope) to S. DeRenne Coerr, 479 34th St., San Francisco, Calif., 94121, whose two-volume book, *Art By Women: An Index of Artists, of U.S. Public Museums and Collections,* should be ready soon for publication.

8. Fair warning: at the Frick all researchers must comply with the dress code imposed by the family, i.e., *skirts* (but no spike heels) for women and blazer or coat and tie for men. You may prefer to correspond with the museum instead.

9. For more information and for the names and addresses of regional representatives, write directly to Clarke Chambers and Andrea Hinding, Women's History Sources Survey, Social Welfare History Archives, University of Minnesota Libraries, Minneapolis, Minn. 55455.

10. Natalie Zemon Davis and Jill K. Conway, *Society and the Sexes: A Bibliography of Women's History in Early Modern Europe, Colonial America, and the United States* (New York: Garland Publishing, 1977). *Signs* 3, no. 2 (Winter 1977) contains a helpful, though by no means complete, listing of bibliographies for research on women in a number of different fields.

11. One of the women artists slide sets distributed through Harper & Row is devoted to Third World American women artists and with it is included a bibliography, with names of helpful scholars in the field, to get people started; there is work enough for several lifetimes. See also note 30, chapter 7 in *Women Artists: Recognition and Reappraisal.* (Harper & Row, 1976).

12. Just some of the examples of what we also call the "Mozart's sister" syndrome are: Tintoretto, Fragonard, Brueghel, Copley, Peale, Eakins, John, Calder, Rivera, Ernst, Duchamp, and Tanguy. Read also Virginia Woolf's *A Room of One's Own* for a (fictional) account of the tragic life of Shakespeare's sister.

13. Eola Willis, "The First Woman Painter in America," *International Studio* (July 1927): 13.

14. A famous example is the so-called David at the Metropolitan Museum in New York, which is now thought to be the work of Constance Marie Charpentier.

15. The Modern Languages Association, 62 Fifth Ave., New York, N.Y. 10011, has developed an excellent model for doing such regional research on women writers, much of which would be adaptable to art.

16. See chapter 5 in *Women Artists: Recognition and Reappraisal* and also the exhibition catalog from Vassar College edited by William H. Gerdts, *The White Marmorean Flock* (Poughkeepsie, N.Y., 1972).

17. *Women Artists News*. Cynthia Navaretta, editor (Midmarch Associates, Box 3304, Grand Central Station, New York, N.Y. 10017) regularly publishes information about panel discussions held in New York City and other places.

8

Sex as a Status Characteristic in the Visual Arts

JEAN GILLIES

Women's studies courses are a valid and viable addition to traditional academic offerings. More and more campuses across the country are including them. With the founding of a National Women's Studies Association, it appears that these courses will be sanctioned as acceptable and established components of academia. Furthermore, women's studies are not consigned to higher education alone. One of the goals of the new association will be to disseminate information to precollege levels of education, for feminism is an attitude that should be learned through an evolutionary rather than a revolutionary process.

Since the interest in and growth of women's studies have not abated, it is appropriate to look at what has been offered in the visual arts. Even a cursory examination of listings from colleges and universities throughout the nation reveals that a feminist perspective on the visual arts is not widely represented and has been limited in scope. The relatively few courses that are being taught are historical revisions of the contributions of women artists and, in some cases, iconographical examinations of female images. These are necessary and valuable, but there are other directions in women's studies that might be used in courses on the visual arts, enriching or expanding what is now being offered. One such approach advocates crossing disciplinary boundaries, incorporating research and methodologies from other fields, to uncover interdisciplinary correspondences and generate new insights.

An avenue for the pursuit of this possibility is in the area of the social sciences, where scholars have been addressing a matter of concern to all women, one that is not inherent in the two directions now being followed by art historians and educators. For that reason alone it warrants attention. Currently social psychologists have been reexamining normative patterns of behavior and attitudes in order to understand the persistent perpetuation of sex-linked role behavior among individuals. No longer is it justifiable to explain these patterns as contingencies of biological functions; much more is involved, and researchers in this and related fields are seeking to identify other causative and/or contributory factors.

In the literature that addresses sex-linked role behavior, one of the most controversial issues among social scientists seems to be women's lack of high achievement. In conjunction with this problem, sex-role socialization differences between women and men are recurrent considerations. It appears that women do not expect to achieve as much or reach to the professional heights of men. Here the notion of "feedback," which is inferred during one's social interactions, is introduced as a process that affects both sexes and helps determine an individual's self-image in terms of expectancies and achievement.

In "Conceptualizing Sex as a Status Characteristic: Applications to Leadership Training Strategies," Marlaine E. Lockheed and Katherine P. Hall commented on the interactions of women and men in mixed-sex groups of colleagues.[1] Women tend to contribute less, take fewer initiatory actions, and have less influence than men in such situations. However, the authors' explanation for these characteristics differs from other theories by proposing that they are concomitants of status, as posited by Berger, Cohen, and Zelditch in their "theory of diffuse status characteristics and expectation states."[2] These three researchers believe that under specific conditions "the relative power and prestige of group members will be determined by their relative status."[3] The hypothesis of Lockheed and Hall, then, is that sex is a status characteristic that determines expectancies. Interaction between women and men depends on the status each holds in relation to the other; women are seen in and accept the lower rank; and feedback from male-female interaction teaches women to expect and achieve less than men.

The role of visual imagery in art may not seem pertinent to the problem of assigned positions of status, yet it is precisely this consideration that brings the visual arts and social psychology together.

Indeed, the humanist may be able to help the scientist identify why
and how such positioning is perpetuated, for status is best understood visually. Unlike role behavior, which can be explored in the
temporal arts of literature, theater, and film, status or rank is conceived as a hierarchical positioning of persons within a defined environment. This is a visual concept. Therefore, it may be proposed that
the perception of status in mixed-sex group interactions can be compared to the perception of rank in paintings and sculpture. Art, then,
may constitute a silent but powerful form of feedback that communicates and perpetuates societally accepted notions of sex as a characteristic of status.

Exploring these notions in a women's studies course could be
fruitful and exciting to the art historian or an educator who is familiar
with and can explain the formal conventions that convey rank in art.
The conventions themselves are obvious when pointed out, but cor-
relative principles should be presented also. First, it must be emphasized that the effectiveness of artistic devices depends on the
entire visual context and the way in which the viewer relates not just
to figural images but their spatial setting. Any teacher of art knows
that the average viewer primarily attends to subject matter, assuming
it to be the most important part of a work. The fact is, less obvious
compositional elements have predetermined the relationship of all
parts and, therefore, the viewer's response.

The total visual image, then, is an arrangement of still figures,
positioned in some kind of space. This space is defined by the figures
and in turn exists as their context. And experience indicates that the
status of figures depicted in paintings and sculpture is inferred from
the kind of arrangement used by the artist.

Next, some of the basic conventions governing rank in art may be
explained. A distinction needs to be made between works that depict
a single image and those with two or more figures. If only one image
is represented, the viewer is usually asked to relate to it personally.
Its size will tend to suggest its importance relative to the viewer. The
larger the figure is in relation to the defined perimeters of space, the
more important one assumes it to be. In a painting, the closer the
figure is to the plane of the two-dimensional surface, the more im-
pressive will be her or his visage in its immediacy to the viewer. If the
gaze of an image is directed outward from a frontal pose, the figure
seems to mandate attention and authority. Any "state" portrait will

give evidence of these points, demonstrating how the viewer perceives her or his own subordination to the person portrayed.

When two figures are represented, status is inferred from the ordering of the images themselves and the pictorialized relationship between them. Whether one or the other is seen as having a higher rank again depends on certain conventions. In those artistic traditions that ordinarily use a horizontal base line for all figures, the more important one will invariably be depicted on a larger scale. If the figures are the same size, it is assumed they have the same or equal rank. In traditions that do not place figures on a base line but instead penetrate the two-dimensional surface of a painting with an illusionistic third dimension, status is just as evident. One figure may be larger than another, set forward in the illusionistic space or placed above the other. These are all indications of rank. In addition, a figure is perceived as more important when it occupies the center of the composition, so that another must be placed to the side in a less prominent position.

Indeed, rank has been an important factor in art throughout documented history. The conventions that determine its legibility to and interpretation by the viewer were well established with the depictions of religious and royal images in ancient art. It is an axiom in the representation of deities that the more elevated the divinity, the higher or larger she or he must be in the composition. This principle, of course, has applied to both female and male deities and has been used with royal images as well to indicate that the viewer owes them obeisance and respect.

So deeply ingrained has been this axiom that the implications of its application to secular figures has gone virtually unnoticed. However, it may be that the transition from religious and regal rank ordering to secularized status positions was not made without a shift in meaning. Instead of connoting hierarchical status as a condition that warrants subordination out of respect, conventions that denote rank may now be associated with the importance of figures as they relate to each other—or the viewer—individually, societally, or, indeed, sexually.

This raises the question of whether sex in secular art has been shown as a status characteristic. If that be so, then it corresponds to the premise on which Lockheed and Hall based their article. Presumedly this can be answered by examining works of art for the use of status conventions, allowing for variables that might affect the positioning of figures, such as attributes or gestures that have specific iconographical meanings. If sex appears to be a status characteristic, then one may pursue the questions of (1) whether it is reasonable to assume that art has contributed to the persistence of rank ordering of women and men in mixed-sex interactions, and (2) whether the impact of visual imagery is sufficiently forceful to constitute a subliminal indoctrination of both women and men that affects achievement expectancies.

Answers to these questions cannot be given yet, but certainly they can be sought by feminists who are involved with visual images, especially those in women's studies programs. The notion that the depiction of rank in art may be intimately related to the persistence of sex as a characteristic of status has implications that are too far-reaching to be ignored.

It may be instructive to look at two paintings with the same subject matter to see how compositional differences affect the perception of status and, therefore, meaning in art. The subject of Oedipus and the Sphinx was painted by several artists during the nineteenth century. A comparison of one by Jean Auguste Dominique Ingres (1827) with that executed by Gustave Moreau in 1864 is especially interesting. Ingres placed a young, muscular Oedipus in the center of his vertical composition. The Sphinx, creature of power through her gift of prophecy, is shadowed on the left, foreboding but not intimidating to Oedipus, whose self-confidence is indicated by his firm stance as he leans toward and directs his gaze at the monster. One understands that he is unaware of danger. Moreau, on the other hand, placed the female creature in the center of his composition, with a slim Oedipus on the viewer's right, caught between the Sphinx's claws, which grab at vulnerable parts of his body, and the wall of rock, which blocks his exit and contains him within the painting. His head is down; he uses the rock for support, appearing off-balance because of the weight and aggression of the monster. There is no question that Oedipus' fate is inescapable. The Sphinx has him "in her clutches," and Oedipus is doomed.

There are similarities as well as differences between these two works that accentuate the importance of artistic choice. Both are vertically composed, and both depict the same two characters from the same episode of the famous Greek myth. The compositional devices that govern rank operate in the same way in both paintings, but the application of those devices differs. In the earlier work status is given to the male figure; in the later one, it is given to the female. Therefore, the viewer makes different inferences about the images and perceives a different meaning from each painting. In Ingres' painting one sees a stalwart young hero who seems to exemplify "manly virtues" and self-assurance. The viewer of Moreau's version sees a destructive, emasculating female monster, a dangerous predator. When Oedipus is given the higher rank, one perceives prestige and exemplary traits; when the Sphinx outranks him, one recognizes a power that is negative and threatening.

While it is probably true that external factors operating in the nineteenth century influenced the selection of this episode from the Oedipus story as subject matter, the contrast between the kind of power given to the male as opposed to that granted the female is compelling. Value judgments are implicit in the contrast. Ingres' Oedipus exhibits characteristics that are understood as positive, masculine traits. When the Sphinx controls the painting through the pictorial arrangement, her domination is recognized as a negative, female power. Conversely, the subordinate male in Moreau's version is seen as helpless, trapped, perhaps weak and effeminate; while the lower ranking Sphinx in the earlier painting is not an overt threat. These images, then, are value-loaded as status signifiers, and it is clear that men are supposed to have higher status and more power than women. She who deviates from her dependent status is dangerous and evil.

Similar types of female power images appear often in late nineteenth century art, so Moreau's Sphinx is not unique. *Femmes fatales*, sirens, and destructive monsters are frequent motifs. Rossetti's Pandoras, Beardsley's Salome, and Munch's vampire are obvious examples. In all cases these females tend to dominate the compositions with pictorialized rank. The message is clear—women who wield power are dangerous, and their power is sexual. If it is not controlled by both women and men, it will destroy.

In conclusion, the working hypothesis for a new line of inquiry in the visual arts applies information from social psychological investigations and proposes that works of art with human figures perpetuate status relationships between women and men that are understood as fixed because they are determined by sex. The visual evidence seems to positively reinforce higher status as a male attribute, and deviations from assigned rank are presented negatively. The corollaries are: (1) this kind of content contributes to the persistence of rank ordering of women and men in mixed-sex group interactions as a tangible expression of a visual concept, and (2) this kind of content constitutes feedback that is forceful enough to affect expectancies and self-valuation because it is perceived unconsciously from traditional artistic conventions that are received subliminally by the naive viewer repetitively and frequently.

The application of this line of inquiry to women's studies courses is self-evident. Using standard methodology, aesthetic principles and artistic conventions can be examined. Content and meaning in relation to style and artistic choice can be demonstrated, and the implications of the perpetuation of images that carry valuative connotations regarding sex-related status and traits can be explored.

NOTES

1. Marlaine E. Lockheed and Katherine Patterson Hall, "Conceptualizing Sex as a Status Characteristic: Applications to Leadership Training Strategies," *The Journal of Social Issues* 32:3 (Summer 1976): 111–124.
2. Joseph Berger, Bernard P. Cohen, and Morris Zelditch, Jr., "Status Conceptions and Social Interaction," *American Sociological Review*, 37:3 (June 1972): 241–255.
3. Lockheed and Hall, "Conceptualizing Sex as a Status Characteristic," p. 115.

II
FEMINIST
REEXAMINATIONS OF ART,
ARTISTS, AND SOCIETY

9

The Pink Glass Swan
Upward and Downward Mobility in the
Art World

LUCY R. LIPPARD

The general alienation of contemporary avant-garde art from any broad audience has been crystallized in the women's movement. From the beginning, both liberal feminists concerned with changing women's personal lives and socialist feminists concerned with overthrowing the classist/racist/sexist foundations of society have agreed that "fine" art is more or less irrelevant, though holding out the hope that feminist art could and should be different. The American women artists' movement has concentrated its efforts on gaining power within its own interest group—the art world, in itself an incestuous network of relationships between artists and art on the one hand and dealers, publishers, and buyers on the other. The public, the "masses," or the audience is hardly considered.

The art world has evolved its own curious class system. Externally this is a microcosm of capitalist society, but it maintains an internal dialectic (or just plan contradiction) that attempts to reverse or ignore that parallel. Fame may be a higher currency than mere money, but the two tend to go together. Since the buying and selling of art and artists is done by the ruling classes or by those chummy with them and their institutions, all artists or producers, no matter what their individual economic backgrounds, are dependent on the owners and forced into a proletarian role—just as women, in Engels' analysis, play proletarian to the male ruler across all class boundaries.

Looking at and "appreciating" art in this century has been understood as an instrument (or at best a result) of upward social mobility

in which owning art is the ultimate step. Making art is at the bottom
of the scale. This is the only legitimate reason to see artists as so
many artists see themselves—as "workers." At the same time,
artists/makers tend to feel misunderstood and, as *creators*, innately
superior to the buyers/owners. The innermost circle of the art world
class system thereby replaces the rulers with the creators, and the
contemporary artist in the big city (read New York) is a schizophrenic creature. S/he is persistently working "up" to be accepted, not
only by other artists, but also by the hierarchy that exhibits, writes
about, and buys her/his work. At the same time s/he is often ideolog-
ically working "down" in an attempt to identify with the workers
outside of the art context and to overthrow the rulers in the name of
art. This conflict is augmented by the fact that most artists are originally from the middle class, and their approach to the bourgeoisie
includes a touch of adolescent rebellion against authority. Those few
who have actually emerged from the working class sometimes use
this—their very lack of background privilege—as privilege in itself,
while playing the same schizophrenic foreground role as their solidly
middle-class colleagues.

Artists, then, are workers or at least producers even when they
don't know it. Yet artists dressed in work clothes (or expensive
imitations thereof) and producing a commodity accessible only to the
rich differ drastically from the real working class in that artists control their production and their product—or could if they realized it
and if they had the strength to maintain that control. In the studio, at
least, unlike the farm, the factory, and the mine, the unorganized
worker is in superficial control and can, if s/he dares, talk down to or
tell off the boss—the collector, the critic, the curator. For years now,
with little effect, it has been pointed out to artists that the art world
superstructure cannot run without them. Art, after all, is the product
on which all the money is made and the power based.

During the 1950s and 1960s most American artists were unaware
that they did *not* control their art, that their art could be used not
only for esthetic pleasure or decoration or status symbols, but also as
an educational weapon. In the late 1960s, between the Black, the
student, the antiwar, and the women's movements, the facts of the
exploitation of art in and out of the art world emerged. Most artists
and artworkers still ignore these issues because they make them feel
too uncomfortable and helpless. Yet if there were a strike against

museums and galleries to allow artists control of their work, the scabs would be out immediately in full force, with reasons ranging from self-interest to total lack of political awareness to a genuine belief that society would crumble without art, that art is "above it all." Or is it in fact *below* it all, as most political activists seem to think?

Another aspect of this conflict surfaces in discussions around who gets a "piece of the pie"—a phrase that has become the scornful designation for what is actually most people's goal. (Why shouldn't artists be able to make a living in this society like everybody else? Well, *almost* everybody else.) Those working for cultural change through political theorizing and occasional actions are opposed to *anybody* getting a piece of the pie, though politics appears to be getting fashionable again in the art world and may itself provide a vehicle for internal success; today one can refuse a piece of the pie and simultaneously be getting a chance at it. Still, the pie is very small, and there are a lot of hungry people circling it. Things were bad enough when only men were allowed to take a bite. Since "aggressive women" have gotten in there too, competition, always at the heart of the art world class system, has peaked.

Attendance at any large art school in the United States takes students from all classes and trains them for artists' schizophrenia. While being cool and chicly grubby (in the "uniform" of mass production), and knowing what's the latest in taste and what's the kind of art to make and the right names to drop is clearly "upward mobility"—from school into teaching jobs and/or the art world—the life-style accompanying these habits is heavily weighted "downward." The working-class girl who has had to work for nice clothes must drop into frayed jeans to make it into the art middle class, which in turn considers itself both upper and lower class. Choosing poverty is a confusing experience for a child whose parents (or more likely mother) have tried desperately against great odds to keep a clean and pleasant home.[1]

The artist who feels superior to the rich because s/he is disguised as someone who is poor provides a puzzle for the truly deprived. A parallel notion, rarely admitted but pervasive, is that people can't understand "art" if their houses are full of pink glass swans or their lawns are inhabited by gnomes and flamingos, or if they even care about houses and clothes at all. This is particularly ridiculous now, when art itself uses so much of this paraphernalia (and not always satirically); or, from another angle, when even artists who have no visible means of professional support live in palatial lofts and sport beat-up $100 boots while looking down on the "tourists" who come to SoHo to see art on Saturdays. SoHo is, in fact, the new suburbia. One reason for such callousness is a hangover from the 1950s, when artists really were poor and proud of being poor because their art, the argument went, must be good if the bad guys—the rich *and* the masses—didn't like it.

In the 1960s the choice of poverty, often excused as anticonsumerism, even infiltrated the esthetics of art.[2] First there was Pop Art, modeled on kitsch, advertising, and consumerism, and equally successful on its own level. (Women, incidentally, participated little in Pop Art, partly because of its blatant sexism—sometimes presented as a parody of the image of woman in the media—and partly because the subject matter was often "women's work," ennobled and acceptable only when the artists were men.) Then came Process Art—a rebellion against the "precious object" traditionally desired and bought by the rich. Here another kind of co-optation took place, when temporary piles of dirt, oil, rags, and filthy rubber began to grace carpeted living rooms. The Italian branch was even called *Arte Povera*. Then came the rise of a third-stream medium called "conceptual art," which offered "anti-objects" in the form of ideas—books or simple Xeroxed texts and photographs with no inherent physical or monetary value (until they got on the market, that is). Conceptual art seemed politically viable because of its notion that the use of ordinary, inexpensive, unbulky media would lead to a kind of socialization (or at least democratization) of art as opposed to gigantic canvases and huge chrome sculptures costing five figures and filling the world with more consumer fetishes.

Yet the trip from oil on canvas to ideas on Xerox was, in retrospect, yet another instance of "downward mobility" or middle-class guilt. It was no accident that conceptual art appeared at the height of the social movements of the late 1960s nor that the artists were sympathetic to those movements (with the qualified exception of the women's movement). All of the esthetic tendencies listed above were genuinely instigated as rebellions by the artists themselves, yet the fact remains that only rich people can afford to (1) spend money on art that won't last; (2) live with "ugly art" or art that is not decorative, because the rest of their surroundings are beautiful and comfortable; and (3) like "non-object art," which is only handy if you already have too many possessions—when it becomes a reactionary commentary: art for the overprivileged in a consumer society.

As a child, I was accused by my parents of being an "anti-snob snob" and I'm only beginning to see the limitations of such a rebellion. Years later I was an early supporter of and proselytizer for conceptual art as escape from the commodity orientation of the art world, a way of communicating with a broader audience via inexpensive media. Though I was bitterly disappointed (with the social, not the esthetic achievements) when I found that this work could be so easily absorbed into the system, it is only now that I've realized why the absorption took place. Conceptual art's democratic efforts and physical vehicles were cancelled out by its neutral, elitist content and its patronizing approach. From around 1967 to 1971, most of us involved in conceptual art saw that content as pretty revolutionary and thought of ourselves as rebels against the cool, hostile artifacts of the prevailing formalist and minimal art. But we were so totally enveloped in the middle-class approach to everything we did and saw, we couldn't perceive how that pseudo-academic narrative piece or that art world-oriented action in the streets was deprived of any revolutionary content by the fact that it was usually incomprehensible and alienating to the people "out there," no matter how fashionably downwardly mobile it might be in the art world. The idea that if art is subversive in the art world, it will automatically appeal to a general audience now seems absurd.

The whole evolutionary basis of modernist innovation, the idea of esthetic "progress," the "I-did-it-first" and "it's-been-done-already" syndromes that pervade contemporary avant-garde art and criticism, are also blatantly classist and have more to do with technology than with art. To be "avant-garde" is inevitably to be on top, or to become upper-middle-class, because such innovations take place in a context accessible only to the educated elite. Thus socially conscious artists working in or with community groups and muralists try to disassociate themselves from the art world, even though its values ("quality") remain to haunt them personally.

The value systems are different in and out of the art world, and anyone attempting to straddle the two develops another kind of schizophrenia. For instance, in the inner city community murals, the images of woman are the traditional ones—a beautiful, noble mother and housewife or worker, and a rebellious young woman striving to change her world—both of them celebrated for their courage to be and to stay the way they are and to support their men in the face of horrendous odds. This is not the art-world or middle-class "radical" view of future feminism, nor is it one that radical feminists hoping to "reach out" across the classes can easily espouse. Here, in the realm of aspirations, is where upward and downward mobility and status quo clash, where the economic class barriers are established. As Michele Russell has noted,[3] the Third-World woman is not attracted to the "Utopian experimentation" of the left (in the art world, the would-be Marxist avant-garde) or to the "pragmatic opportunism" of the right (in the art world, those who reform and co-opt the radicals").

Many of the subjects touched on here come back to Taste. To a poor woman, art, or a beautiful object, might be defined as something she cannot have. Beauty and art have been defined before as *the desirable*. In a consumer society, art too becomes a commodity rather than a life-enhancing experience. Yet the Van Gogh reproduction or the pink glass swan—the same beautiful objects that may be "below" a middle-class woman (because she has, in moving upward, acquired upper-class taste, or would like to think she has)— may be "above" or inaccessible to a welfare mother. The phrase "to dictate taste" has its own political connotations. A Minneapolis worker interviewed by students of artist Don Celender said he liked "old art works because they're more classy,"[4] and class does seem to be what the traditional notion of art is all about. Yet contemporary avant-garde art, for all its attempts to break out of that gold frame, is equally class-bound, and even the artist aware of these contradictions in her/his own life and work is hard put to resolve them. It's a vicious circle. If the artist-producer is upper-middle-class, and our standards of art as taught in schools are persistently upper-middle-class, how do we escape making art only *for* the upper-middle-class?

The alternatives to "quality," to the "high" art shown in art-world galleries and magazines have been few and for the most part unsatisfying, although well-intended. Even when kitsch, politics, or housework are absorbed into art, contact with the real world is not necessarily made. At no time has the avant-garde, though playing in the famous "gap between art and life," moved far enough out of the art context to attract a broad audience—that audience which has, ironically, been trained to think of art as something that has nothing to do with life and, at the same time, tends only to like that art that means something in terms of its own life or fantasies. The dilemma for the leftist artist in the middle-class is that her/his standards seem to have been set irremediably. No matter how much we know about what the broader public wants, or *needs*, it is very difficult to break social conditioning and cultural habits. Hopefully, a truly feminist art will provide other standards.

To understand the woman artist's position in this complex situation between the art world and the real world, class, and gender, it is necessary to know that in America artists are rarely respected unless they are stars or rich or mad or dead. Being an artist is not being "somebody." Middle-class families are happy to pay lip service to art but god forbid their own children take it so seriously as to consider it a profession. Thus a man who becomes an artist is asked when he is going to "go to work," and he is not so covertly considered a child, a sissy (a woman), someone who has a hobby rather than a vocation, or someone who can't make money and therefore cannot hold his head up in the real world of men—at least until his work sells, at which point he may be welcomed back. Male artists, bending over backward to rid themselves of this stigma, tend to be particularly suscep-tible to insecurity and *machismo*. So women daring to insist on their place in the primary rank—as art makers rather than as art house-keepers (curators, critics, dealers, "patrons")—inherit a heavy bur-den of male fears in addition to the economic and psychological discrimination still rampant in a patriarchal, money-oriented society.

Most art being shown now has little to do with any woman's ex-perience, in part because women—rich ones as "patrons," others as decorators and "homemakers"—are in charge of the private sphere, while men identify more easily with public art—art that has become public through economic validation (the million-dollar Rembrandt). Private art is often seen as mere ornament; public art is associated with monuments and money, with "high" art and its containers, in-cluding unwelcoming white-walled galleries and museums with clas-sical courthouse architecture. Even the graffiti artists, whose work was unsuccessfully transferred from subways to art galleries, were all men, concerned with facades, with having their names in spray paint, in lights, in museums. . . .

Private art is visible only to intimates. I suspect the reason so few women "folk" artists work outdoors in large scale (like Simon Rodia's Watts Towers and other "naives and visionaries" with their cement and bottles) is not only because men aspire to erections and know how to use the necessary tools, but because women can and must assuage these same creative urges inside the house, with the pink glass swan as an element in their own works of art—the living room or kitchen. In the art world the situation is doubly paralleled. Women's art until recently was rarely seen in public, and all artists are voluntarily "women" because of the social attitudes mentioned above; the art world is so small that it is "private."

Just as the living room is enclosed by the building it is in, art and artist are firmly imprisoned by the culture that supports them. Artists claiming to work for themselves alone, and not for any audience at all, are passively accepting the upper-middle-class audience of the internal art world. This is compounded by the fact that to be middle-class is to be passive, to live with the expectation of being taken care of and entertained. But art should be a consciousness-raiser; it partakes of and should fuse the private and the public spheres. It should be able to reintegrate the personal without being satisfied by the *merely* personal. One good test is whether or not it communicates, and then, of course, what and how it communicates. If it doesn't communicate, it may just not be very good art from anyone's point of view, or it may be that the artist is not even aware of the needs of others, or simply doesn't care.

For there is a need out there, a need vaguely satisfied at the moment by "schlock."[5] And it seems that one of the basic tenets of the feminist arts should be a reaching out from the private sphere to transform that "artificial art" and to more fully satisfy that need. For the art-world artist has come to consider her/his private needs paramount and has too often forgotten about those of the audience, any audience. Work that communicates to a dangerous number of people is derogatorily called a "crowd pleaser." This is a blatantly classist attitude, taking for granted that most people are by nature incapable of understanding good art (i.e., upper-class or quality art). At the same time, much ado is made about art educational theories that claim to "teach people to see" (consider the political implications of this notion) and muffle all issues by stressing the "universality" of great art.

It may be that at the moment the possibilities are slim for a middle-class art world's understanding or criticism of the little art we see that reflects working-class cultural values. Perhaps our current responsibility lies in humanizing our own activities so that they will communicate more effectively with all women. Hopefully we will aspire to more than women's art flooding the museum and gallery circuit. Perhaps a feminist art will only emerge when we become wholly responsible for our own work, for what becomes of it, who sees it, and who is nourished by it. For a feminist artist, whatever her style, the prime audience at this time is other women. So far, we have tended to be satisfied with communicating with those women whose social experience is close to ours. This is natural enough, since this is where we will get our greatest support, and we need support in taking this risk of trying to please *women*, knowing that we are almost certain to displease men in the process. In addition, it is embarrassing to talk openly about the class system that divides us, hard to do so without sounding more bourgeois than ever in the implications of superiority and inferiority inherent in such discussions (where the working class is as often considered superior to the middle class).

A book of essays called *Class and Feminism* written by The Furies, a lesbian feminist collective, makes clear that from the point of view of working-class women, class is a definite problem within the women's movement. As Nancy Myron observes, middle-class women:

> can intellectualize, politicize, accuse, abuse, and contribute money in order not to deal with their own classism. Even if they admit that class exists, they are not likely to admit that their behavior is a product of it. They will go through every painful detail of their lives to prove to me or another working-class woman that they really didn't have any privilege, that their family was exceptional, that they actually did have an uncle who worked in a factory. To ease anyone's guilt is not the point of talking about class. . . . You don't get rid of oppression just by talking about it.[6]

Women are more strenuously conditioned toward upward cultural mobility or "gentility" than men, which often results in the woman consciously betraying her class origins as a matter of course. The hierarchies within the whole span of the middle class are most easily demarcated by life-style and dress. For instance, the much scorned "Queens housewife" may have enough to eat, may have learned to consume the unnecessities, and may have made it to a desired social bracket in her community, but if she ventures to make art (not just own it), she will find herself back at the bottom in the art world, looking wistfully up to the plateau where the male, the young, the bejeaned seem so at ease.

For middle-class women in the art world not only dress "down," but dress like working-class *men*. They do so because housedresses, pedal pushers, polyester pantsuits, permanents, and the wrong accents are not such acceptable disguises for women as the boots, overalls, and windbreaker syndromes are for men. Thus, young middle-class women tend to deny their female counterparts and take on "male" (unisex) attire. It may at times have been chic to dress like a native American or a Bedouin woman, but it has never been chic to dress like a working woman, even if she's trying to look like Jackie Kennedy. Young working-class women (and men) spend a large amount of available money on clothes; it's a way to forget the rats and roaches by which even the cleanest tenement dwellers are blessed, or the mortgages by which even the hardest working homeowners are blessed, and to present a classy facade. Artists dressing and talking "down" insult the hardhats much as rich kids in rags do; they insult people whose notion of art is something to work for—the pink glass swan.

Yet women, as evidenced by the Furies' publication and as pointed out elsewhere (most notably by Bebel), have a unique chance to communicate with women across the boundaries of economic class because as a "vertical class" we share the majority of our most fundamental experiences—emotionally, even when economically we are divided. Thus an economic analysis does not adequately explore the psychological and esthetic ramifications of the need for change within a sexually oppressed group. Nor does it take into consideration that women's needs are different from men's—or so it seems at this still unequal point in history. The vertical class cuts across the horizontal economic classes in a column of injustices. While heightened class consciousness can only clarify the way we see the world, and all clarification is for the better, I can't bring myself to trust hard lines and categories where fledgling feminism is concerned.

Even in the art world, the issue of feminism has barely been raised in mixed political groups. In 1970, women took our rage and our energies to our own organizations or directly to the public by means of picketing and protests. While a few men supported these, and most politically conscious male artists now claim to be feminists to some degree, the political *and* apolitical art world goes on as though feminism didn't exist—the presence of a few vociferous feminist artists and critics notwithstanding. And in the art world, as in the real world, political commitment frequently means total disregard for feminist priorities. Even the increasingly Marxist group ironically calling itself Art-Language is unwilling to stop the exclusive use of the male pronoun in its theoretical publications.[7]

Experience like this one and dissatisfaction with Marxism's lack of interest in "the woman question" make me wary of merging Marxism and feminism. The notion of the non-economic or "vertical" class is anathema to Marxists, and confusion is rampant around the chicken-egg question of whether women can be equal before the establishment of a classless society or whether a classless society can be established before women are liberated. As Sheila Rowbotham says of her own Marxism and feminism:

> They are at once incompatible and in real need of one another. As a feminist and a Marxist, I carry their contradictions within me, and it is tempting to opt for one or the other in an effort to produce a tidy resolution of the commotion generated by the antagonism between them. But to do that would mean evading the social reality which gives rise to the antagonism.[8]

As women, therefore, we need to establish far more strongly our own sense of community, so that all our arts will be enjoyed by all women in all economic circumstances. This will happen only when women artists make conscious efforts to cross class barriers, to consider their audience, to see, respect, and work with the women who create outside the art world—whether in suburban crafts guilds or in offices and factories or in community workshops. The current feminist passion for women's traditional arts, which influences a great many women artists, should make this road much easier, unless it too becomes another commercialized rip-off. Despite the very real class obstacles, I feel strongly that women are in a privileged position to satisfy the goal of an art that would communicate the needs of all classes and sexes to each other, and get rid of the we/they dichotomy to as great an extent as is possible in a capitalist framework. Our sex, our oppression, and our female experience—our female culture, just being explored—offer access to all of us by these common threads.

NOTES

1. Charlotte Bunch and Nancy Myron, eds., *Class and Feminism* (Baltimore: Diana Press, 1974). This book contains some excrutiating insights for the middle-class feminist; it raised my consciousness and inspired this essay (along with other recent experiences and conversations).
2. Actually nothing new; the history of modern art demonstrates a constant longing for the primitive, the simple, the clear, the "poor," the noble naif, and the like.
3. Michele Russell, "Women and the Third World," in *New American Movement* (Oakland, Calif.: June 1973).
4. Don Celender, ed., *Opinions of Working People Concerning the Arts* (St. Paul, Minn.: Macalester College, 1975).
5. Bernard Kirchenbaum, in correspondence. Celender, *Opinions of Working People*, offers proof of this need and of the huge (and amazing) interest in art expressed by the working class, though it should be said that much of what is called art would not be agreed upon by the taste dictators.
6. Bunch and Myron, *Class and Feminism*.
7. This despite their publication of and apparent endorsement of Carolee Schneemann's "The Pronoun Tyranny," in *The Fox*, 3 (Wellesley, Mass.: Shiryoku, 1976).
8. Sheila Rowbotham, *Women: Resistance and Revolution* (London: Allen Lane, 1972; New York: Pantheon, 1972).

10

Female Experience in Art
The Impact of Women's Art in a Work Environment

RUTH E. ISKIN

In early summer of 1975 I was asked by the Women's Committee and the Office of Equal Opportunity of Aerospace Corporation to curate an exhibition of women's art on the subject of female experience. This seemed to me to offer the potential of reaching a broad audience and avoiding the defensive reactions often attached to "feminist art" or "female sensibility" in the art world.[1] This art has been at the heart of an ongoing, often heated controversy that has clouded the issues and obstructed direct perception of the work.

Female experience has been the starting point for the new art created by feminists since 1969. Consciousness-raising and other forms of women's communication, sharing and group action initiated as a result of the women's movement, made female experience a rich source of subject matter and sparked the fresh energy with which women are making art. For the show I selected the work of 15 Los Angeles artists[2] to represent both a broad scope of women's experiences and a diversity of media, ranging from large environmental pieces to paintings, drawings, photography, prints, collage, assemblage, and artists' books. In an attempt to build a bridge between the art and the creators' intentions, I requested written statements from the artists, which, along with biographical information, were available in a folder in the exhibition area.

The exhibition was on view from August 18th through September 5th in the cafeteria conference dining rooms of the Aerospace Corporation. It was the first exhibition of professional art on the company's ground, preceded only by shows of art by employees. Although sponsored and funded by the corporation, the show was initiated by feminist employees who conceived it to offer "insight into the emotional aspects of contemporary women."[3] They scheduled it to coincide with Women's Week, a program featuring prominent speakers and entertainers.

The management of Aerospace Corporation ("a non-profit research and development corporation, which provides technical direction of general systems of engineering, primarily for the Air Force"[4]) had been forced to develop new policies for hiring women to meet affirmative action requirements for receiving government funds. Women are in the minority, constituting only 25 percent of the roughly 3,200 Aerospace employees. Most of them (80–85 percent) are in lower echelon clerical and secretarial positions; only a few rank among the engineers, scientists, or chief administrators. The company was, no doubt, hoping that the art exhibition and the activities of Women's Week would go on record as testimony to their newfound good will toward women. Much to my surprise, and to the dismay of the sponsors, the exhibition became the focal point of hot debate. Violent emotional reactions, protests, and support quickly assumed the dimensions of a local scandal and echoed for months in letters to the editor in *The Orbiter*, the company's newspaper.

The art in the exhibition offered a feminist point of view on subject matter usually treated from a male perspective. Though one might assume that the controversial responses arose out of an alienation from contemporary art forms, it seems that the conflict stemmed primarily from feminist content.[5] None of the works included were blatantly political protest art, yet they all reflected, to varying degrees, a new feminist consciousness. It was this consciousness—judging from the reactions of many of the female viewers—that was unfamiliar and threatening.

We are accustomed to think of political art as crude, illustrative, or plainly propagandistic, in contrast to "good/serious/modernist" art. It has, of course, been pointed out that no art is entirely disconnected from its historical, political, cultural, and geographical environment and that, therefore, any art reflects these conditions. However, feminist art is often labeled political art because the consciousness it reflects is held by a minority, and it is at odds with the tacit beliefs of those in power. The label "political art" is used to demean the work rather than to evaluate its artistic significance.

In a recent interview with Judy Chicago, the artist articulated her thoughts and feelings about these issues:

> The issue of politics for me arises at the point where my work interfaces with culture; it does not arise at the point of origin in my studio. I never think about politics when I make my art; rather I think about being true to my own impulses, and for a woman to be true to her own impulses is, at this point in history, a political act. . . . What I challenge is the idea that masculinity is inherently better than femininity; that hardness is better than softness, that defensiveness is better than vulnerability, and that violence is better than sharing. The assertion of womanhood is a challenge to all these values that allow war, dehumanization, rape, and art that lacks relationship with reality.[6]

Faith Wilding elaborated on the relation between personal and political change:

> It has always been a tenet of the feminist movement that the personal is political. It is political because when a person becomes transformed, enters into public experience, and infuses her own experience into the public, the world becomes transformed for her, but in addition she then has the possibility of transforming the world. . . . We have witnessed too many people who are in politics who have never experienced any kind of personal change or real vision.

What specifically triggered the controversy? The art in the exhibition included a wide range of feminist work: parodies on public images of women (Helen Alm Roth and Carole Caroompas); private images of women and interior spaces (Margaret Neilson); women's self-images integrated with their historical and mythological references (Judy Chicago and Faith Wilding); references to women's vulnerability, powerlessness, and powerfulness (Astrid Preston); relics of admired female figures as magic talismans (Hazel Slawson); communal efforts (Maria Karras); and the quilt/grid pattern and color pink seen as tributes to women's collaborative forms (Sheila de Bretteville).

In her tableau environment, *Remnants in Homage to Lily Bart from Edith Wharton's House of Mirth*, Nancy Youdelman "reconstructed" a scene from the book with theatrical grandeur and presence. The tableau represents the climax of Wharton's novel, when Lily Bart, having lost her wealth and status, kills herself. Hauntingly life-like, her full-size figure, bearing the artist's own features, reclines in bed. Her skin tone is grayish, and the sleeping drops that caused her death are by the side of her bed. The floor is cluttered with remnants of her life: letters, photographs, delicate laces, dresses, corsets, and veils. Youdelman creates metaphors (sleep, passivity, death) for what have been essential aspects of female experience: economic dependence on others, lack of ultimate control over one's own life, victimization by circumstances. In the guise of a nineteenth-century tragedy, Lily Bart's story is emblematic for women who have remained powerless in society.

In Youdelman's photographic series *Leaves: A Self Portrait*, the artist is lying on the ground, gradually being covered with leaves (from photograph to photograph) until she is entirely buried:

> It represented ways I felt; I felt numb all over, or like a sleepwalker, something that could just disappear, and I think that is that powerlessness in female experience, sleep. There is also something esthetic about it; I love the color of the leaves; it is about death, and one could suppose that it might also mean renewal.

Youdelman treads on precarious ground in presenting the passive female figure, lying unconscious, as horizontal female figures have so often been used in the history of (male) art to entice the spectator by reminding him of his vertical superiority. However, Youdelman's tableau successfully evokes the solemn empathy of the viewer, who is confronted with the *victim's* feelings about her powerlessness.

In Jan Lester's tableau environment, *Cats Enamoured Kits: Helpless Tom and Merciless Sex Kitten* (1974), two cats are anthropomorphized to enact a sexual encounter scene. The human environment, dress, and behavior patterns throw into relief the stereotyped patterns of men and women, only the roles are reversed. The female cat plays the determined "attacker," the seducer, while the male cat withdraws with some apprehension. At the same time, Lester sees her work as a manifestation of how women are perceived when they take an active role in a situation.

> The tableau had to do with sexual politics and with the female taking power. It goes further than just one sexual encounter; it goes out into the world in general. It is *one* situation like a snapshot that makes it clear that this goes on in all situations in society.

Sherie Scheer's series, *Heavenly Visions*, depicts Fragonard-inspired images of her own baby as a cherub floating in an infinite blue California sky. "Wherever they go, they have no choice in it. . . . The heavenly vision in which they appear is both ideal and it is limbo." This reflects Scheer's own experience as a first-time mother:

I found the child very sensual. It was unexpected to me what a strong female biological experience it was to have a child, and then to be absolutely in love with the child. In the course of using her as a model, however, I made her cry, sometimes neglected her, and in a way I *used* her, both as a model and as inspiration. . . . I was aware that the art that makes it in L.A., or made it at the time was nonimage-oriented, and I am very image-oriented. I was also entirely aware that showing babies in one's art was really outrageous, and it gave me a devilish pleasure, because I think that a lot of art that makes it is empty formula and doesn't have any blood in it; it is not daring and it is not a turn-on either. So it was like breaking a taboo, and especially for a woman artist.

Like Scheer, Gilah Hirsch deals with female power within its traditional domain. She uses the imagery of food as "a secret biography, a metaphorical code:"

The shape and color of food itself was so completely right and ripe for my own feelings that it became a symbol for me; especially the tomato, strawberry, and egg became symbols for myself. These are expressed in scale and potency; it is a strange word to use in relationship to an egg, a potent egg. . . . The strawberry is one of the few fruits that carries its seed on the outside, it is a vulnerable fruit; it is juicy and has strength and vulnerability at the same time. . . . Rather than feminist, these paintings are, I think, more expressive of femaleness. It was a personal statement for me. . . . I can't separate my experience from a female experience; I feel powers in me, very specifically in certain centers in me.

Suzanne Lacy's book *Rape Is* (1972) has a white cover that becomes bloody red on the inside. To open the book one must tear apart a red sticker labeled "rape."[7] Lacy's book names 21 instances of rape—not only as a sexual violation but also a series of psychological assaults:

Rape is when you are skipping home from school and are surrounded suddenly by a gang of large boys. Rape is when the man next door exposes himself and you feel guilty for having looked. Rape is when you're walking alone, thinking your own thoughts, and a man driving by shouts, "Hi Sweetie!"

The traditional representation of rape in art (with the exception of Kollwitz[8]) represents the experience of the rapist by focusing on his strength, activity, and beauty and further removes rape from a realistic experience through mythological disguise. Lacy first forces the viewer to enact a metaphorical rape ("deflowering" the book by tearing the sticker) and then confronts the viewer with what rape means to its victim.

In Karen Carson's drawings of beds (1971–75) woman *is* the bed. The drawings are expressionistic in style and imagery, powerful as well as satirical statements about the myth of happiness in sexual relationships. In this case, too, the "disturbing" feminist content of Carson's drawings arises from the historical art tradition of reclining female figures on beds and sofas. Many of these women become an integral part of the inanimate, passive, yet sexually inviting surface on which they are reclining. Unlike males, Carson identifies with the oppressed—the woman-bed—and at the same time, as artist, she takes active charge of that surface, penetrates it with a giant screw *(Screw)*, converts it into a carton of eggs *(Easy Lay)*, severs it with a saw blade *(Edge of Night)*, or crowns it with a giant camera *(Easy Shot)*.

These surreal visualizations are take-offs on popular puns, which function as titles and were often the starting points for the drawings. The series began as a macabre, though humorous, comment on popular sexist-consumerism. What emerges is a violent denunciation of sexual roles, until finally the bed—former haven of consumer pleasure—disintegrates from *within (Cracking Up* and *Shattered Dreams),* smashing any illusions we might still have about bed and woman. In these most recent drawings the formerly inanimate object erupts uncontrollable, and its fragments fly into space. What is commonly labeled women's liberation is, in fact, as Carson expresses it, an excruciatingly painful process beginning with the recognition of exterior oppression, leading to the experience of oppression from within, and finally building toward a complex reintegration—represented by the artist's new work—collages in which the torn and mutilated fragments are reunited on a cohesive surface.

I would say that these drawings were intentionally propagandistic. . . . It had to do with consumer and sexual politics. . . . The frame of mind that I was in when I did these drawings was severe frustration over treatment by men. . . . The drawings were also politically charged for me because I talked about them to all kinds of groups from Valley housewives to a continuation high school culture-hour class; I thought people would be bored by these drawings and they weren't. They seemed to have a good time and related to the drawings immediately. Now, it is not necessary to have a good time when viewing art, but there was blanket recognition of the issues.

When I looked in the newspaper, I noticed that you could apply sexual politics, directly or indirectly, to almost every image in the advertisement world; every image implies sexual promises. My original fantasy was that I would have enough money to take out a full page ad in the *L.A. Times* and just change the images a little bit. Obviously the most political thing about that was my fantasy about how many people I could reach that way. It is the nature of good political art to be recognizable and understandable by a lot of people and maybe at a visceral level too. . . . Political art is often satirical and probably most effective at that level.

The Aerospace exhibition provided an opportunity to witness the heightened impact of contemporary feminist art when viewed by a "nonart" audience—a cross-section of middle America who normally would not encounter art, and specifically by a female audience alienated from feminism. (The negative response came primarily from women.[9]) It can also be seen as a test case for implementing a long-desired goal—bringing art into a public daily work environment.

Had the show been exhibited in any number of established or alternative gallery spaces, it probably would not have caused unusual debate, and certainly it would not have promoted any doubt about the artistic merit of the work.[10] In the cafeteria conference rooms of Aerospace, however, the exhibit infiltrated a male environment that ordinarily would not display women's work made from a feminist perspective and certainly would not give it public acclaim. The work was predominantly considered scandalous; it engendered passionate objections and firm negative judgments. The show was labeled *pornography* rather than *art* by people who were unlikely ever to have considered what is or isn't art.

This disclaimer was the protesters' attempt to dismiss such threatening and upsetting material. Casting it as pornography im-

plied that the art lacked any real esthetic value and therefore need
not be taken seriously. The level of naiveté of the critical
responses—when opposed to the more sophisticated criticism to
which we are accustomed from much of the art world—was refreshing in its directness. One letter of protest stated:

> I object to the Art Exhibition. . . . I find it degrading. As a woman, and
> hopefully a lady, I find it extremely offensive. . . . I am unable to lower
> my sights to the gutter level of this exhibit. In my opinion, it is lewd,
> vulgar, obscene and immoral. Since when did good taste and modesty go
> out-of-style?[11]

In another letter, signed by 36 people—almost a petition—the art
was called:

> in poor taste, bad character, and a definite infringement on the rights of
> all women and men who give sex the dignity, respect and honor that was
> intended for the human race.
>
> The Aerospace Corporation has drastically changed its practices since
> the 1960s to allow this type of "smut" to be exhibited, and the employees
> were encouraged through desk-to-desk distribution and advertising to
> view the exhibition.
>
> We are sure that with much less expense to the Company, the repre-
> sentatives . . . could have arranged for a display of pornography, pictures
> and books from one of the adult bookstores in the Los Angeles Area, and
> at a lower insurance premium. . . . The Aerospace Women's Committee
> does not speak for all of the female employees, as there are those of us
> who still adhere to the old principle that we were liberated immediately
> when we were born in America, we enjoy being treated as a woman and
> we are definitely Miss or Mrs. and not Ms.[12]

Clearly these female viewers at Aerospace "saw" in the art their
own worst fears of feminism. Their objections, though focused on
the exhibition, were rooted in their alienation from the organized
women's movement. Confronted by art that dealt with an oppression
familiar in most of their lives, real images that did not correspond to
the illusion of the American dream presented a powerful threat.
The art was perceived as offensive precisely because it was not
placed in a neutralizing environment like a gallery, where viewers
can easily hide behind anonymity. The art invaded their own daily
working sphere where it threatened how they were viewed in their

professional positions. Brought into the work context, the art reflected more directly upon them. The heightened emotional reactions caused a strong need to disassociate themselves verbally from the picture of womanhood presented in the show.

While identification with female experiences and values is threatening in any situation in a patriarchal society, such identification may be virtually impossible when introduced into a work environment dominated by male values and power. Such an environment, by implication and as a condition for the possibility of working there, demands a woman's identification with patriarchy over a recognition of her own oppression. To admit that what was expressed in the art is real—women's powerlessness and powerfulness, their sexual feelings and experiences, and the fact that women are rape victims—is to shatter the very myth that has sustained traditional womanhood all along. It is admitting publicly to an embarrassing, private part of woman's experience, which she has attempted to conceal even from herself in an effort to preserve the "human dignity" of which she is robbed daily. This response is one we all felt during initial stages of our femininism, when we first became conscious of the shame and self-dislike we had buried for so long, before we were ready to reshape our own feelings by taking pride in ourselves, other women, and art that dealt with these subjects.

The reactions of the women at Aerospace are not, I suspect, uncommon. I doubt very much that a minority of Black workers in a predominantly white work environment would find it any easier to respond to an exhibition of art exposing painful aspects of the experience of being Black in American society; or that Detroit factory workers, for example, readily identify with the realistic presentation in Rivera's mural of the hardships of factory work.[13] There is, however, an important difference between the situation of women and other workers. Regardless of their status, women are subject to oppression as women, which crosses class boundaries. In addition to their job or profession—whether factory worker, teacher, nurse, doctor, engineer, or scientist—women still do the unpaid, endless, menial labor of housework, bear children, and carry the sole responsibility of raising them. All women are potential rape victims, and all women live in a male-dominated society, which is based on various cultural versions of enslavement and denies women's culture.[14]

Those women who had not attempted to step out of female role conditioning in their jobs at Aerospace were more oppressed than other workers because they received lower wages and had lower professional status. They were the most offended by the show. The middle-class women who rebelled against female role conditioning in their jobs at Aerospace (the engineers, programmers, scientists) were the only ones who had developed a feminist consciousness and reacted favorably to the exhibition. For example, in a letter of support, one woman expressed her response to the exhibition and the protesters' views:

> That women have suffered personally and professionally from conditions ranging from lack of opportunity to manipulation and even exploitation on the basis that they are women is uncomfortable to face.
>
> The Art Exhibition, a high quality collection of some very honest and courageous works, was unusually rich in content for those of us who in some way or another have "been there." Although there was a deliberate intent to shock, it was as a means to focus emotionally on the art; it was not propagandistic. These are personal and esthetic interpretations of some of the hard truths encountered by women, and the obscenity lies in the fact that these wrongs arise because of wide-range departure from good human values.
>
> Those who want to oppose smut should look for it in our politics, in our mores, in the management of our corporations, in our personal relationships.[15]

In her review of the exhibition, Melinda Worz concluded:

> The Female Experience in Art offers a wide panorama of contemporary women's attitudes. . . . It is gratifying to see such a high quality show outside the established sacred halls of art, as part of a working environment.[16]

In thinking now about this exhibition, I realize that it was unrealistic to expect an enthusiastic reception, or even acceptance, for art like this among female viewers who were not already feminists, or somewhat sympathetic to feminism. It might have seemed that the work was not perceived for what it was—but on the contrary, it was in fact accurately perceived and found objectionable. Such response is typical when feminism is introduced into a male-dominated culture.

For those women at Aerospace who were sympathetic to feminism, the exhibition was a positive experience providing a new awareness of the existence of women's culture created by contemporary feminists. In that sense the exhibition did broaden the audience for contemporary feminist art. For some of these women who previously had no particular interest in art, the exhibition was a beginning of what has since become an ongoing interest and commitment to women's art.

> I am still thinking about one piece in the show, which I would like to own if I had money. I decided that if I bought art, it would be women's art because of my commitment to feminist artists.[17]

Earlier that same summer, my colleagues and I in the Feminist Studio Workshop[18] had come to a collective definition of feminist art based on our goals, experiences, and observation of our students' work. We defined the function of feminist art as raising consciousness, inviting dialogue, and transforming culture. It became clear to me that both the individual art exhibited at Aerospace and the exhibition as a whole in fact realized these goals to the extent that was possible in that time and space.

NOTES

1. The exhibition also provided a good starting point for sorting out my own views on the more complex issues of feminist content and female sensibility in art, though I prefer the term "female form language" to "female sensibility" or "female imagery" because the latter have come to be identified with one specific, biologically oriented theory.
2. Funding limitations did not permit the inclusion of works by artists who resided outside of the Los Angeles area.
3. *Orbiter* 15, no. 20(1975): 2, from a letter to the editor by the Women's Week Planning Committee.
4. Glenda Madrid (of the Aerospace Office of Equal Opportunity and Women's Planning Committee) in conversation with the author.
5. Though some of the nonfeminist viewers more familiar with contemporary art forms did not share the protesters' offense, it is very unlikely

that a "neutral" exhibit of contemporary art would have caused similar negative reactions. In addition, none of the protesters mentioned any criticism of art *forms*; all their comments tended to focus on *content*, and most of them made reference to a general distaste for feminism.

6. All the quotations from artists are from recent interviews conducted for this article.

7. The precedent for this feminist use of the sticker is Susana Toree's exhibition catalog for *Twenty-Six Contemporary Women Artists* (Ridgefield, Conn.: Aldrich Museum, April, 1971), in which tearing the seal implied not only physical violation in order to "enter" the long hidden works of women artists, but also the destruction of a square cold black seal on a white cover, which represented the prevalent Minimal art, to reach the warm inside covers, colored red.

8. Kollwitz's etching *Raped* is unique in its complete focus on the experience of the raped woman: she is lying on the ground, dead or unconscious. Neither the rapist nor his act are in the picture.

9. The men seemed to react neutrally to the show, probably because the art did not expose *their* experience and possibly, as was suggested to me by Glenda Madrid, because they are more prone to intellectualize and thus were more removed from the level of emotional response the show raised for women.

10. When I curated the Aerospace exhibition, I did censor myself at one point. I did not include Chicago's *Red Flag* lithograph even though, dealing with menstruation, it would have fitted well into an exhibit on female experience in art. Its literal character prevented me from exhibiting it in that context, as I anticipated that it would be shocking to the audience.

11. *Orbiter* 15, no. 17 (1975): 2.

12. Ibid.

13. Joanne Parent (one of the authors of "The Fourth World Manifesto") told me the following incident. While she was working in a factory, experiencing first-hand the hardships involved, she understood how well Rivera's mural portrayed those; but when she commented on that to her fellow workers, they negated or at least minimized their own experience of oppression compared to its heightened portrayal in the mural. The similarity to women's situation is that workers who (consciously or unconsciously) feel powerless in their jobs deny the pain of their experiences if its expression would jeopardize the only wage-earning option available to them. It is no accident that women all over the country first explored their oppression in the *private, safe,* and *supportive* context of consciousness-raising groups, removed from the institutions in which they experienced oppression in their daily lives.

14. It is for this reason that feminism and feminist art have validity for all women. For the same reason, the Marxist model of workers' oppression does not ultimately address itself to women's oppression, beyond that of working-class women. For an extensive analysis of these issues see "The Fourth World Manifesto," reprinted in *Radical Feminism,* eds. Anne Koedt, Ellen Levine, and Anita Rapone (New York: Quadrangle, 1973), pp. 332–357.
15. *Orbiter* 15, no. 20 (1975): 2.
16. *Art Week* 6, no. 29 (Sept. 6, 1975).
17. Glenda Madrid, in a recent conversation with the author. Madrid was also a major source of information for the responses to the exhibition and the statistics and position of women employees at Aerospace.
18. The Feminist Studio Workshop is the first alternative institution for women in the arts and humanities; it is housed in the unique context of the Woman's Building in Los Angeles. Since it was founded in 1973, over one hundred women have received their education at the Feminist Studio Workshop, and several thousand students have participated in the Extension Program at the Woman's Building.

11

The Male Artist as a Stereotypical Female

JUNE WAYNE

We artists complain about the same old problems year after year, no matter how obscure or famous we may be. We ask each other how to get a show, or a better gallery, or how to move our dealers to promote our works more vigorously. We gossip a lot about the museums too: how a certain trustee collects the art of so-and-so, which explains his retrospective at the Modern, or a certain balding young curator is mounting a whole exhibition to prove his pet esthetic gimmick. Every year yet another lawyer-dealer combination is reported to be raiding yet another artist's estate. And obviously every issue of every art magazine proves anew how stupid critics can be.

Sooner or later one of us casually drops the word that Joseph Hirshhorn just blew into town and "bought out the studio," but no mention is made of the prices he paid—nor do we ask. We know the idiosyncracies of all the collectors, and we'd just as soon not be reminded what "making it" can mean. Artists lick their wounds for nourishment, not for healing.

Over the years I have pondered why guilds and royalties, which work fairly well for actors, writers, and composers—even for scientists and inventors—never developed for visual artists too. Perhaps because we are unwordly about the practical matters of sales and careers? Neither art schools nor university art departments provide courses in business and the professional problems of being an artist. A master's degree may qualify a student to replace the teacher but not to bargain with a dealer. Anyhow, who could teach such courses? Art professors cannot hack it either in the art market so new artists fare no better than preceding generations.

A union or a guild needs an industry *against which* to organize, but the art scene has no single nexus of power to bargain with. As for public agencies, they dissolve into lay committees, which have neither the concern nor authority to address the grievances of artists. The art world lives in an ebb and flow of guerilla warfare. Such citadels of power as there are—museums, foundations, arts councils, the National Endowments—are held by *them*, not us, and only rarely can one find that an artist is a member of one of *their* committees. So we learn very early to see ourselves as esthetically unique and morally superior—which is a palatable way of saying isolated and powerless.

But neither the hostile ecology of the art mileiu nor the inadequacies of art department curricula fully explain why artists, who have as much common sense as other people, fail to use even the most elementary protections when it comes to their art. For instance, why do so many artists consign their work to obviously inept or venal or fly-by-night dealers without asking so much as a receipt, let alone a contract or a credit reference? I could list many examples of idiot behavior by otherwise intelligent artists. Why does our cynicism, which is based on painful experience, only express itself in hostile passivity instead of prideful self-protection?

In recent years, the many freedom movements have sharpened my awareness of similarities between the behavior patterns of artists and other minority groupings. There is a direct relationship between the power of any oppressor and the self-esteem and self-evaluation of those who are held in check. In this context feminist literature set me thinking about the relation between women artists and sexual stereotyping. The practical utility of treating the male artist as though he were a woman struck me forcefully for it would explain much that puzzled me about the interface of artists with the rest of the art world's professionals.

It appears to me that society unconsciously perceives the artist as a female and that artists act out the feminized stereotypical patterns projected onto them. Inasmuch as these patterns are self-destructive and profoundly inhibiting to independent action, the ease with which artists are maintained in a state of disenfranchisement endures for generation after generation. It becomes profitable to many people to view the artist as one unable to cope with the real world of money and trade, although a pedestal is where the artist, like the woman, waits while others are alleged to cope in his behalf.

Although there always have been artists of both sexes, only males survived into art history. Yet even for male artists one is more apt to believe that Leonardo and Michelangelo were homosexual than that Peter Paul Rubens was a diplomat. For the ancient but still powerful demonic myth prepares us to accept the warped and bizarre personality to be an indicator of talent and even as proof of genius. Some of the characteristics that artists are given in the demonic myth are, surprisingly, almost identical with characteristics described by Betty Friedan in *The Feminine Mystique*. So profound is the stereotype of the artist as the inchoate, intuitive, emotional romantic, that both the public and artists themselves find it difficult to imagine that we can be anything else.

The demonic myth presents the artist as one possessed of mysterious forces that well up during creative seizures as it were. The work of art is alleged to be produced without the exercise of the artist's will and may even seem to be unmodified by knowledge itself. The artist "can't help it" or "doesn't know how it happened" or whence came the inspiration. Should the artist try to analyze, control, even to think peripherally about the creative moment, it may be vitiated or even destroyed. The artist is thought to be a sort of medium through whom creative miracles are manifest and unless one is BORN an artist, neither effort nor intelligence (not even surgery) makes one into one. So the demonic myth presents the artist as biologically determined—born with Promethean fires as it were.

The feminine mystique also is based on biological determination. The woman is alleged to be born to procreate and to spend her life in servicing her procreation. No effort of will or intellect is needed to reproduce her kind. She is a sort of medium through whom the procreative miracle is manifest. If one isn't born a woman, no effort of will or intelligence (not even surgery) can transform one into one. The biology of the woman, like that of the artist, is proposed to be her destiny.

Obviously the artist makes art and the woman make babies, but the word *create* is commonly used to describe both processes. That will and brain are said to be unnecessary and even antithetical to the function of women and of artists encourages the elision of the male artist into perception as a female by the public. Semantic confusion causes operational distortion in many kinds of human experience: this is why the do-it-yourself hobbyist tells you he loves being "creative" and shows you a book shelf to prove it. Creativity, procreation, and "making something" are used interchangeably in our society as though synonymous.

Lurking just below the surface of public consciousness is a pervasive assumption that any man whose feelings, intuitions, and purposes are inchoate in source and unusual in product must be a homosexual. Even the most *macho* of male artists faces this problem, and the recent tributes to José Limon particularly emphasized as remarkable that he brought a masculine aspect to the art of the dance. Do *real* men "go for" ballet, poetry, and pictures or do they go for sports? Isn't the culture sector the province of the ladies' committees? Aren't the arts seen as girlish frills in the educational system? What papa is pleased that his son wants to be an artist? Why are art reviews published on the woman's page (between the cranberry sauce and the Simplicity patterns) in nearly every newspaper in this country?

Many authorities have insisted that womanhood is incompatible with profundity of thought, intellectual discipline, or worldly accomplishment, but none puts this position more succinctly than does Helene Deutsch, Freud's eminent but submissive disciple. She writes that: "Woman's intellectuality is to a large extent paid for by the loss of feminine qualities. Her intellectuality feeds on the affective life and results in its impoverishment." Change only two words and Deutsch's formulation will sound as though it had been written about artists: "The *artist's* intellectuality is to a large extent paid for by the loss of valuable *creative* qualities. The *artist's* intellectuality feeds on the *creative* life and results in its impoverishment." A perfect fit.[1]

That critics, art historians, and even artists accept the cliche that the brain is a threat to creativity would explain why, if an exhibition is reviewed as "cerebral" or "intellectual," the words are understood as pejorative, not complimentary. There is a special limbo for Robert Motherwell, who often is called the most intellectual of contemporary artists. Who envies Motherwell that niche? Not that he surely is the MOST intellectual of the artists; there are others who may be more so. But Motherwell lets himself be seen as such whereas most artists hide their mind under a bushel. Richard Diebenkorn, during a conversation with me, once called it "maintaining a low profile." Reaction to a brainy artist is like reaction to a female intellectual—neither is quite to be believed.

After I had noted the interchangeability of "artist" with "woman," I played with feminist literature, substituting artist for woman, and found myriad examples where the substitution worked perfectly. (I won't take time or space to illustrate here since you can verify this easily for yourself.) Next I rearranged the actors of the art milieu according to sexual roles: artists as women regardless of actual gender: dealers, collectors, curators, patrons, critics, public functionaries, et al., as men regardless of actual gender. Now the passivity of artists and the aggressiveness of these other categories became logical and predictable.

How natural that artists are stereotyped as inept, unworldly, insecure, gossipy, cliquish, capricious, flirtatious, indirect, devious, manipulative, overimaginative, emotional, intuitive, unpredictable, colorful, and overly aware of costume and image. Why expect artists to understand money, contracts, or business? Why indeed. One must *help* artists, *support* them; they cannot cope. Accordingly we artists look for help not equality, support not self-determination. We expect "them" to take care of us, get us into the fashionable collections, and make us famous. And we await results of their efforts while grousing in the studio or rapping at Barney's Beanery or sunning on the beaches at the Hamptons in the summertime. We might as well be Lana Turners awaiting stardom at Hollywood soda counters.

Nor are our fantasies so inappropriate. What dealer does not claim to know more about nearly everything (including art) than does the artist? What curator is unsure of superior judgment of what the artist is *really* doing? What critic or reporter feels obliged to ask an *artist* what the work is all about? What collector sees the artist as anything but a freak, however lovable?

But if all this is true, why are *women* artists discriminated against? If male artists are acceptable as quasi-females in female postures, why not women artists too? Because the male artist is camouflaged by the demonic myth, not the feminine mystique. He rides motorcycles, not subways; pops drugs, not iron supplements. Groupie girls with pale sheafs of stringy hair trail after him, not his kiddies. A hundred romantic props comprise his demonic image, and most are macho to the hilt. But the woman artist is only understood to be a woman by the feminine mystique. She is an instant Mrs. So-and-so living in a tract house with hubby and the babies. She is thought to dabble in oils in the family den, which only she refers to seriously as her studio.

And her art is assumed to be a matter of tight little landscapes and flower arrangements or decorative, derivative abstractions displayed over the couch in an all too dreary and domestic living room. To be a wife, a mother, and forty is to suffer a fatal syndrome; no matter what the truth or how large the talent or accomplishment, she is only a woman trying "to pass" as an artist.

A few of us have achieved some recognition, but we clearly carry demonic markings that hide our female stigmata. We live in lofts and storefronts and other wildly unconventional spaces just like the male artists do. We dress in unisex or as fantastic eccentrics: Nevelson and O'Keeffe do not shop at Peck and Peck. As successful (women) artists, we *must* prefer lovers to husbands and be on guard every moment against conventionalized female gestures. If one is lesbian, so much the better; this demonizes the image and gains one the wife that every artist needs to do the scut work of a career.

For an artist's wife, whether an artist herself or not, holds the outside salaried job that pays the studio rent. She also assists within the studio, looks after the framing and shipping, writes the letters, and does the phoning. She may even verbalize "his" esthetic too, while HE maintains the demonic posture of not knowing what he is doing when he is creating in the studio. She plans the cocktail parties to which collectors and curators and critics are invited, and she also will stand patiently aside while a female collector (that *she* fished in) exercises the male prerogative of seducing her husband. What man would do as much for an artist wife?

But all these efforts, no matter how devotedly performed, are seldom to much avail. The reality is that only a few artists at a time can be promoted in the art market as it presently functions. The art market is a secretive, unregulated, labile arena, which the jargon of the Security Exchange Commission would describe as untidy. Although it is a young market insofar as contemporary American artists are concerned, already it's incestuous and even sclerotic in some respects.

When women and minority artists clamor to share the recognition and rewards available till now to a few white males, they merely add themselves to an overcrowded talent pool, which art marketeers cannot serve in any case. Although no formal studies have been performed on the size and nature of the artist population, some careful estimations suggest that *there are something more than 300 esthetically valid artists without dealers for every artist of comparable quality* with one. Furthermore, I doubt that more than one artist in 50 who do have galleries, lives from the sales the dealer generates. Every industry needs a labor reservoir from which to draw its talents, but a ratio of 12 percent of unemployed for teachers and engineers, for example, is extremely high. Unemployment of 25 percent to 50 percent among Black males under the age of 25 is the worst ratio in the nation. So you can see that 300 artists for every gallery slot is a redundancy of intolerable proportion.

Some would say there are too many artists, but I believe these figures represent the underdevelopment of the market system and that the galleries serve neither the general public around the nation nor the artist population. The art dealers cluster in a few big cities where they cater to each other in alliances of ownership of particular works of art and sell these to an interchangeable clientele of moneyed urbanites. Like the two men with one diamond who sell only to each other at constantly rising prices, much of the traffic in art involves a small circle of international dealers and collectors. Since collectors have limited ability to absorb works of art (some museums have reached their limits too), sooner or later they begin to trade, and their collections reenter the market to compete with newer works. So the word collector is fast becoming another word for trader—as in stocks.

Unfortunately the tax deductible structure, which was intended to encourage support for cultural institutions, can now be seen to encourage art speculators by providing downside protection against risk. Much more needs to be written about taxes, the museums, the market, and the problems of artists, but I only refer to them here as a frame of reference for my comment that it is profitable to some people that artists remain demonized—that is, feminized—that is, lobotomized.

The future of the art world in this country will, I believe, be profoundly influenced by the self-reevaluation of women and minority artists who are reversing a previously passive acceptance of outside pressures. Many women artists note that half of nothing is nothing and that to share what the male artist has been getting is to move from our harem to his. By contrast, such militancy as male artists are beginning to express these days concerns itself more with the loss of teaching jobs on campuses than with changes in fundamental attitudes toward participation *as equals* in the art milieu.

The shape of the art scene of the future depends on how profoundly, how philosophically, and yes, how *cerebrally*, artists come to understand themselves. Will we reject romantic stereotypical behavior that serves to keep us down? Will we use those intellectually creative aptitudes for problem solving that we artists possess, actually, in somewhat higher measure than most other people?

Obviously if the battle for the freedom of the press and the restoration of checks and balances in the Congress are lost, artists will go down the tubes like everybody else, but if the nation makes a new commitment to freedom and life enhancement, then many options open up for artists that we did not have before. Assuming peace and freedom, in the 1980s the art marketing apparatus we know will have enlarged somewhat but will have been largely by-passed by self-help activities by artists. The opening of studios to the public, now in evidence, will expand, I believe, into substantial artist-owned cooperative corporations comparable to the cooperative structure used by the Canadian Government in behalf of Eskimos and similar to the consumer co-ops that have a long tradition in this country. I do not mean the simplistic "share-the-rent, share-the-cleaning" cooperation we see among artists just now, but rather the professionally run, business cooperatives that have considerable tax and legal muscle within our society. Artists probably will be showing and selling through their own coops and may also share housing, studio facilities, medical care, insurance, and many kinds of professional services as well. I refer to P.R., accounting and legal, even catalog and mailing services.

Everywhere artists are talking about organizing themselves one way or another. I believe the best approach will be the formation of a guild something like the Screen Writers Guild rather than a "membership" grouping for various social action purposes. A guild with a full-time professional staff could lobby out the terrible tax inequities that burden artists and ruin our families when we die. Such a guild also could lobby for (and win, I have no doubt) the right for artists to pay their income taxes with their art—as is a norm in Mexico. Such a right would then permit the government to start an art bank or library from which every sort of tax exempt institution could borrow works of art for use at the community level in schools, hospitals and public buildings.

It would take such a guild to implement residual rights for artists and police the implementation of such rights and collect our royalties for us. But all this depends on whether we ourselves decide to form a guild; residual rights will not arrive as a fancy gift from the "johns" who feel they have been keeping us, like aging call girls, as an act of charity. Once artists form a power block, our guild will be able to work with other arts institutions to open up the news media to the culture sector, to provide arts news to the people, and to end the blackout of creative people. The arts should have visibility comparable to that afforded sports. Perhaps in the next few years we will see the appearance of a cultural news wire service, which, like AP and UP and the Farm News Wire Service, will provide teletyped professionally written stories to all media, printed and electronic. When will arts reporters be a norm on every TV news team?

I believe that within the next few years museums will be at least partially financed by the federal government and that, as a result, there will be a forced clean-up of many of the conflicts of interest now rife within museum operations. I trust the interlocking boards of trustees will be broken up and that an artists' guild will have its representatives sitting on all museum policy making boards. But, of course, with federal money will come the increasing danger of political interference in the culture sector. It could happen that the museums, theaters, opera companies, and the like could find themselves cannibalized by politicians as now is happening before our very eyes to educational television.

I believe that artists must intensify discussion as to our own functions beyond the role of makers of objects as a sort of cottage industry. Art is more than product, and I can see how self-determination could lead directly to the formation of a national civil service of creative people of every kind to perform those life enhancement services that reevaluation of the quality of life suggests is necessary to the survival of the species.

Freed of the hopelessness that our own banal and stereotyped behavior of the past imposed on us, both the possibilities and the responsibilities of the future take on new and daring dimensions. I wish I had more confidence that we artists will meet the challenge. For the moment, I will be content if more of us accept ourselves as

the intellects we are. This first step could lead us almost anywhere—
and anywhere is up from where we are.

NOTES

1. Helene Deutsch, *The Psychology of Women*, vol. 2 (New York: Greene and Stratton, 1944), p. 290.

12

"Of Men, Women, and Art":[*]
Some Historical Reflections

MARY D. GARRARD

Two years of public activity on behalf of the Women's Caucus for Art have persuaded me that, to paraphrase Shirley Chisholm, I suffer discrimination as much or more through my identification with the arts than through my identity as a woman. In October 1976, I had an encounter with the United States government that confirmed a growing suspicion that the problem for women in art lies not only in being female, but in the condition of art itself. Let me begin by describing that experience.

The occasion was a panel sponsored by the National Commission on the Observance of International Women's Year, one of a series during which the Commission heard of women's problems in various fields. Diane Burko, Lila Katzen, June Wayne, and I were to testify on the visual arts that morning, to be followed by representatives of the performing arts in the afternoon. Considering the ceremonial significance of the hearings—a blue-ribbon committee under a presidentially appointed commission had invited us to the State Department to tell them what should be done about women in art—the actual event seemed absurdly inconsequential. We gathered in a small room, committee members and panelists together around a long table, with a few guests in a line of chairs around the perimeter. Evidently, I thought, this was primarily for the record, as one could tell from the microphones on the table and the tape recording equipment visible on one side of the room. But as we warmed to our

---

*I should like to acknowledge my quotation of Linda Nochlin's title for her 1976 College Art Association convocation address. It is too good to be used only once.

Terri Whitesel

subjects, filling the air with statistics and points of view, suddenly we were told that the tape recorder was not working and, later, that it would not be working at all that day, since no one was on hand to repair it. A man in the room muttered audibly, "that wouldn't be tolerated if this were a Congressional committee on the Hill!"

We resumed our perorations, following embarrassed assurances from kind ladies that notes would be taken, drafts prepared, and recommendations carefully preserved. Yet I suspect that each of us there felt that the importance of our testimony had been subtly diminished. Clearly, what was occurring in Room 1205 of the State Department was small-scale and insignificant, hardly to be compared to whatever Henry Kissinger was doing upstairs or wherever he was. But was this because the hearing involved women, or art? A glance at the sheet describing the overall committee structure showed the Arts and Humanities Committee to be strangely unique. It was the only committee of the ten to represent a specific profession, or collection of related professions. Others included Child Development, Homemakers, Women in Employment, Women in Power, Women with Special Problems. One was not certain whether to be disturbed or amused. We were neither in power nor employed, but at least we did not have special problems.

Or did we? Why indeed were the arts and humanities singled out as a category of special female concern, analogous to homemaking, if not for the obvious historical association between women and the arts? I had even alluded to this point unwittingly in my own testimony, explaining that since art has often been stigmatized as a womanly pursuit, men in the field have taken great care to preserve appropriately virile images for the roles of artist or art historian and to ensure that the more prestigious work is done by males, lest the profession become female-dominated and hence weak in image. Yet because at the time I was thinking more about women and less about art itself, it was only after the hearings that the more fundamental point became clear—that the status of art in our society closely parallels the status of women.

Like women, the arts are simultaneously cherished for their purifying, uplifting value even as they are regarded as frivolous and a luxury in the larger social scheme. In the priority of values, the arts occupy both the lowest and highest positions—lowest when it comes to funding, highest when it comes to lip-service praise. But either way, they are not really central to the workings of society and are typically thought of as one of its fringe amusements. Thus recently a state representative in Arizona, on filing a bill to abolish the Arizona Commission on the Arts and Humanities on the grounds that it is a "nonessential agency," said: "Culture is fine in a time when the state is in good financial condition, but when you try to pinch pennies, you have to cut the frills."[1] (One wonders what she would think of Louis XIV bankrupting the French treasury to pay for Versailles.) Yet if the share of the Arizona budget given to the arts is anything like its national counterpart, the savings will be pitifully small. Throughout the IWY hearings we were reminded time and again how little of the federal budget goes to the arts. The 80 or so million dollars given annually to the National Endowment for the Arts represents something like a day's worth of the annual defense budget. Between 1967 and 1976, only 474 artists had received NEA grants. The United States spends one-eighth as much per capita on the arts as does Great Britain, and one-sixteenth as much as West Germany.[2] We women had come to the government to demand a larger slice of a pie so small that its subdivision was scarcely worth bickering about.

Like women, viewed historically, the arts are poor, have no legitimate place of their own in society, and are dominated and overshadowed by the "necessary" masculine fields of economics, political science, the military, and business. They do not pay their way, do not produce income (though some murmur that the performing arts sometimes show a profit), and while no one ever asks whether the war machine pays for itself, the purposes of defense spending and international diplomacy being self-evident, national spending for the arts is perceived either as a dole or a tithe, but in any case, as an outlay for which no estimable return is expected. It comes under the heading of charitable contributions. One gives to the arts as one gives to the needy or to a cancer fund. By some curious inversion of values, the areas of endeavor that are linked to our loftiest or more humanitarian values are carried on through charity and volunteer work. The things that we theoretically hold most dear do not warrant federal support.

This seeming paradox is best understood through the analogy of the double standard of value typically applied to women. The connection between art and women is intricate. On the one hand, they share a similar fringe status in relation to society as a whole; yet on the other hand, art and femininity have been intimately linked in other ways, at least in modern history. June Wayne's incisive analysis of a closely related subject, the power interaction between the modern artist and his or her patrons, critics, and dealers in terms of stereotypical male and female roles[3] brilliantly illuminated a murky area, and her insights have found broad application. I would like to take her concept one step further and to show that it can be applied not only to the artist but to art itself and to develop the historical picture in support of this point.

The image of art outside the arts has changed considerably from age to age, and a short essay is no place to outline its history. Yet it is appropriate to take as a point of departure the founding of the American nation, when circumstances called for a self-conscious redefinition of the proper role of art in a democratic society. Benjamin Henry Latrobe, in his oration delivered at the dedication of the Pennsylvania Academy in 1807, expressed the view that art was indispensable to the functioning of a democracy, providing healthful recreation, a means to elevate public taste, and political luster for the nation.[4] His implicit assumption that art had a certain inherent power beneficial to the strength of the country proved to be a relic, increasingly old-fashioned, of earlier European attitudes, for there was from the beginning of the nation a more wide-spread opinion that the arts were a luxury. Benjamin Franklin regarded them as "necessary and proper gratifications of a refined society," but urged postponing their encouragement until such tastes could be satisfied by a stronger national economy.[5] This point of view is echoed in the celebrated remark of John Adams:

> I must study politics and war, that my sons may have liberty to study mathematics and philosophy. My sons ought to study mathematics and philosophy, geography, natural history and naval architecture, navigation, commerce and agriculture, in order to give their children a right to study painting, poetry, music, architecture, statury, tapestry and porcelain.[6]

Writing in 1824, the historian Jared Sparks gave Adams's view a different emphasis: "When we grow older, and have more leisure, more wants, and more wealth, we can afford to indulge in luxuries," and "the American soil . . . [will] be found not less fertile in the products of fancy and taste than it now is in the fruits of practical invention and wise maxims of political science."[7] Now that "fancy and taste" have been pitted against practicality and wisdom, the cultivation of art is no longer a matter of delayed gratification, of saving the best for last, but of taking care of important matters first and leaving capricious and impractical pursuits to come as afterthoughts.

Value distinctions have set in, with the arts acquiring attributes characteristically assigned to the female sex. The distinction between usefulness and luxury can, of course, be traced to Puritan roots (as in the often quoted, "The Plowman that raiseth Grain is more serviceable to Mankind than the Painter who draws only to please the Eye"). Yet the history of attitudes toward women also offers parallels too striking to dismiss. One argument often expressed, that art weakens the moral fiber of the nation, was stated in terms oddly analogous to a preacher's warning of the seductive nature of women. Mark Hopkins' opinion of the arts, for instance, as stated by a reviewer of *The Connexion Between Taste and Morals*, was that the fine arts were immoral, "because they often pander directly to vice, because the pleasures received from them . . . are of a sensuous character . . . and because they have flourished among corrupt and degrading nations."[8]

Just as women in the nineteenth century were perceived as coming in two varieties, seductive and virtuous, the *femme fatale* and the Good Woman,[9] so the view of art as corruptive was rejected by those who saw exactly the opposite properties. Far from seducing men away from their sterner purposes, art could improve the mind and soul, provide agreeable and welcome distraction from material pressures, and heighten one's virtue and morality. Exactly like a good wife. As the "nationalist apologia" was formulated in the early nineteenth century, the characteristics ascribed to art often seemed identical to those ascribed to women. The arts provided "rational enjoyment" for wealthy men who might otherwise succumb to gambling or other base temptations. According to De Witt Clinton, the "cultivation of the liberal arts will not allow men to relapse into ferocity." William Tudor, prominent Bostonian, extending the argument to the national level, claimed that the tendency of the arts is to "purify, adorn and elevate every country where they are cherished."[10]

Matthew Arnold, though not American, must be mentioned, for in his classic beleaguered defense of the arts in an age of growing materialism and scientific postivism, he assigns to art another attribute related to man's relationship with woman—its "undeniable power of engaging the emotions."[11] Unlike John Adams, who saw art's appeal to the emotions as a pre-Englightenment vestige of superstition and despotism,[12] and also unlike the do-gooder claims of the American nationalists for art's self-improving benefits, Arnold rejects for one brief moment the false dichotomy between art as temptress and as domestic helpmate, seeing it, as he said elsewhere, "steadily and whole," as an authentically powerful, authentically good force that renders strong men stronger (as opposed to strong men weaker or weak men stronger) by helping to connect their thought with their feeling.

Yet even Arnold, in his efforts to counter T. H. Huxley's claim for the superior value of science in education, is forced to acknowledge, "the reproach which is often brought against the study of *belles lettres* . . . .: that the study is an elegant one, but slight and ineffectual, a smattering of Greek and Latin and other ornamental things, of little use for anyone whose object is to get at truth and to be a practical man."[13] Though Arnold goes on to resist this reproach, the adjectives go unchallenged, and we are left with the same lingering ties between art and femininity—"elegant," "slight and ineffectual," and "ornamental."

In his parenthetical admission of the impracticality of the arts and letters, Arnold notes the modern value accorded to work and trade, especially in the United States, where he observes, quoting Emerson, "the modern majesty consists in work."[14] To the degree that business and science shared the popular characterization as practical, productive, and essential to the progress of society, they could be seen interchangeably as the masculine counterparts of impractical, ornamental, feminine art. (One wonders what Arnold and Huxley might have thought to see science itself join the *belles lettres* in the 1970s, shrinking in the eyes of both government contractors and prospective students as it declines in immediate practical usefulness.)

As the work ethic rose in the nineteenth century to provide the primary measure of achievement, the arts themselves slipped deeper and deeper into the feminized role, and, *horribile dictu*, women themselves increasingly took up the arts. The dangers for young men of too much interest in the arts are perfectly illustrated in Charles Butler's moral instruction book for young men, written in 1836. In a section proclaiming the virtues of "Solid Accomplishment," he sets the following direct advice in a dialogue: "Ornamental education, or an attention to the graces, has a connexion with effeminacy. In acquiring the gentleman, I would not lose the spirit of a man."[15]

The connection between art and "ornamental education" was confirmed by James Jackson Jarves. In the *Art Idea*, offering a characterization of art, he proposes it as a "counter-weight or balance" to science:

> Art adorns science. Science is the helpmeet of art. . . . Art [is] the ornamental side of life, as Science is its useful. . . . We build, manufacture, classify, investigate and theorize under [Science]. . . . But our pleasure is more intimately related to art as the producer of what delights the eye and ear and administers to sensuous enjoyment.[16]

Jarves does not here link these distinctions with sexual stereotypes, yet notice how in a different context he uses the rational-emotional polarity to explain the efflorescence of women sculptors and to reveal an association between men, reason, and science, and between women, feeling, and art. In an 1871 review of American sculpture in Europe, he observes that: "Few, if any, American women have won a reputation in painting, [though] several have acquired some distinction in sculpture." He suggests as a possible reason that: "Modern painting is essentially scientific in its system of instruction. It requires much mental and manual toil," and since:

> few women as yet are predisposed to intellectual pursuits . . . naturally they turn to those fields of Art which may seem to yield the quickest returns for the least expenditure of mental capital. Having in general a nice feeling for form, quick perceptions, and a mobile fancy, with, not infrequently, a lively imagination, it is not strange that modeling clay is tempting to their fair fingers.[17]

When later in the same passage Jarves praises the works of Harriet Hosmer as having a "robust, masculine character, even in details, as if wrought out by hard headwork and diligent study of models by a mind that had forced itself, as with a manly energy, to achieve a mechanical mastery of a profession for which it has no supreme aesthetic predilection," he is simultaneously able to declare Hosmer an exception to her sex and art itself as masculine in its more cerebral aspects. How this is to be reconciled with his earlier definition of art as sensuous, pleasurable, and nonintellectual is not entirely clear. The discrepancy can, in fact, only be understood as a consequence of the gymnastic efforts of the art-identified nineteenth century male to preserve an image of virility for his field, in the face of the threat posed by the increasing presence of women in that field.

Another tactic employed by the male artist seeking to escape the stigma of feminization was to separate the arts into high and low, the fine arts versus the crafts, and to claim for himself the higher reaches, which were asserted to be beyond the scope of the female mind. The clearest instance of this approach is seen in an anonymous author's claim in *The Crayon* of February 1860, that women might be educated in the arts they were best suited for—painting porcelains and ivory, making jewelry or "simple ornament," for:

> Where shall we find, except among women, the patience and carefulness required in the coloring of botanical plates and every description of illustrative art? . . . . man is not made for a sedentary life; woman, on the other hand, conforms to it without inconvenience. . . . It is only in *womanizing* (italics his) himself, in some degree, that man succeeds in obtaining the development of these faculties so contrary to his physical constitution, and always at the expense of his natural force.[18]

Now art is virilized by characterization as a profession best practiced by physically energetic people, creatively impatient with mere detail, concerned only with the grander concepts.

But there was another trap concealed down this avenue of escape for male artists on the run, for the more they claimed the higher, nobler ground of art for themselves, leaving the menial crafts for female execution, the wider they were making the separation between art (at least the better part of it) and the practical mainstream of life.[19] Once the first cries of art-for-art's-sake were heard and images associated with aestheticism had acquired a distinctly feminine character, whether in the exquisitely delicate nocturnes of Whistler, the vapid etheral beauties of Dewing, or in the pastel hues of the American Impressionists—not to mention the outrageous dandyism of Whistler or Wilde—it had become clear that the public image of art itself, always precarious, was now in great danger.

This background, overdrawn as it is, helps explain the extraordinary insistence of the Ash Can School painters upon life and virility (Henri's mystic notions about Brotherhood through art), crudeness of technique (Luks' boast of painting with a shoestring dipped in pitch and lard), and the deliberate choice of such thoroughly masculine subjects as boxing and wrestling, as a kind of rescue operation for art's image. Even their critics seemed relieved. A New York *Sun* reviewer of George Bellows exhibition in 1909 observed:

> His boxing pictures . . . call them brutal if you will, they hit you between the eyes with a vigor that few living artists known to us can command. Take any of these Parisian chaps, beginning with Henri Matisse, who make a specialty of movement—well, their work is ladylike in comparison with the red blood of Bellows.[20]

Even allowing the importance of Teddy Roosevelt as a virility exemplum, the artists of the Henri circle pressed their case rather hard, putting as much distance as possible between themselves and Whistler (whom they parodied in mock theatrical productions) and insisting upon restoring the good (virile) name of art itself. Put in modern terms, it amounted to a *macho* takeover of the art world. The irrational superiority accorded to "toughness" and "vigor" in American painting could be exemplified throughout the twentieth century, but it may suffice to cite one example of the ever present danger of femininity for the male artist. Paul Rosenfield wrote of Charles Demuth in 1921:

> Always, his work has airiness, daintiness, charm. Only the artist appears to be a trifle too much the gentlemanly Johnny of his profession. . . . There is always the suspicion of an almost feminine refinement in his work.[21]

Inasmuch as the reviewer's opinion of Demuth is likely to have been colored by the knowledge that Demuth was homosexual, we might as well face this notorious "problem" for the arts head-on. It seems to be commonly understood that all the covert warning signals that society regularly sends to young men who express an interest in the arts originate in the danger that he in joining a profession associated in the popular imagination with homosexuals. Yet it is questionable whether there are, in fact, more homosexuals in the arts than in other fields, or whether they are not simply more visible in the arts, flamboyant or outrageously antisocial behavior having been historically more highly tolerated by society in the arts than in other fields, since art is, as we have seen, perceived as a less socially normal, less serious pursuit. The latent danger for men entering the arts is not so much that they will be thought to be gay as that art itself is thought to be gay.[22] The arts are not perceived as feminine because many artists are homosexual, but rather because the arts are so deeply associated for many other reasons with female stereotypes, reflecting values and images that attract some male homosexuals, even as they also attract nonhomosexual males who do not find these associations threatening, and repel males who resist being linked with femininity. Men can more easily protect their personal images as straight than they can defend the virility of the entire profession. The problem, such as it is, does not involve the association between homosexuals and art, but the association between each of those with women and the consequent demeaning of each as a factor of the historical second-class status of women.

Men, then, are historically justified in their concern that the arts are regarded as female. The connection is both *symbolic* and *functional*. It is symbolic in that the very qualities and attributes of the arts are analogous, in sterotype, to female qualities. In this sense it is not surprising that the personification of painting is female, the muses are female, and the whole network of allegorical pairs finds art, peace, and culture pitted against war, industry, and commerce. Indeed, in an excessive moment, Emerson even asserted that women *are* art.[23] The association between women and art is functional in that women, having had far more leisure time than men under social structures normal until the present, have virtually cornered the market of art activity, if we discount the status of that activity and measure only time spent at it. Women presently make up a majority in most art schools, a trend initiated in the later nineteenth century, have played a significant role as patrons of the arts, and fill nearly all of the army of volunteers who offer their services to museums. If we now look briefly at the latter two areas, the pictures will be rounded out.

Even as one states that women have been important patrons of the arts, it becomes obvious that modification is necessary. For one Isabella d'Este, there were handfuls of Alfonso d'Estes, Federigo da Montefeltros, and Medicis. For a few Mme. de Pompadours, du

Barrys, or Marie Antoinettes, there were far more Crozats, Algarot-
tis, or Louis XVIs. For every Gertrude Stein, a Leo Stein. Even when
the female was the influence behind the patronage, as in the case of
Louisine Elder Havemeyer, it was the husband who actually paid and
had his name recognized. Why, then, do we mindlessly repeat:
"Women have been important as patrons of the arts"? Can it be that
they stand out distortedly because patronage itself is (despite its
etymology), in the stereotypical view, feminine and not masculine?

In rearranging the actors of the art milieu along sex lines, June
Wayne pits against the artist, who is passive and female, an entire
cluster defined as aggressive, manipulating, and male: dealers, collectors, curators, patrons, critics, and the like. Yet perhaps some distinctions are in order, because while money is manifestly the *sine qua
non* of patronage, those who commission, purchase, or otherwise
deal in art do not all have the same relationship to money. It has been
generally true since the eighteenth century that patronage of art has
borne a parasitic relationship to a society's basic economic system, in
that money spent on the commissioning or purchasing of art was not
working capital, but what might be called "loose money," diverted or
leftover from the cycle of making, investing, and spending. Certainly
this has been the case in the United States, whether one thinks of
private patrons such as Robert Gilmor or Thomas Handasyd Perkins
in the nineteenth century, or John Quinn or Peggy Guggenheim in
the twentieth. Money given to supporting art is not funneled through
ordinary social channels and thus does not figure directly in the
economy. In this sense, art patronage bears more a symbolic than
functional relationship to women, in playing a female role in the
larger economic family.

Art as investment is, of course, drawn into a working relationship
with the economy, since there are real profits as well as immense tax
advantages for the high-powered collector-investor. Yet when paintings and sculptures are treated as just another commodity, like grain
or tin, we are really not talking about art as a creative enterprise, but
as free enterprise, marketable under the rules of demand created by
diminishing supply. The art dealt with is not drawn from the outset into an organic relationship with society, as Arts-and-Crafts Movement
or Bauhaus theorists envisioned, but is instead haggled over like a
corpse, the artist ignored until the creation is "dead," or more literally, the creation ignored until the artist is dead, at which time, under

present tax laws, the work in the studio is transformed from materials into a commodity with a price tag. In a perverse way, art becomes sterotypically virilized through this form of association with money, even as a man's sense of masculinity may be shored up by a prostitute. Deliberate flouting of conventional morality has an ancient association with virility—one recalls the *machismo* of badmen from the Old West to the Mafia—and in a context such as modern finance, where operations are conducted with a wink at ethics or morals, and pieties are out of place, the take-over of cultural objects, which trail associations with virtue, acquires a peculiar quality, not of femininity, but of hypervirility. It is almost like seducing a nun.

If art investors are, then, masculine in these terms, and patrons are feminine, what of the museums, institutions that exist in this country primarily as a consequence of high-powered marketplace art acquisition mixed with leisurely building of personal collections that result in monuments to rich people's hobbies? Isabella Stewart Gardner had engraved on her palace in Fenway Park in Boston, *"C'est mon plaisir,"* a motto that effectively symbolizes both the spirit in which major American art collections were formed and the spirit in which the museums that house them are typically approached. Only for scholars and art students is museum-visiting an engagement in work. For everyone else, tourists, tired executives, and the like, it is strictly a leisure pursuit. And not only is museum-going a peripheral, not functional, part of these people's lives, but only a small segment of the total population appears to regard going to look at art as a significant part of their lives—according to a 1974 Associated Councils of the Arts report, it is something like 4 percent.[24] Art involvement, as expressed through museum-going, can fairly be defined as "ornamental" in comparison to most people's serious, work-life pursuits, and it is not even necessary to mention the poor showing that art would make when compared to other leisure pursuits like professional sports and television.

Yet advocates of the American museum have seen it as playing an important social role through education. The charters of the Metropolitan Museum in New York and the Boston Fine Arts Museum, both founded in 1870, each state that one of the museum's purposes is to furnish instruction in the fine arts.[25] This purpose was fulfilled in a fairly modest way, chiefly through practicing art schools, before the recent growth of museum education departments and programs. But the emphasis on education has increased so rapidly that most of the nation's museum directors now consider, according to a 1974 survey, "providing educational experiences for the public" to be a museum's most important function, with conservation and preservation of works of art following as a poor third.[26] This attitude is not merely a modern aberration from what one would expect directors to regard as a museum's basic function, but seems to be rooted in nineteenth-century ideas. First, education programs seem to positively reinforce the lingering concept that art-is-good-for-you (instilling virtue, improving morals, and adding to the general good). The tenacity of this idea is shown in contemporary rhetoric. George Heard Hamilton asks: "Is it not the fundamental moral imperative basic to the development of museums in the nineteenth and twentieth centuries, that they have an essentially educational function to perform in a modern democratic society?"[27]

Thus the museum acquires utilitarian justification, even as it assumes a more active social role, and it becomes in a sense de-feminized as a result. Yet from society's viewpoint, the virilization is illusory. Museum education is relatively harmless, since it is not "real" education at all, not being a part of the schools and universities and having no formal program. Such "education" has at best an adjunct relation to other forms of study; it is ornamental rather than fundamental, in the same sense that nineteenth-century writers saw all of art. That museum education is carried on more by women than men in America, and to an incredible extent by nonpaid volunteers,[28] follows as much from the limited importance that society assigns such work as from the traditional concept of both art and education as female preserves.

Museums will continue to play the stereotypical role of female in American society as long as they continue to depend so heavily on private funding. According to the 1974 National Endowment for the Arts survey, art museums produce only 42 percent of their total income from their own revenues; the rest comes from private and government support. Seventy-nine percent of the revenue of art museums comes from the private sector, with private donations making up 32 percent of that figure. In both cases, the percentage of private support is higher in art museums than in other types of museums.[29] Some of the consequences of this financial picture are familiar. The museum director is obliged to play a supplicant role with prospective donors, compromising at every turn for the sake of obtaining the hoped-for gift—familiar strategems to the female who depends upon the moneyed male for her livelihood. As former National Gallery Director John Walker cheerfully described in his autobiography, using other people's money to indulge one's private tastes can be a great deal of fun,[30] but, like wives and mistresses, one is always dependent upon and plays to the caprices of the Man.

Now that the great collections have long been acquired, mainstay support for museums continues to be provided by the wealthier upper classes through donations, service on Boards of Trustees, local arts committees, and as volunteer docents. For obvious reasons, this visible, personal support is largely offered by women, who on these social levels have more free time. Perhaps the most surprising statistic to be discovered in the NEA survey is that two-thirds of the total number of employees in American art museums are unpaid volunteers.[31] It need hardly be emphasized that an overwhelming majority of these volunteers are women. We may draw predictable inferences from this information about the traditional value of women's work as nil, financially. Yet we must not ignore the equally clear indication of the degraded status of art in American society.

But if all this is so, then what? Does the solution lie in increased federal funding for the arts? Certainly it is tempting to suggest this, particularly so that museums might pay for the work they are getting from volunteers. Yet there is always a question of constraints accompanying government intervention, and artists reasonably wonder whether they really want federal controls and surveillance, or whether, as June Wayne said at the IWY hearing, they aren't better off as "free-wheeling monkeys."[32] And a larger arts budget for the sake of more of the same will not automatically change the public estimation of art's value. We do not need more art; what is needed is that art itself become more important in our national life—but not as entertainment, ornament, or frill. Perhaps we could even settle for Jarves' notion of the counterweight or balance to science and industry, if art were assured of equal footing. Yet we sorely lack nonsexist metaphors to express such a relationship.

I do not presume to offer a new utopian scheme for the proper relation between art and society, much less to blueprint the escape of art from the specific dilemma I have described. It simply has seemed worth pointing out that art has suffered from its association with sterotypical femininity, just as women have suffered from the same identification. Women, however, have begun to detach themselves from their crippling, limiting image and are beginning to acquire a new image as well as a more equal position in society. As women artists become more prominent, they present, paradoxically, a *less* feminized image for the profession than men, because becoming a serious artist is for a woman (with her housewife-amateur trappings) a step *into* professionalism rather than out of it. Further, a look at the successful tactics of the feminist movement, while not providing a solution for art, may yet give an intimation of how its lost territory might be reclaimed. Basic questions might be asked, such as whether art *should* be on the dole, or whether it does not have a rightful, natural place in a free society. Yet even if no conscious effort is made, perhaps there is still reason for optimism. If the status of art is in some historical and inescapable way bound up with the status of women, then it may fairly be expected that art's fortunes, like women's, will be improving.

NOTES

1. Reported in *Art Workers' News* (March 1976): 11.
2. These statistics were provided by several speakers at the State Department hearings. See also *Artists Equity Association National Newsletter* (Fall 1975): 4–5, in which similar testimony given to a Senate subcommittee in July 1975 is reported.
3. June Wayne, "The Male Artist as Stereotypical Female," reprinted in the preceding chapter in this book.
4. See Joshua C. Taylor, "The Art Museum in the United States," in *On Understanding Art Museums*, ed. Sherman E. Lee (Englewood Cliffs, N.J.: Prentice-Hall, 1975), p. 35.
5. Quoted by Lillian B. Miller, *Patrons and Patriotism: The Encouragement of the Fine Arts in the United States, 1790–1860* (Chicago: University of Chicago Press, 1966), p. 12.
6. John Adams, *Letters of John Adams Addressed to His Wife*, ed. Charles F. Adams (Boston: C. C. Little and J. Brown, 1841), pp. 67–68.
7. Sparks' review of C. J. Ingersoll's *Discourse Concerning the Importance of America on the Mind* (Philadelphia: A. Small, 1823) appeared in *North*

American Review 18 (January 1824): 162, and is cited by Miller, *Patrons and Patriotism*, p. 13.

8. Miller, *ibid.*, p. 236. The review appeared in *North American Review* 54 (January 1842): 232–33.

9. On this now familiar concept in feminist literature, see: H. R. Hays, *The Dangerous Sex: the Myth of Feminine Evil* (New York: Pocket Books, 1964); Katherine M. Rogers, *The Troublesome Helpmate: a History of Misogyny in Literature* (Seattle: University of Washington Press, 1966), chapter VI; and Martha Kingsbury, "The Femme Fatale and her Sisters," in *Woman as Sex Object: Studies in Erotic Art, 1730–1970, Art News Annual* 38, ed. Thomas B. Hess and Linda Nochlin (New York: Newsweek, 1972).

10. Clinton's address of 1816 to the American Academy and Tudor's essays of the same period are cited by Miller, *Patrons and Patriotism* p. 12 and 21–22. Her chapter "The Nationalist Apologia" is an invaluable source for American attitudes toward the arts in the nineteenth century.

11. Matthew Arnold, "Literature and Science" (an essay prepared for his American lecture tour of 1883), in *Major British Writers* ed. G. B. Harrison (New York: Harcourt, Brace, 1954), vol. 2, p. 490.

12. Miller, *Patrons and Patriotism,* p. 13.

13. Arnold, "Literature and Science," p. 485.

14. Ibid., p. 484, quoting Emerson's essay "Literary Ethics."

15. Charles Butler, *The American Gentleman* (Philadelphia: Hogan and Thompson, 1836), p. 116. The advice is repeated in the summary, p. 287. I am grateful to Josephine Withers for calling my attention to this source.

16. James Jackson Jarves, *The Art Idea: Sculpture, Painting and Architecture in America* (New York: Hurd and Houghton, 1865), pp. 5–6.

17. J. J. Jarves, "Progress of American Sculpture in Europe," *Art Journal* n. s. 33 (1871): 7.

18. *The Crayon* 8, part 2 (February, 1860): 28.

19. The widening gap between the fine and the useful arts was, of course, a matter of growing concern to many nineteenth century writers, not the least of whom were Ruskin, Greenough, and Emerson. Emerson's somewhat less familiar opinion may be quoted to stand for the rest: "Art makes the same effort which a sensual prosperity makes, namely, to detach the beautiful from the useful . . . (but) this division of beauty from use, the laws of nature do not permit. . . . Beauty must come back to the useful arts, and the distinction between the fine and the useful arts forgotten." ("Art," in *Essays,* 1st series; London: J. Chapman, 1853), pp. 190–91.

20. *New York Sun*, 1909, quoted in Charles H. Morgan, *George Bellows, Painter of America* (New York: Reynal, 1965), p. 104.

21. Quoted by Henry McBride, foreword to *Charles Demuth Memorial Exhibition Catalogue* (New York: Whitney Museum of American Art, 1937–38).

22. I use the word deliberately for its feminine connotations. While it is not clear exactly when "gay" entered our language as slang for homosexual (the Oxford English Dictionary does not admit the definition), it is telling that all nineteenth and twentieth century synonyms for "gay" pertain to the world of women—chic, charming, whorish, etc. The homosexual application may have originated in a mid-nineteenth century usage, "leading an immoral life," as in prostitution.

23. "The felicities of design in art, or in works of nature, are shadows or forerunners of that beauty which reaches its perfection in the human form. . . . All men are its lovers. . . . It reaches its height in woman. 'To Eve,' say the Mahometans, 'God gave two thirds of all beauty.' " *Culture, Behavior, Beauty* [Boston: J. R. Osgood and Co., 1876], p. 97.

24. The study, *Americans and the Arts* (reported by Charles Parkhurst in *On Understanding Art Museums*, p. 93), discloses that 48 percent of the adult public has gone at least once to a museum; of that group, 30 percent were moderate or frequent attenders. Yet the survey covers all museums, and only 25 percent of the public surveyed preferred art museums to other kinds. Thus I obtain the figure of about 4 percent who regularly go to art museums.

25. Related by George Heard Hamilton in *On Understanding Art Museums*, p. 106.

26. *Museums USA: A Survey Report* (Washington, D.C.: The National Endowment for the Arts, 1975), table 9, p. 23. "Providing aesthetic experiences" rated second in importance.

27. Hamilton, in *On Understanding Art Museums*, p. 104.

28. *Museums USA*, table 146, p. 289. While the overall male-female ratio for art museum personnel is 60 percent male to 40 percent female, in education departments it is 44 percent male to 56 percent female. The nonprofessional education department ratio is 14 percent male to 86 percent female.

29. *Museums USA*, table 202, p. 412.

30. John Walker, *Self-Portrait with Donors* (Boston: Little, Brown, 1974).

31. *Museums USA*, pp. 184, 277 and 282. In 1971–2, the base year for the study, there were 35,600 art museum employees, of which 11,700 were paid, and 35,600 were unpaid volunteers.

32. Following the publication of this article, I received the following cor-

rective comment from June Wayne (personal letter, June 29, 1976): "Incidentally, in the quote of me, I intended it to be *'performing monkeys'*—*i.e.,* the organ grinder as patron and the monkey as artist. . . . If pressed, I would have to conclude that we are about as free wheeling as epileptics during a seizure."

13

Stereotypes and Women Artists

CINDY NEMSER

We all know that there is a body of myth about the "true" nature of womankind. These myths have hardened into stereotypes so deeply ingrained in the consciousness of society as to scarcely bear questioning. Now these time honored assumptions are at last being reinvestigated and demolished. The activities and accomplishments of womankind in every area of life are being reassessed and refined. Therefore, it is only right—in fact, it is essential—that this reexamination be undertaken in the field of art, the area of humankind's highest endeavor.

Along with art history, art criticism has played a vital role in measuring and evaluating the extent of the achievements of women artists. Art critics of both sexes, however, being no different from other human beings, have stereotyped notions as to what constitutes women's art. My intention is to uncover these stereotypes and to bring them into the open. Perhaps when exposed to the clear light of reason, they will be laughed out of existence. Then we can begin anew to judge women's art.

In examining these stereotypes, I will first build up a composite picture of the various attributes that art critics believe go into making up a female artist's work. In other words, I want to find out what is the supposed nature of women's art. Then I plan to investigate an area of writing Mary Ellman in her book *Thinking About Women* calls phallic criticism. In this kind of writing, women's work is always evaluated in relation to men's; it will be interesting to see how women come out when these comparisons are made. I have deliberately limited myself to the criticism written in the nineteenth and twentieth centuries because until then few women had independently entered the art field as professionals.[1]

FEMININE STEREOTYPES

Though many different stereotypes have been formulated about women artists and their work, they all seem to stem from one common source, the biological functions of the female sex organs. According to George Moore, writing in 1900 in *Modern Painting:* "Women's nature is more facile and fluent than man's. Women do things more easily but they do not penetrate below the surface."[2] Moore does not reveal on what grounds these conclusions have been formed, but their biological sources are evident. Facile and fluent immediately conjure up images of the lubricity of the internal female sex organs and, of course, the menstrual cycle. Inability to penetrate below the surface is a reference to women's lack of a penetrating organ, which at that time was supposed to be the prime instrument of creation. Indeed the lack of this organ is the essential basis for many critics' continued inability to view women as creative artists. George Moore unequivocally asserts that: "Women have created nothing."[3] Arthur Bye in *Art and Decoration* (1910) maintains that the "man's sphere is that of creation . . . woman's that of preservation and nourishment,"[4] while J. C. Holmes in the *Dome* (1899) confirms that "the true genius of the sex is observant, tasteful, and teachable, but not creative."[5] Echoes of this attitude are to be found in James Fitzsimmon's general evaluation of an exhibition of the National Association of Women Artists in *Art Digest* of 1952. He declares that: "The work is earnest and competent, but seldom attains originality."[6] (Interestingly enough, Louise Nevelson had a piece in this show, but her work is not singled out as an exception to this rule.)

Since many critics have accepted the idea that women artists are noncreative, it is natural for them to believe that any work produced by a woman is the result of having imitated some man. Art history and art criticism are almost unanimous in assuming that if a woman artist has any contact with a male artist, be he husband, lover, friend, or acquaintance, she must either be his pupil or deeply under his influence. Up to today most critical accounts of impressionism designate Mary Cassatt and Berthe Morisot as the pupils of Degas and

Manet respectively, although neither participated in this relationship.[7]

Despite the general consensus that women artists lack creativity and, as George Moore has so beguilingly put it, are "best when confined to the arrangement of themes invented by men,"[8] women like Cassatt and Morisot did persist in painting pictures that were distinguished. How to explain such distinction in beings supposedly excluded from originality by their biology? Nietzsche in his *Will to Power* came up with a solution to this problem that has kept male chauvinist critics happy for the past hundred years. He maintained that women did have one artistic impulse, the impulse to captivate.[9] As we shall see, this captivating quality has released an avalanche of critical adjectives that have been applied to female art with the most monotonous regularity for the past century. George Moore strings quite a few of the most popular ones together when he remarks that: "Women have carried the art of men across their fans charmingly, with exquisite taste, delicacy, and subtlety of feeling."[10] For Apollinaire, feminine art is "courtesy, joy, bravura." It is full of "grace," "youth," and "freshness." The most characteristic word he can find to describe it is "serpentine."[11]

Interestingly enough, when used by women even visual components such as color, line, and form, as well as the use of various techniques of paint application, have captivating feminine qualities. Camille Mauclair Faust, writing in 1911 of the French Impressionists, says that Morisot has "stated the femininity of this luminous and iridescent art."[12] Apollinaire admires Marie Laurencin's feminine arabesques,[13] while B. H. Friedman in his *Art News* article of 1966 commends Helen Frankenthaler's staining techniques as appropriate for her "free, lyrical, and feminine nature."[14]

Included in the category of captivation is, of course, the concept of witchery. Female artists are often referred to as witches and associated with occult powers and practices. Vivian Raynor, reviewing Nevelson in *Arts*, is glad that the artist grew up in Rockland, Maine, rather than in Salem, Massachusetts, in the seventeenth century.[15] Dorothy Gee Seckler tells us that Nevelson's art has been associated with "subterranean mysteries and magic rites."[16] All this sounds rather complimentary until one remembers that the witch is a wielder of black magic.

Witchery aside, captivating impulses are primarily positive if not entirely laudable. However, when other aspects of women's biological nature form the basis for her artistic attributes, the character of women's art becomes less and less praiseworthy. Because woman is looked upon as either the receiver or preserver of life rather than its creator, anything she *does* originate is believed to come out of a "passive, unconscious" kind of creativity. Harold Rosenberg remarks on this particular aspect of the female when he writes in *Vogue* that: "Women, poets, and heroes are involved in passivity. They do not exactly grasp what they are doing or who they are."[17] Hilton Kramer, describing Mary Frank's works in *Arts*, says "a kind of passivity encloses these sculptures,"[18] while James Schuyler in *Art News* sees a Frankenthaler painting as a "river reflecting clouds and evening."[19]

Since woman by nature is consigned to passivity, conversely she is viewed as open to attack from all external elements. This vulnerability explains the use of such words as emotional, sensitive, immediate, spontaneous, nervous, and hysterical, words that are sprinkled so overgenerously throughout the art criticism of women's work. According to Donald Judd, Frankenthaler's paintings are "verified by emotion."[20] André Salmon sees Suzanne Valadon's art "at the service of a pure spontaneity,"[21] while Hilton Kramer labels Margaret Israel's achievements as "hysterically gay."[22]

Women artists are not always to be found in a state of distraction. Yet when they revert to their natural passivity, a worse danger besets them. They are likely to turn narcissistic, and critics view this unpleasant female tendency with great severity. Sidney Tillim makes his disapproval evident when, in his review of Frankenthaler's exhibition in May 1959, he states that: "She yields to the inevitable narcissistic temptation of finding every spot significant."[23]

The woman artist's basically womb centered nature is also said to influence her choice of subject matter. J. K. Huysmans in *L'Art moderne* (1833) maintains that "only a woman is capable of painting children,"[24] while Alfred Werner in *Arts* praises Morisot because in selecting subjects like Sunday picnics, playing children, and young women preparing to look their best, "she drew abundantly upon the femininity she felt in herself."[25] John Baur sees the same conformity to female nature in O'Keeffe's choice of subject matter. He notes that she has "preferred to trace the sensuous curves of flowers, bleached bones on the desert and other natural objects in which she discovered a wealth of feminine symbolism."[26]

Technique and style are also seen as heavily influenced by the woman artist's enclosed female nature. In the *Crayon* (1860), J. Durand notes that woman is "best suited to all kinds of engraving techniques because she easily conforms to the sedentary life, . . . that motionless activity which the engraver's pursuit demands."[27] James Thrall Soby in a piece called "To the Ladies" finds Surrealism a style well suited to female artists because its main characteristics are "an unrelenting and naked introspection."[28]

Viewed as narcissistic and limited in range, women artists are also seen by many critics as unwilling or unable to make the great sacrifices supposedly necessitated by devotion to one's art. George Moore declares "in art woman is always in evening dress . . . her mental nudeness is parallel to her low bodice . . . she will make no sacrifice for her art."[29] James Fitzsimmons confirms this notion when he writes in an unpublished letter that: "Up until today, few women have been (or are) serious about art in the right way. High art is not 'something one does' or a 'spare time avocation.'"[30]

Categorizing women artists as captivating, emotional, narcissistic, and narrow in scope, critics are hard put to explain their worthy achievements. This predicament explains the frequent use of the word intuitive in dealing with women's art. The *Webster's New World Dictionary* defines intuition as the "immediate knowing or learning of something without the use of conscious reasoning." Granting women intuition is the perfect means whereby her solid attainments can be acknowledged without giving her full credit for them.

All in all, the woman artist emerges as a kind of primitive being, unformed and underdeveloped. Sometimes she is viewed as childlike; at other times she is merely childish, as when R. H. Wilenski charges in the *London Observer* that 90 percent of all women artists are immature.[31] Some critics, however, greatly prize this "essential being" quality in women artists. It relates to the idea of Rousseau's noble savage, unspoiled by corrupting civilization. Carl Zigrosser in his book on Käthe Kollwitz stresses over and over that she "has the plainspokenness of the elemental woman—the matriarch—on whom the tactics of subtle indirection have not yet been imposed by society."[32] Critics also realize that loss of this pure essence leads to one of the woman artist's most despised defects: affection, the ruination of both her style and temperament.

As we examine the various biologically engendered stereotypes critically associated with women artists, we discover a personage who is classified as noncreative, imitative, captivating, passive, emotional, narcissistic, narrow minded, selfish, intuitive, and elemental. Though some of these qualities are highly desirable, by now our picture is so confused and contrary it is laughable.

PHALLIC CRITICISM

The art of men has also been defined, to a large degree, by critical clichés derived from male physiognomy and sexual biology. Strong, grand, powerful, forceful, assertive, bold, rigorous, creative, direct, tough—these are words that abound in critical accounts of men's art works. Male artists also get the benefit of being designated as intellectual, intelligent, conscious, logical, and structured. Now, as we have seen, women's art is seldom described in terms of this male-oriented vocabulary; yet our male-dominated society values these qualities most of all. Therefore, it is not surprising to discover that when woman's art is compared to man's in such phallic criticism, woman is always the loser.

There are various forms of phallic criticism, but they all have one factor in common—they are all built on a premise David Bourdon states quite succinctly in an unpublished letter written in 1971. He declares that: "Women artists have always been inferior to men artists."[33] Not all critics are as blunt as Bourdon. Some like to play the separate-but-not-equal game. Walter Sparrow, writing in 1905, fancies himself a champion of women's rights when he says of Vigée-Lebrun: "Her paintings may not be the highest form of painting, but highest they are in their own realm of human emotions."[34] John Bauer in 1951 also shows great gallantry towards O'Keeffe's art, but he pronounces it "a little apart from the mainstream, not for technical or stylistic reasons but because of the very personal and feminine character of her art."[35]

Nor is it necessary for a critic to use specifically the words male, female, or the like, to make feminine inferiority clearly understood. Donald Judd's review of Frankenthaler's paintings of 1963 in *Arts* accomplishes these gender distinctions solely by means of the appropriate stereotyped adjectives. He states: "Frankenthaler's softness is fine, but it would be more profound if it were also hard. Bonnard and

Watteau's paintings, for example, are soft, essentially almost as soft and sensuous as Frankenthaler's, but their work is also tough and the softness is one aspect."[36]

A recent variation on this theme of inequality is to maintain that when it comes to female art, sex is of no consequence. Writing of Georgia O'Keeffe's painting in the *Artforum*, Peter Plagens testily observes that: "Whether or not there are sexual parts lurking in the pictorial configurations may never get affirmation one way or the other, but in the light of her whole work the idea is painfully trivial."[37] However, there is nothing trivial in Plagen's inability to fend off the image of artist Richard Serra as a penis invading the vagina of the Pasadena Art Museum.[38]

Now, since woman's art can never be as good as man's, the only way for her to make any progress, according to another form of phallic criticism, is to attempt to make an art that looks like his. Baudelaire bestowed his highest praise upon the painter Eugénie Gautier when he said: "She paints like a man."[39] The same sentiment is expressed without specifically referring to the artist's sex when John Rewald commends Morisot for "lacking neither assurance nor temerity."[40] A rather bawdy variation on this theme occurs when Arthur Cravan, in *Exhibition of the Independents* (1914), suggests that Marie Laurencin should learn to paint with her vagina. He writes: "Marie Laurencin . . . now there's one who needs to have her skirts lifted to get a sound . . . some place to teach her that art isn't a little pose in front of a mirror."[41]

Conversely, if an artist improves as she comes closer to assuming male qualities, it follows that the more "female" her art becomes, the more offensive it is. Katherine Kuh cannot bear the idea of a woman artist named "Grandma Moses." In the *Saturday Review*, she vitriolically inquires: "Though Titian lived to be 91, can one imagine calling him 'grandpa'?"[42]

Critics will praise a woman striving to paint like a man as long as she does not succeed too well. If her emulation comes too close for comfort, then the woman artist will be condemned for denying her female nature. George Moore reports mockingly that a woman attempting to penetrate the surface of art is "but a clumsy masquerade in unbecoming clothes."[43] Bye is even more severe. He insists that Rosa Bonheur, who never married or had children but put all her energy into her career, was, "what in German is called a 'Urninge' [an asexual] and scarcely can be classed among women painters at all."[44] Recently John Perreault, in his review of Nancy Graves, expresses the same male disapproval of a woman too manlike in her abilities. Critical of her intellectual approach, he speculates: "Perhaps it is the fact that Graves is a woman that makes her emphasize her intelligence to such a degree. . . . She reads too much."[45]

Women artists who are viewed as willing to accept male instruction and apply it to an art that reflects the stereotyped version of feminine nature are most acceptable to male chauvinist critics of both sexes. They are usually dismissed with a pat on the head or a playful slap on the rump (though often the pat turns into a cuff). Here is George Moore's kindly appraisal of Angelica Kauffmann's work: "Though her work is individually feeble, . . . she was content to remain a woman in her art; . . . she imitated Sir Joshua Reynolds to the best of her ability and did all in her power to induce him to marry her. How she could have shown more wisdom it is difficult to see."[46]

These docile women are also useful as switches with which to whip the more rebellious of their sister artists. Albert Ten Eyck Gardner commends Mary Cassatt for not using the mural space at the World's Columbian Exposition in Chicago in 1893 for "the feminist propaganda then rampant."[47] David Shirey applied this same strategy in his review of Loren MacIver in the *Times*. Speaking with forked tongue, he gushes: "What is particularly pleasant about Miss MacIver's pictorial visions and palette in this age of 'gimme' aggressions and women's liberation movements, is that Miss McIver gets her pictorial rights not through mugging onslaughts but through subtle and persuasive brainwashings."[48]

Various types of masculine criticism can be combined to put down the work of men as well as that of women. Clement Greenberg uses this tactic to take a swipe at the Minimal art he so thoroughly dislikes. In discussing Anne Truitt's pieces of 1963 he says "had they been monochrome, the objects in Truitt's 1963 show would have been qualified as the first examples of orthodox Minimal Art. And with the help of monochrome the artist would have been able to dissemble her feminine sensibility behind a more aggressively far-out, non-art look, as too many masculine Minimalists have *their* rather feminine sensibilities."[49] Greenberg first insults the Minimalists by calling their sensibilities feminine. Then he imputes to them the need to dissemble their feminity, which makes them sneaky and even more feminine. But Truitt is willing to stake herself on the truth of her sensibility, feminine or not; she at least openly acknowledges her female nature and therefore is more admirable than those unmanly Minimal deceivers, and she does this in her painting, the aspect of her work of which Greenberg most approves.

If we look back on the image of the woman artist presented to us by the art critics cited in this essay, we see that she has been typecast in accordance with the accumulated clichés associated with her female biology. Some female artists no doubt have succumbed to these stereotypes and have produced the sexually clichéd art expected of them. However, this capitulation on the part of certain women artists does not give critics carte blanche to view women's work, or men's either, with any prejudged set of criteria based on a set of outworn sexual prejudices. There is still no conclusive data on the part of scientists and behavioral psychologists as to whether or not the so-called male and female character traits or physiological gestures are the results of biological or cultural influences.[50] Therefore, until we know a great deal more about the workings of the human body, I must take great exception to John Canaday's claim that he can recognize the feminine in a work of art and enjoy it in the same way as he would "Fragonard's high spirits" or "Botticelli's curious melancholy."[51] Moreover, knowing as we do that when the word feminine appears in art criticism some form of discrimination is being practiced, we must conclude that Mr. Canaday is not being as impartial as he believes himself to be.

One hopes "feminine" will not always continue to retain its pejorative connotations, but these associations will only be altered when society as a whole alters its attitude toward women in general.

NOTES

1. Most women painters and sculptors came into art as assistants to their more famous fathers and husbands. Elisabeth Vigée-Lebrun and Angelica Kauffmann did attain independent reputations as accomplished artists, but they were the exceptions rather than the rule.
2. George Moore, *Modern Painting* (New York: Charles Scribner, 1900), p. 226.

3. Ibid., p. 227.

4. Arthur Bye, "Women and The World of Art," *Art and Decoration* 10 (1910): 87.

5. J. C. Holmes, "Women as Painters," *Dome* 3 (1899): 6.

6. James Fitzsimmons, "All Woman Annual," *Art Digest* 6, no. 16 (May 15, 1952): 15.

7. Adelyn D. Breeskin, who has devoted much of her career as an art historian to championing Mary Cassatt, insists that the artist was neither Degas's pupil nor his disciple but rather his respected ally. See Adelyn D. Breeskin, *Mary Cassatt* (Washington: National Gallery of Art, 1970), p. 13. See also Lloyd Goodrich, "Cassatt and Morisot," *Arts* 17, no. 2 (November 1930): 115.

8. Moore, *Modern Painting*, p. 227.

9. Friedrich Nietzsche, *The Will to Power*, trans. Anthony M. Ludovier (New York: Russell & Russell, 1964), vol. 2, p. 261.

10. Moore, *Modern Painting*, p. 227.

11. Guillaume Apollinaire, *The Cubist Painters* (Paris: 1913); trans. Lionel Abel (New York: Wittenborn, 1944), p. 27.

12. Camille Mauclair Faust, *The French Impressionists*, trans. P. G. Konody (London: Duckworth, 1911), p. 143.

13. Apollinaire, *Cubist Painters*, p. 25.

14. B. H. Friedman, "Towards the Total Color Image," *Art News* 65, no. 4 (Summer 1966): 32.

15. Vivian Raynor, "Louise Nevelson and Martha Jackson," *Arts* 35, no. 10 (September 1961): 40.

16. Dorothy Gee Seckler, "The Artist Speaks: Louise Nevelson," *Art in America* 55, no. 1 (January 1967): 35.

17. Harold Rosenberg, "The American Woman's Dilemma: Self Love, No Love," *Vogue* 149, no. 9 (May 1967): 163.

18. Hilton Kramer, "The Possibilities of Mary Frank," *Arts* 37, no. 6 (March 1963): 54.

19. James Schuyler, "Helen Frankenthaler Exhibition," *Art News* 59, no. 3 (May 1960): 13.

20. Donald Judd, "Helen Frankenthaler Exhibition," *Arts* 34, no. 6 (March 1960): 55.

21. André Salmon, "Letter From Paris," *Apollo* 11 (January 1930): 48.

22. Hilton Kramer, "Margaret Israel," *New York Times*, February 27, 1971, p. 23.

23. Sidney Tillim, "In the Galleries," *Arts* 33, no. 8 (May 1959): 56.

24. J. K. Huysmans, *L'Art moderne* (Paris: G. Charpentier, 1883), p. 232.

25. Alfred Werner, "Berthe Morisot, Major Impressionist," *Arts* 32, no. 6 (March 1958): 45.

26. John I. H. Baur, *Revolution and Tradition in Modern American Art* (New York: Frederick A. Praeger, 1951), p. 60.
27. J. Durand, "Women's Position in Art," *Crayon* 8 (1860): 25.
28. James Thrall Soby, "To the Ladies," *Saturday Review of Literature* 29, no. 27 (July 6, 1946): 14.
29. Moore, *Modern Painting*, p. 229.
30. James Fitzsimmons, unpublished letter to Cindy Nemser, January 14, 1971.
31. Cited in "Women's Art," *Art Digest* 5, no. 13 (April 1, 1931): 7.
32. Carl Zigrosser, *Prints and Drawings of Käthe Kollwitz* (New York: Dover Publications, 1951), p. xviii.
33. David Bourdon, unpublished letter to Cindy Nemser, 1971.
34. Walter Sparrow, *Women Painters of the World* (London: Hodder & Stoughton, 1905), p. 11.
35. Baur, *Revolution and Tradition*, p. 60.
36. Donald Judd, "Helen Frankenthaler," *Arts* 37, no. 7 (April 1963): 54.
37. Peter Plagens, "A Georgia O'Keeffe Retrospective in Texas," *Artforum* 4, no. 9 (May 1966): 29.
38. Peter Plagens, "Los Angelos, Richard Serra," *Artforum* 8, no. 8 (April 1970): 86.
39. Charles Baudelaire, *Art in Paris, 1845–1862*, trans. Jonathan Mayne (London: Phaidon Press, 1965), p. 18.
40. John Rewald, *Impressionism* (New York: Museum of Modern Art, 1961), p. 292.
41. Arthur Cravan, *Exhibition of the Independents* (Paris: 1914), p. 12.
42. Katherine Kuh, "Grandma Moses," *Saturday Review* 43, no. 37 (September 10, 1960): 16.
43. Moore, *Modern Painting*, p. 226.
44. Bye, "Women and the World of Art," p. 87.
45. John Perreault, "Art," *Village Voice*, February 4, 1971, p. 13.
46. Moore, *Modern Painting*, pp. 229–30.
47. Albert Ten Eyck Gardner, "A Century of Women," *Metropolitan Museum Bulletin* 7, no. 4 (December 1948): 116.
48. David Shirey, "Loren MacIver," *New York Times*, November 28, 1970, p. 17.
49. Clement Greenberg, "Changer: Anne Truitt," *Vogue* 15, no. 9 (May 1968), p. 281.
50. Ray L. Birdwhistell, *Kinesics and Context* (Philadelphia: University of Pennsylvania Press, 1970), pp. 39–46. Also see Naomi Weisstein, "Psychology Constructs the Female," in *Sisterhood Is Powerful*, ed. Robin Morgan (New York: Vintage Books, 1969), pp. 205–20.
51. This is a paraphrase of an unpublished letter from John Canaday to Cindy Nemser, December 22, 1971.

14

Why Do We Speak of Feminine Intuition?

MARGARET MEAD

The term *intuition* is used to describe knowledge that seems to appear full-blown. It is knowledge that appears in a nonrational way, the steps leading to which are unrecognizable and difficult to articulate, either for the knower or for those who watch the knower. *Feminine intuition* is used to describe those intuitive understandings that seem to come more easily and quickly to women by virtue of their sex. While the term usually applies to some aspect of human relationships, when used without the qualifier *feminine* it may apply to any kind of knowledge, the source of which is obscure.

Following its use in everyday life in our own society, one can often detect the term's comic element. For instance, a man, coming home tired and disgruntled, slams the car door shut, kicks a misplaced boot away from the door, slams the door, walks into the living room, and throws down his coat in an inappropriate place. His wife asks: "What's the matter, dear?" and he answers in wonder: "How did you know anything was the matter?" By extension, men who pay attention to the moods of others or pick up minimal cues from the behavior of others are said to have an "almost feminine type of intuition."

Although cultures differ in the extent to which they articulate comments on gender differences in perception, certain universals seem evident. Girls not only learn to talk earlier than boys, but they also learn to talk about different things; they learn the names for relationships and learn to comment on the behavior and motives of those around them. Even if, as in Samoa, speculation about the motives of others is discouraged and masked under the blanket diag-

167

nosis *musu* (unwilling), girls still made the diagnosis earlier. Little girls also imitate their mothers' tone of voice, nag, cajole, and insinuate (often with comic effect) in tones that are fully identifiable as those of women.

Methodologically, as a cultural anthropologist, I look first at available cross-cultural behavior and do not turn to psychological explanations until the cultural ones are exhausted. If girls seem universally to display this kind of behavior, the next question may be, are there any cultures in which boys also display this behavior? We do not have extremely detailed studies investigating this point, but the material we do have on prerevolutionary Russians—both males and females—suggests that both displayed an extremely alert sense of the unavowed intentions and motives of others; this seems to be related to their generalized expectation that children of both sexes identify temperamentally with both parents and that children of each sex could internalize characteristics of the other. Thus, it was said that a boy learned tenderness from his mother, and a girl learned a masculine-type bravery from her father. While certain qualities of personality were thought to be gender-linked, these could also be learned; but a lively alertness to the undeclared or unrecognized motives of others was still felt to be a feminine attribute that could be learned by men.

Fortune telling, an occupation that requires tremendous attention to the small cues given by strangers, tends to be regarded as a female occupation. When comparing methods of reading the future as practiced by men versus women, the male methods tend more often to be supported by props—dice, divining bones, harpiscopy—while women are able to "see" the future in tea leaves, in the palm, or in handwriting. But all of these techniques can be, and sometimes are, practiced by men, whether they are gender-linked or not.

Another occupation in which a high degree of sensitivity and attention to small, imperfectly verbalized or nonverbalized cues is necessary is child psychiatry or child psychoanalysis. Because the ordinary approach to the patient by way of speech is often not available in dealing with children, toys, tools, and test objects are used instead to allow the child to be active, to run away, cower on the floor, batter the analyst with his fists, or manipulate miniature objects, thereby allowing communication where no words are possible. One stylized form of such communication procedure is an objective test called the Lowenfeld World Technique.[1] Here, a child (or an adult) is presented with a set of miniatures of the real world (horses, cows, motor cars, houses, people, post boxes), a few fantasy objects (witches, dragons), a box of sand, and a pail of water; the child is then told to make a world. The therapist watches, records, and assists (when skill or the search for an appropriate animal fails) as the patient communicates to himself or herself, feelings and views of the world hitherto inaccessible to both therapist and patient. This procedure is related to the kind of self-illumination that comes from a daydream or a dream or (for someone skilled in self-analysis) from a poem or a painting. The finished creation embodies the same kind of knowledge that, when apprehended in the behavior or expressive work of another, we call intuition.

In my long and articulate relationship to child analysts, it has been my experience that women find this kind of therapeutic or psychological enterprise more congenial and less tiring than do men, that men tend to abandon it earlier and turn to analyzing adults who deal with children, rather than children themselves. It appears that male and female analysts use different approaches to observing and participating communicably in the behavior of small children; males identify with the child, try to feel what the child feels, and respond in terms of postures and attitudes that, having experienced themselves, they can analyze. In this respect, their behavior is much like the behavior they are taught when they become aware of a countertransference. Women, on the other hand, can watch small children as one of them or in the role of mother or nurse, alert to the smallest indication of a child's needs. In tracing back, I have found that those men who are as successful as women in being able to tolerate long periods of watching children have learned this from women—either from women analysts, women anthropologists, or, as in two striking cases (in childhood and adolescence), from twin sisters.

There is also some cross-cultural evidence that considerable differences exist in the types of gender-linked behavior that can be tested with instruments and the extent to which test results can be modified by immediate experience. Thus, Kate Franck, in her gender test, found that boys who had been recently chastised tended to emit the same type of passive responses to the test stimuli that were usually associated with those of girls.[2] I found that among the Tchambuli of Chambri Lake, in New Guinea, where women play a

much more active role than is customary and men are more dependent upon display and responsiveness, the small girls and small boys
also behaved in opposite ways. Whereas among the other South
Pacific peoples I have studied, small girls are usually absorbed in the
care of babies by the time they are ten and are less curious and
interested in the world about them, less willing than the boys to
participate in the unfamiliar activities of the field anthropologist,
among the Tchambuli it was the small girls who maintained their
curiosity and alertness to the outside world, while the boys withdrew
into an emphasis on their own bodies and their own feelings.

Thus, the material we have suggests that although males can learn
to show and to use "feminine" intuition, and girls can learn to inhibit
it, as a rule girls and boys learn to apprehend the behavior of others
(as well as the "meaning" of some products of behavior) in different ways.

This difference can be ascribed to the difference in the way in
which male and female children experience the early period in life
when they are cared for almost exclusively by women. Women, if
watched carefully, handle, bathe, feed, caress, lull, and stimulate
male and female babies differently; although wide individual, temperamental, class, and caste differences are also found (for example, a
lower-class nurse will differentiate between upper-class nurslings and
her own children).

But with all due allowance for such differences, women tend to
treat female infants as like themselves and males as different—as
small creatures who should be taught different kinds of activity.
Correspondingly, male and female infants respond to the difference
in gender of those who are holding and caring for them early in life
(as early as two months), but here again, it is difficult to tell whether
this is an instinctive response to smell, or style of movement, or
rather a response to the difference in the child-directed behavior of
the caretaker.

A recurrent example of differential treatment of infants by women
is that while girls are encouraged to lean passively against their
mothers, boys are encouraged to face their mothers actively and later
to move away from them. (Erikson found that in analyzing children's
play productions, girls tend to build a back or supporting wall, while
boys built towers or scenes of activity in open spaces.[3]) Stated simply, female infants are cared for primarily by others like themselves,

males by others who are unlike themselves; girls are encouraged to identify, in posture and pace, with their female nurses, boys are forbidden to make this identification—are pushed off their mothers' laps and encouraged to move out and away. Girls learn on their mothers' laps and by their sides; boys learn to leave their mothers' laps to explore and master the environment around them.[4]

In cases where drawing or painting have been introduced experimentally from outside the culture (as I did among the Manus[5]) or by stranger artists (as was done in Bali[6]), girls draw as women do, while boys' drawings are immediately recognizable as male (girls drawing beadwork or cake, boys drawing fishermen, warriors, or *kris* dancers). Where, however, traditional styles of drawing exist, these spontaneous differences do not appear. Thus, among the Latmul, where there are highly developed and stylized ways of representing males and females, both boys and girls alike drew in an adult male style. On the other hand, among the Arapesh, where women amuse themselves by drawing stick figures on bark, both boys and girls drew in a female style.[7]

Thus, while girl children learn to identify with their mothers, boys learn *not* to identify with their mothers. Furthermore, girls actually identify with the process of mothering—a process that paradoxically means a lack of identification with the nursling being mothered. Successful mothering requires that a woman (or a man who plays this role) learn not to identify with the infant needing care; not to project his or her own needs on the infant, but to be alert to the infant's actual needs.

When a boy is pushed off his mother's lap, he is also pushed away from identifying with the needs of others. He is given the message: be yourself; do not respond to the arms that have held you. As a result, we have the paradox that a female child learns from her mother (or nurse) how to be attentive to the needs of another, while a male child is left with identification as his only access to these needs. The psychic cost of this difference in upbringing is vividly apparent in the case of male versus female analysts of children; the male analyst attempts to understand child patients by identification, involving expensive regression and the struggle to overcome it, while the female analyst has available either identification or the position of a watchful, attentive nurse or mother.

So far I have suggested that the capacity to be attentive to the other is a function of the way children are reared in the care of women. It may be, however, that the capacity to attend to another is a function of a much deeper process related to a woman's experience of the process of gestation during which she must physiologically relate to a being that is other—sometimes very much other—than herself. It need not be that the actual experience of pregnancy is necessary for the development of feminine intuition, for although many women do not bear children, all women were born of women and almost all have been reared by women who have borne children—their own mothers. The permission to lean back and identify with her mother, which is given to a girl, may well be, therefore, the permission (or the invitation) to identify with a mother's capacity for relating to another in the deepest possible way.

If it is merely the postnatal experience that is operative in shaping the capacities of male and female children, then a change in life style in which young fathers take as much care of infants as do young mothers should make it possible for both boys and girls to identify with a like parent and differentiate themselves from the opposite gender parent. This might be accompanied by less of a need (on the part of mothers) to push their sons away from them, as sons instead would be drawn towards their fathers. The mothering behavior, even if rooted at the very deepest level in the process of gestation, would become at least partly available to male children also.[8] But these are speculations about the future.

In the world humankind has known for the last million years or so, infants have been breastfed, carried, and cared for primarily by women; it is from females that males and females learn different things. Under primitive conditions of child rearing, the child of a mother who cannot relate successfully to her child, or whose child cannot thrive on her milk, will die; children of women who cannot see their child as "other"—hungry, sleepy, and thirsty in its own rhythm, not in hers—would not survive.[9] Thus, feminine intuition, as the capacity to attend to (rather than identify with), would be perpetuated from generation to generation whether structurally related to women's child bearing functions or not.

There is a further theoretical possibility. Given that some temperaments (of which there are both male and female versions) are innately responsive to the needs and desires of others, while other temperaments are not, if both men and women are expected to conform to a nonresponsive temperamental style, intuition would be less pronounced as a characteristic of feminine behavior.[10] But the sheer necessity of caring for an infant whose needs are different from her own might still force the unresponsive woman, or the woman who was fitted (by cultural pressure) into an unresponsive mold, to attend to infants and children and so learn to be attentive to the needs and desires of others.

A further speculation involves the way in which men and women have treated the external world; while men impose their wills upon it, bending it to their purposes, women's greater historical tendency is to adapt to the environment within which they find themselves. The historical division of labor between hunting and gathering did, of course, predispose women to watch where the berries and bulbs grew and where to return to find them; men were occupied in the pursuit of game. Here again we cannot be certain that even 50,000 years of one type of food producing practice rather than another would result in the selection of men and women who differed from one another. Similarly, the fact that women in our society have done best in those areas that require listening and looking, while men have excelled in those areas where they impose a form upon the world, may reflect some basic difference, or may be merely a historical residue of earlier ages. We do know women in many cultures are more field dependent than men.[11]

From a different angle, we might ask how is intuition preserved and cultivated? Can it be extinguished in women? Can it be cultivated in men? If, at present, it is habitual behavior for women reared by women, what kind of childrearing and teaching by women of boys or young men might open the way for males to have more access to intuitive types of behavior? Is recognition of pattern in fact a form of feminine intuition, which when practiced by males, is something that they have learned from women? Could intuitive behavior, once freed from its anchorage in maternal behavior, be made readily available to both boys and girls?

Is the fear of using intuition (among Euro-American scientists, for example) simply a fear of being feminine, of surrendering to the nature of an observed set of phenomena instead of building up information from carefully devised logical steps? I have known brilliant men who felt somehow guilty when they arrived at some important insight intuitively. They have felt constrained to return laboriously to an assumed ignorance and reconstruct, step by step, the knowledge they already had.

This was, in fact, the history of the enormously expensive study on the authoritarian personality. When all the complicated instruments had been applied and analyzed, we were right where we first started when Else Frenkel-Brunswik wrote her "intuitive" article.[12]

These are all possibilities that need exploration. We also need to know more about transexuals—those who appear to be male children who have so closely and physically identified with their mothers, and have been so closely identified as female by their mothers, that their feelings and movements are feminine rather than masculine.[13] We need information on children who have been cared for by members of both sexes from birth. We need much more material on the way in which small infants learn to distinguish sex, on the appearance of the earliest forms of sex-typed behavior, and to correlate these with the kind of work that John Money is doing.[14] We need to look at the work of Alan Lomax, who has found that differences in musical style vary with the role of women in food production.[15]

Until we know a great deal more, we won't be able to say much that is definite about feminine intuition.

NOTES

1. Margaret Lowenfeld, "The World Technique," *Topical Problems in Psychotherapy* 3(1960): 248–263.
2. Kate Franck, "Preference for Sex Symbols and Their Personality Correlation," *Genetic Psychology Monographs* 33, no. 2 (1946): 73–123.
3. Erik H. Erikson, "Sex Differences in the Play Configurations of American Adolescents," in *Childhood in Contemporary Cultures*, eds., Margaret Mead and Martha Wolfenstein (Chicago: University of Chicago Press, 1955), pp. 324–341.
4. Margaret Mead, *Male and Female: A Study of the Sexes in a Changing World* (New York: Morrow, 1949).
5. _____, *Growing Up in New Guinea: A Comparative Study of Primitive Education* (New York: Morrow, 1930).
6. _____, "Research on Primitive Children," in *Manual of Child Psychology*, ed., Leonard Carmichael (New York: Wiley, 1946), pp. 667–706.

7. _____, "The Bark Paintings of the Mountain Arapesh of New Guinea," in *Technique and Personality in Primitive Art*, Museum of Primitive Art Lecture Series No. 3 (New York: The Museum of Primitive Art, 1963), pp. 8–43.

8. _____, "A Note on the Evocative Character of the Rorschach Test," in *Toward a Discovery of the Person: The First Bruno Klopfer Memorial Symposium, and Carl G. Jung Centennial Symposium* (Burbank, Calif.: Monograph of the Society for Personality Assessment, 1974), pp. 62–67.

9. _____, "Changing Patterns of Parent-Child Relations in an Urban Culture" *International Journal of Psycho-Analysis* 38, part 6 (1957): 369–378.

10. _____, *Sex and Temperament in Three Primitive Societies* (New York: Morrow, 1935); Mead, Margaret. *Blackberry Winter: My Earlier Years* (New York: Morrow, 1972).

11. Helen Lewis, *The Psychic War in Men and Women* (New York: New York University Press, 1976).

12. T. W. Aderno et al, *The Authoritarian Personality* (New York: Harper & Row, 1950).

13. Robert Stoller, *Sex and Gender: On the Development of Masculinity and Femininity* (New York: Science House, 1968).

14. John Money and Anke Ehrhardt, *Man and Woman, Boy and Girl* (Baltimore: Johns Hopkins University, 1972).

15. Alan Lomax, "A Note on Feminine Factors in Culture History," in *Being Female: Reproduction, Power and Change*, ed., Dana Raphael (The Hague: Mouton, 1975).

15

The Myth of Masculine and Feminine Polarity

BARBARA WHITE KAZANIS

Today there is an equivocal semantic value to the term "myth." We use it in the sense of a fiction—an illusion, a false belief, a fable. We use it also in the sense of a primordial revelation or a sacred tradition. Well into the nineteenth century traditional Western scholars treated myth as the leftover vestiges of a prescientific viewpoint, a symptomatic expression of a primitive and poorly developed mind. However, for at least the past 70 years, scholars have approached the study of myth from a point of view different from their predecessors.

Myth as used in this chapter does not mean a false belief, a pseudoscientific account, nor an account of ritual or cult. Myth here is understood, as Alan Watts, the great discussant of East and West has described it, as a unique experience. He says: "Myth is to be distinguished from religion, science, and philosophy because it consists always of concrete images, appealing to imagination, and serving in one way or another to reveal or explain the mysteries of life. . . . Mythic image at once reveals and conceals. The meaning is divined rather than defined, implicit rather than explicit, suggested rather than stated."[1] Mark Schorer says: "Myths are the instruments by which we continually struggle to make our experience intelligible to ourselves. A myth is a large controlling image that gives philosophical meanings to the facts of ordinary life; that is, which has organizing value for experience."[2]

This chapter will explore the images of women as found in the myths of masculine and feminine polarity. We are concerned with how these myths are large controlling images that give meaning to the facts of our ordinary life.

What, exactly, do we mean by masculine/feminine polarity? Alan Watts says it is something much more than simple duality or opposition. Masculine and feminine are the extremities of a single whole. He tells us that: "Polar opposites are inseparable opposites, like the poles of the earth or a magnet, or the ends of a stick or the faces of a coin." He goes on to say that "though what lies between the poles is more substantial than the poles themselves—since they are the abstract 'terms' rather than the concrete body—nevertheless man thinks in terms and therefore divides in thought what is undivided in nature." Watts concludes "that when anyone draws attention to the implicit unity of polar opposites, we feel something of a shock. For the foundations of thought are shaken by the suspicion that experiences and values which we have believed to be contrary and distinct are, after all, aspects of the same thing."[3]

In a culture such as ours, which has lost touch with the sources of its images, the symbols of masculine and feminine polarity have come to be treated as solid, opaque objects, and the differences between men and women have become "things." Therefore, in reexamining the feminine and masculine principles we must be willing to shift our awareness to that area of unity that lies between the poles. It is more substantial than the forced choice between either the male or female pole. We need to create for ourselves the possibility of a new myth, an image, one more appropriate to our present history.

TELLING AGAIN THE MYTHS OF MASCULINE AND FEMININE POLARITY

In China polarity is represented by the fundamental forces of Yin (female) and Yang (male). The *I Ching*, an ancient book of Chinese wisdom says: "One Yin and one Yang, that is the Tao." Tao roughly translates as "oneness." Early Chinese authors tell us that the Yin/Yang principles never become fully separated. The image is that of cyclical changes of nature where only one principle is manifest and dominant while the other is latent and recessive, as in the contrast between winter and summer. Thus when the energy of one principle achieves fulfillment, it automatically transforms into its opposite. The Tao is considered as descriptive of all forms of existence. Male and female reflect the same wavelike operations of the basic Yin/ Yang forces as does nature. Throughout all discussions no undertone of "good" and "evil" is implied, rather harmony, happiness, and health are assured through the attainment and maintenance of a balance between the Yin and Yang, the male and female forces.

While polarity in China is characterized by the image of "harmony," in Japan the polarity is one of "tension." Amaterasu, the female sun goddess, characterized by tender features, and Susanoo, the storm god, characterized by stern and harsh aspects, symbolize polarity. According to legend their relationship is strained. While nobility adopted the female pole as their guiding principle, and the warrior class took the male as their guiding principle, this social distinction meant no ethical rejection but rather a distinction of function.

In the whole of Indian thinking, the principles of male and female have always been assumed to be intrinsically positive. Guenther, scholar of Eastern thought, selects a quotation from the Brhadaranyaka-upanishad that demonstrates this:

> In the beginning, this (the universe) was the Viraj alone in the shape of a person . . . became the size of a man and woman in close embrace. He divided the body into two. From that (division) came husband (pati) and wife (patni). He united with her. From the (union) human beings were born.[4]

Thus, the Viraj, the Indian equivalent to the Chinese Tao, has within its original unity the polarity of maleness and femaleness. When it breaks up, each of its parts retains the divine; one part is not valued over another. The whole universe is taken as an embodiment of the divine, and copulation is seen as the reenactment of the original cosmic creation. The sculpture of Siva as Ardhanarisvara (half-man/ half-woman) expresses the understanding that maleness and femaleness each possess divine qualities.

In Vajrayana Buddhism the existential aspect is emphasized against the epistemological discussion. Experience and meaning are each embodied in both ideas and action. Guenther says: "The polarity of 'appreciative discrimination' and 'meaningful action,' in philosophical terms, of 'male' and 'female' in worldly and poetic form, expresses the fundamental tendencies of humanity." He goes on to say: "There is perpetual movement, a continuous change of states, and, at the same time, a constant removal of contraries by states of relative equilibrium." He concludes that: "Human reality is just this state of suspended tension between maleness and femaleness, in which both are 'open,' nothing as such, and only their incessant interaction, their becoming, is real."[5]

The presupposition of the essentially divine and positive quality of both the masculine-feminine poles remains the major difference between Western Christian and Eastern imagery. In the Eastern view, reality is an interactive tension between maleness and femaleness. These two polarities are two kinds of formulated energies, perhaps we could say two kinds of knowledge differing in their symbolic forms. In contrast, the Western approach to polarity begins to establish the idea of mutual exclusivity. It goes on to establish arbitrarily one principle as good and the other as evil. It thus creates a hierarchy between the principles and assigns a moral value to the terms masculine and feminine, establishing male as good, female as evil.

In the Western world we may trace the break in the mutuality of the images of male-female polarity to Plato. Plato, in taking up the question of polarity of experience, distinguished between two ground principles; the logos (which was rational, mathematical, and formal and which he called the male) and eros (which was intuitive, emotional, and aesthetic and which he called female). To the ethical distinctions of logos and eros he added the male and female principles, ethically exalting the male principle and denigrating the female principle. The logical modes are considered acceptable, while the erotic, emotive, and aesthetic modes become suspicious. This distinction confirmed male dominance, sustained the social conditions of a patriarchal slave society, and legitimized the suppression of intuitive, emotive, and aesthetic modes of knowledge, which posed a threat to the abstract "order."

Christianity further dissolved the original unity of the polarity principle when the church fathers further exalted the rational principle. Taking up the images of the dualism of light and dark, good and evil, matter and spirit, they made the battle between opposites the central thesis of Christianity. From the logical/intuitive, logos/eros principles applied to male and female bodies, we find the ethical questions of good and evil raised by Plato transformed by the church into moral judgments. The church fathers turned Plato's epistemology into metaphysical principles. The feminine became evil; the masculine, good.

In summary, note that the images of polarity begin historically in the East with the inner unity of opposites. As human kind moved forward in historical time and westward geographically, it arrived at the contemporary era and the ultimate dualism that has followed the disappearance of all notions of an inner unity of maleness and femaleness.

THE RESULTS OF THE PRESENT VIEW OF DUALITY

Mythic image establishes meaning on all levels: psychological, anthropological, and cosmological. Therefore, it is important to consider the hidden mythic images within our present art, scholarship, culture, and religious structures. To do this, let us note the assumptive duality in our concepts of scholarship. Remember that the mythic image that grounds our present view of polarity in the West is that of absolute duality, and thus all contraries are ultimately evaluated in ethical and moral terms of good and evil. Consider the implicit values we attach to these terms of polarity taken from everyday language and the current concepts we base our scholarship upon: black/white, female/male, intuitive/rational, aesthetic/scientific, subjective/objective, devil/god, instinct/behavior.

It does not take much imagination to realize that white, rational, male, and scientific are deemed right. By further extension, the objective, the outside, and the environmental forces of behavior are deemed important and correct. Thus, our scholarship reflects scientific objectivism, and our psychology emphasizes behaviorism. We note that the scientific areas are financially and morally supported. We see our art becoming increasingly conceptual.

By further extension, we find the subjective, the instinctual forces of experiences are not evaluated as positive and important to the culture. They are often judged as morally negative. We see scholarship negate empathy and intuition. The arts devalue personal imagery. It is precisely this view of the arts, women, and the imaginal experience as morally suspect and perhaps downright evil, that necessitates the search for a new mythic image. The imprisoning closure that our present view presses upon the vividness and fecundity of our experience is intolerable.

THE CREATION OF A NEW MYTHOLOGY: A THREE-FOLD TASK

The search for a new mythic image may be characterized by the search for the relationship of opposites in union. The three aspects of this might be taken as anthropological, psychological, and cosmological. But we are separating into distinctive disciplines what is whole in a lived life. We would be foolish if we thought there was one linear solution. Also, one does not set out logically to create a new myth, but rather our myths are revealed to us in the images we bring to form in our daily rituals, in the work of our art and our scholarship.

Let us then turn to look at some emergent images that are exemplary of this search for a new myth of masculine and feminine polarity; the anthropological view of Susanne Langer, the psychological view of Carl Jung, and the cosmological view of Alan Watts.

One emergent image may be found in Langer's anthropological redefinition of man from rational animal to image maker. She says: "In the fundamental notion of symbolization—mystical, practical, or mathematical, it makes no difference—we have the keynote of all humanistic problems. In it lies a new conception of 'mentality' that may illumine questions of life and consciousness." This study of symbolization is a new field of study, which does not spring from any traditional discipline. It runs, she says, at least two distinct and apparently incompatible courses: "Yet each course is a river of life . . . and each fructifies its own harvest. . . . One conception of symbolism leads to logic and meets new problems in theory of knowledge; and so it inspires an evaluation of science and a quest for certainty. The other takes us in the opposite direction to psychiatry, the study of religion, fantasy, and everything but knowledge."[6]

In this view we see a new recognition of unity, bifurcation, a new valuing of the terms of polarity, and a call for a new view of *Mind* that will establish a transformed unity.

Carl Jung, the psychologist, provides the basis for a new recognition of our essential unity with the universe in his work on the unity of psyche and matter. In his studies of the dream, the image, the unconscious, and the chthonic aspects of human experience, he reintroduced a valuation of what has come to be associated with the feminine. His work in "active imagination" and "sychronicity" already speak to the fruitful harvest of the study of symbols in differing modes from which Langer points us.

Through his work on the psychic process of differentiation of the apparent contraries within us and the process of individuation, (the achieving of a psychic wholeness, which he calls the Self in contrast to the usual state of self-consciousness we call ego) he points us toward an enlarged understanding of the "differences" we have come to call masculine and feminine.

Jung's imagery has contributed greatly to the balancing of our overly rational psychology. It has served to direct us towards a psychology of the feminine. But Jung's greatest contribution to our contemporary myth making is the clear vision of the subject of psychology being the psyche, the soul. Jung felt that the most significant religious event of the twentieth century was the Papal declaration of the assumption of the Virgin Mary into heaven, which he interpreted as a reuniting of the feminine and masculine into the godhead.

In cosmological terms, the unity of opposites must be carried to all levels and applied in all contexts for there to be a totality, a new union. Here Watts tells us we seek to establish the human ideal in images of the hermaphrodite, the androgynous sage, or the divine person whose consciousness transcends polarity.

For Watts, the concern with Eastern images and practices is a vehicle for the practical transformation of human consciousness. From this perspective the East presents us with a great tradition of nonverbal humanities, experiential procedures that reveal the nature of consciousness in their own distinctive form. He feels that it is in the study of mystical traditions, such as those of Sufism and Buddhism (which do not see themselves as dogmas but as processes of studying consciousness itself), that the mythic qualities of life are reawakened. Watts suggests that this is a concern that is "repugnant to academics, contemptible to businessmen, threatening to Jews and Christians, and irrational to most scientists," but essential to the transformation of our experience into a unity.[7] Yet these traditions contrast with our Western methods of rational intellection in a mutually enhancing way.

Viewing the question of polarities at the cosmological level, it is not difficult to understand the West as one ground principle (the male) and the East as the other (the female). In a very large sense, East and West may be two ways to study the nature of symbolization. If we apply Langer's image we may see that the East and West may be taken as two courses of human symbolization, each with its own harvest, and each with its own methods. The search for a unity of opposites in the form of a new mythic image may well start by the reexamination of cultures as well as the psychology of male and female identity.

CONCLUSION

The most important point to this chapter is that we understand that the issues of male and female are mythic questions, characterized by a multi-dimensional process of consciousness. This process is characterized by the search for a sense of our original unity, an understanding of our differentiation, and the quest for a path to wholeness.

We must acknowledge that myth cannot be deliberately articulated, but is revealed to us from out of the image forms of our lived lives, be they ritual, art or scholarship. Finally, we note that in this view education is about being on a path toward the *experiencing* of wholeness. Failing to grasp this, or mistakenly taking one dimension for the whole, we can never hope to experience ourselves and to permeate what Watts has called the taboo against knowing who we really are.

NOTES

1. Wendell C. Beane and William G. Doty, *Myths, Rites, Symbols: A Mircea Eliade Reader*, vol. 1 and 2 (New York: Harper Colphon, 1975).
2. Alan Watts, *The Two Hands of God: The Myths of Polarity* (New York: Collier Books, Macmillan, 1970), p. 3.
3. Ibid., p. 45–46.

4. Herbert V. Guenther, "The Male-Female Polarity in Oriental and Western Thought," in *Maitreya 4: Woman*, ed. Samuel Bercholz and Michael Fogan (Boulder, Colo.: Shambala, 1973), pp. 51–63.
5. Ibid., p. 56.
6. Susanne K. Langer, *Philosophy in a New Key: A Study in the Symbolism of Reason, Rite, and Art* (New York: Mentor, New American Library, 1973). p. 32.
7. Alan Watts, *In My Own Way: An Autobiography* (New York: Vintage, Random House, 1973), p. 286.

16

The Significance of What Boys and Girls Choose to Draw:
Explorations of Fighting and Helping

SYLVIA GRUBER FEINBURG

Children's drawings are a rich source of information about the ways in which children perceive the world. The drawing process reveals their intellectual understandings as well as their social perceptions, enabling the viewer to consider fears, values, and aspirations as well as predispositions towards particular forms and spatial organizations. Hence, drawings are a powerful tool for examining such a subject as sex role identification. I will discuss some issues related to boys' and girls' preferences for subject matter and the use of space in drawing as well as report the findings of a study that probed similarities and differences in the sexes' responses to the notions of fighting and helping.

Rhoda Kellogg has documented the art work of the preschool child in the most thorough overview that exists in the field. She has identified the evolution of non-objective, as well as objective, forms produced by the very young child and has analyzed such matters as placement on the page, use of media, and ways of assessing competence. Kellogg contends that there are no discernible distinctions between the work of small boys and girls and that neither the specific forms constructed, nor the means used to create them, reveal anything significant that would separate the two groups.[1]

However, once children are well launched into the representational stage (five or six years of age), the subject matter that they depict when given free choice reveals substantial differences between the sexes. Throughout the last century a number of studies have analyzed preferred subject matter. These studies indicate consistently that girls favor subjects of an interpersonal nature, such as friends, parents, and children, while boys show an interest in objects and devices, including vehicles and mechanical equipment. Boys identify with themes of a heroic, extravagant nature and depict subjects associated with motion. These preferences towards subject matter seem rather firmly rooted and have not changed over time. Children from different cultures reflect the same predilections.[2]

None of this should seem surprising when one considers both the nature and relative universality of sex role socialization. It is clear that a culture transmits a very different set of expectations to each of the sexes in terms of what is appropriate behavior. As early as three years of age, children have internalized a firm sense of what is distinctly male or female.[3]

Males are reinforced for high activity and energetic participation. Their infantile curiosity towards exploration and the examination of objects and places is applauded. There is general support for their early aggressive behavior. Assertion and independence are construed as appropriate masculine attributes. Things and how they work are considered fundamental, important learnings for males. Even today, although females are not necessarily dissuaded from investigating objects and devices, they quickly comprehend that activity and accomplishment of a "worldly" nature are considered by others to be less significant for them than pursuits that are related to interpersonal concerns.

One of the most dramatic distinctions in the handling of boys and girls is manifest in the area of aggressive behavior. Physical aggression is not only tolerated but is sometimes actively encouraged in males; quite the reverse is true for females. The boy who strikes out at others is considered to be "all boy," simply testing his sense of self. No such acceptance is conveyed to a girl, who is actively restrained from such physical interactions. Strength, power, and bodily mastery are considered important ingredients for justifying one's masculinity. Being able to stand on one's own two feet, both emotionally and physically, is considered a prerequisite for successful manhood. The female is taught to deny her aggressive drives and to sublimate the desire for power and domination. Hence, she may cultivate the skills of manipulation and verbal attack as counterparts to physical assertion.[4]

In view of all of this, the revelation that small boys draw pictures of objects and vehicles and examine notions of speed and encounter, while females depict people and domestic tranquility seems "logical" and "natural," given the differences in early learning. Art activity for children is, after all, a form of play that reflects the attempt to integrate the values that are perceived within the society.

THEMATIC PREFERENCES

Certain subjects become central to a child's thinking and are examined in art expression with such frequency and intensity as to emerge as dominant themes. Subject matter can be thought of as being thematic when it becomes focused in a very decisive way and is the locus for repeated exploration. A few of the themes that are particularly common for elementary aged children include: dinosaurs and monsters, horses, social encounters, royalty, sports events, and war. These themes are well known by those who work closely with large numbers of children and by parents who have witnessed children's intense involvement with them. Although not all children examine the same themes, it appears that there is a developmental evolution that occurs; this evolution seems clearly sex related. Oedipal and post oedipal boys (between the ages of four and six, in particular) are strongly attracted to the monster and dinosaur theme as well as to vehicles and space ships. Girls of the same age play out their fantasies through the manipulation of kings and queens, princes and princesses, identifying with the glamour and romance of royalty. The horse theme, a most popular and long sustained one, is dominantly female and sometimes extends itself well into the adolescent period.[5] Clearly no single subject remains only within the province of a given sex, for individuality dominates. All children at one time or another examine a variety of possible alternatives. But the deep interest that many children show in relationship to a few notable themes, and the fact that this interest is shared by so many other children of the same age and sex, suggest that something psychologically important is occurring through their repeated manipulations.

In an earlier paper, the subject of war in the art work of young boys was reviewed, and the nature and evolution of this particular theme was documented. The elements of war pictures remain quite constant: situations of combat, usually depicting hordes of men, planes, bombs, ships, and always life threatening danger. The notion of contest, of opposing forces, issues of good guy/bad guy, and winning and losing manifest themselves primarily between six and 12 years of age, although it is at its height during the mid-elementary years and seems to emerge on the heels of the monster stage.[6]

The war theme serves the child in a variety of ways, independently of the most obvious aspect of confronting aggressive feelings. Issues of power and competence, understanding one's role in relationship to others, mastery of tools and equipment, and the importance of collaborative effort on behalf of accomplishment all seem to be intertwined in this early artistic play. For the small boy aggressive activity is frequently perceived and expressed in drawings in an organized manner, involving order, organization, and clear role differentiation. Of additional interest is the depersonalized and collective nature of these combative productions in which individual identity and purpose is clearly subordinated to the larger task of achieving a group goal of mutual concern. It would appear that while a boy engages in aggressive participation in the creation of battle pictures, he also perceives himself as a member of a larger, more significant group, and the subordination of self to this organization is fundamental.

Other subject matters of an aggressive nature that boys explore seem to reflect these same fundamental notions and are less apt to represent conflict of an interpersonal nature, e.g., athletic events, monster and sea encounters, and the like. Fighting, it would seem, is more than just that. It is a means by which the child formulates some fundamental attitudes about interactions among people, about the ways in which they compete, work together, and strive to overcome difficult odds. The young boy's perceptions of aggressive conflict, and the means by which he seeks to examine and comprehend this important aspect of human interaction, become generalized and integrated into a fundamental framework through which he views a larger set of ideas. Small boys' images of conflict are linked to the adult male's preoccupations with competing and succeeding and subordinating one's own personal feelings and concerns on behalf of the task at hand.

But how does the small girl perceive the notion of fighting? It would be naive to think that only boys need to confront aggressive, impulsive feelings and to learn to sublimate them into more socially acceptable contexts. Girls, too, need to confront these same dimensions of human behavior and find the effective means by which to deal with their strong feelings. Yet girls do not appear to make artistic investigations of a comparable nature. The themes that they select—landscapes, domestic scenes, designs, drawings of people and animals—are quite different in quality from those produced by boys. Subject matter for females is more apt to be associated with beauty, nurturance, and tranquility. Although any subject may be treated in a variety of ways, for the most part females produce work that is devoid of the notions of encounter and aggression.

SEX DIFFERENCES AND SIMILARITIES

In an attempt to understand more fully some of the factors that are influential in the production of small boys' war pictures, as well as sex related subject matter in general, a study was undertaken to probe children's reactions to two contrasting aspects of behavior—aggression and lending assistance to others. Lower elementary aged boys and girls were asked to make two pictures, one about fighting, the other about helping. The children included brief written descriptions with their drawings.[7]

The results of this study are of great interest, since they provide information that extends our understanding about the ways in which each of the sexes approaches a given situation. In the case of both fighting and helping, boys and girls differed from one another in the way in which they organized their thinking. Fighting conjures up images of power and competence as they are revealed in organized, depersonal ways for the male. He identifies with events that are removed from home, family, and friends and construes fighting as something that involves teams, armies, and other structured situations requiring rules and order. Quite the opposite is true for the female. Fighting for her is portrayed as interpersonal conflict, specifically two people in direct confrontation. The antagonist is not an unknown individual associated with a rule system, but rather a friend or a relative.

Although both sexes portrayed helping as something that is apt to take place within the home, boys focused primarily upon the task itself as opposed to the girls, who created pictures showing themselves lending assistance to another person—mother, teacher, friend, and so on. Consistently boys' drawings suggested that the situation at hand—the job, the task, the struggle—was central to their concerns, while the girls' drawings suggested that they were preoccupied with their feelings and relationships with significant others. This reinforces the notion that boys are more apt to respond in a depersonal manner, girls in a personal manner, even if aggression is not involved.

Fighting

Contrary to expectations, war was not the most frequently selected subject matter for fighting for boys. Sports themes were, with over one-third of the total population of 90 boys choosing this particular idea. Only 15 percent of the girls selected sports, by comparison. Twenty percent of the boys drew pictures of war, whereas only 4 percent of the girls did so.

The specific subject matter for interpersonal encounters was similar for each of the sexes (two or three people engaged in confrontation), with some small tendency on the part of the boys to include more figures in their drawings (up to five or six). Although a number of boys did create drawings of an interpersonal nature (38 percent), these depictions were frequently of a qualitatively different nature with more instances of significant bodily harm and weapons represented.

Girls also portrayed interpersonal encounters as involving physical fighting but of a less intense nature than the boys. Examples included: "You and your friend have a fight some times because you get mad at each other," and "Me and my sister having a pillow fight, hitting the pillow over each other's heads."

Both groups chose objects as the frequent provocation for fighting and cited dolls, bikes, and toys as instrumental factors, but a few girls identified people as the basis for disagreement, e.g., "The men were fighting over the princess. The man in the blue clothes won her." There is no ambiguity, however, about which sex is primarily identified with fighting, especially when it is associated with physical harm. Large numbers of girls, as well as boys, make reference to boys being involved in aggression, with frequent references to the "boy-hits-girl" syndrome.

Of particular interest is the fact that a number of girls displaced fighting onto animals, such as bunnies, cats, and horses, engaged in disagreement, e.g., "The rabbits are about to start a fight." In none of these instances was there any significant physical aggression expressed, revealing instead a sense of playfulness and affection.

Helping

Both sexes expressed understanding of helping as lending assistance to another person. However, girls' responses to helping another person tended to be more closely allied with family and friends, e.g., "This is me helping my mother put the dishes away," and "I am doing my mother's work for her because she is sick in bed." This contrasted markedly with boys, who said such things as "I am helping the rubbish man to fill the truck." Boys' remarks included numerous responses to rescue and danger. Typical examples are: "This pictures is about a kid sinking in quicksand and another kid is helping him out," and "The boy is helping the girl; the girl is falling off the cliff; the branch is helping, too, and the sun is shining."

Nurturance did not appear for the girls with the same frequency that was anticipated but still reflected an increase over the boys who seldom utilized the idea. Most of the female responses were related to child care and tending the ill at home. Boys were more apt to make pictures related to occupational situations, as one might suspect. They identified with greatest frequency medical, fire, and military situations, whereas girls showed a consistent preference for the medical profession.

Words: A Cohort of Action

Of particular interest was the way in which each of the sexes handled the matter of verbalization within their concepts of fighting and helping. Females often indicated that the characters in their drawings of fighting were talking to one another and shouting disparaging remarks. The boys for the most part omitted this dimension in their depictions of aggression. In the case of helping, however, the situation was somewhat different, with females placing the spoken word within the picture context less frequently than the boys. It appears that females find verbal assault a more appropriate vehicle than physical abuse and feel free to express their anger in this method. The higher use of verbalization within the boys' helping pictures is explained by the numerous rescue drawings in which the rescuer shouts such things as, "Hold on, I'll be there to save you in a moment!" These distinctions would seem to suggest that the use of speech is not in and of itself sex bound but is used by both sexes when it seems contextually relevant.

Spatial Content

An alternate aspect of this study, which examined children's usage of spatial characteristics in drawing, supports other findings that maintain that there are not substantive sex bound distinctions in this realm.[8] With the exception of symmetry, boys and girls were similar in their approaches to picture organization, favoring a central location and a horizontal-vertical axis. Boys indicated a minor additional preference for the all-over placement and girls for the vertical axis. Furthermore, the small distinctions that did emerge were frequently bound to subject matter, representing logical solutions to certain ideas. Apparently there are pervasive ways that all children utilize to portray certain events spatially in the drawing process, and both sexes capture the essential attributes of a particular concept in a comparable manner. Drawings of two individuals angrily confronting one another suggest a central, horizontal-vertical organization regardless of sex; and, conversely, war pictures have a governing skeleton of their own, an all-over location with a mixed axis.

The issue of symmetry offers further documentation of this factor. Many females utilized symmetry in the fighting pictures, as opposed to the males, although the distinctions within the helping pictures were not so pronounced. A combined analysis of the fighting and helping pictures revealed that symmetry occurred more frequently for females than for males. Hence, it is apparent that girls utilized symmetry more than the boys, although the distinction seems to be subject matter based. Interpersonal pictures were frequently depictions of two people confronting one another placed in the central part of the paper. This basic notion is more apt to elicit a symmetrical composition. Since the majority of female pictures about fighting fell into this category, this may explain the high incidence of symmetry for females.

IMPLICATIONS OF THE FINDINGS

This study has confirmed that boys and girls have qualitatively different ways of associating with the ideas of "fighting" and "helping." The fact that each of the sexes is attracted to particular subject matters in their drawings is certainly not new, but the categorization of these subjects into a personal–depersonal dichotomy provides additional information of significance. The fact that in two entirely separate domains, one dealing with aggressive behavior and the other affiliative, cooperative behavior, the two groups responded in a consistently opposite manner suggests that there is a fundamental distinction in the way in which they relate to common events. Boys relate to matters of the group, the task, the challenge, and to situations involving close personal contact.

Why should this be so? If one accepts Maccoby and Jacklin's findings that boys are fundamentally more aggressive than girls, a lot would seem to be explained, particularly those findings that reveal that rescue, physical danger, and acting out are more important to the male than to the female.[9] But the predisposition towards aggression in and of itself does not answer the question of why one sex seems more interpersonally oriented than the other. Perhaps the challenge of mastering stronger aggressive instincts demands of the male greater depersonalization for emotional survival, and the fact that socialization harnesses much of this assertiveness into organized games and events may serve to reinforce a particular quality of interaction.

In any case, the thematic preferences boys and girls have established in drawing (wars and monsters as contrasted with people and domestic scenes, for example) are better understood when the underlying orientation is examined. Small boys' examinations of war and destruction in picture making are not necessarily representations of personal anguish and hostility, as is sometimes documented in the art therapy literature, but instead may reflect the male's drive to channel aggressive energy and to identify with society's expectations for him to accomplish, master, control, and to work collaboratively.[10] Perhaps the reason there is so much conflict of interest between elementary school teachers and small boys who want to examine these themes is because teachers are frequently female and carry with them a different set of associations about the nature and consequences of aggressive behavior. This is not to suggest that because boys are more depersonalized in their approach to experience that they should be allowed to act upon their aggressive instincts without control, but rather that depersonalization enables them to investigate destructive themes with less personal vulnerability. When a girl identifies with fighting, she does so on a personal level and associates it with matters of "getting along" with other people who are important to her. Clearly this involves more personal risk, and not only is fighting discouraged within her by the adult community, but it is not associated with a number of other constructive issues, as is the case with a boy.

Current attempts to diminish any apparent distinctions between the sexes make the findings of this study unpalatable to many. At a time when efforts are being made to equalize opportunities for the female and to diminish stereotypes, it is not satisfying to acknowledge major differences in the ways in which the two groups function. But as has been stated many times in the past, each group, both male and female, needs and can benefit from the obvious strengths that seem to dominate each of the groups. The matter of superiority in terms of personal/depersonal orientation is not the heart of the matter. Obviously the capacity to function from both vantage points is important for all human beings, regardless of sex. Girls have much to learn about the benefits of goal oriented, group directed behavior as it is manifest in a more depersonalized context, and the cultivation of this competence is critical if women are to succeed in a highly competitive gamelike society that is male dominated. But the male, too, needs to cultivate his capacities to function more sensitively on the interpersonal level, to understand the smaller unit, and to behave humanely towards individuals. Neither attribute should be the province of only one of the sexes, and if it appears to be the case at the present time, perhaps it is because society narrowly and rigidly reinforces an initial predisposition.

The fact that ideas govern the ways in which pictures are organized, as opposed to any basic sexual predisposition, is an important issue to consider and introduces the question of whether or not the consistent manipulation of certain subject matters over time ultimately introduces some bias in terms of organizational preferences. For example, does the more frequent use of symmetry on the part of the young female represent an innate tendency in this direction, or is it the ramification of portraying certain ideas frequently enough for them to have become internalized as a dominant way of working, independently of subject matter?

Since the socialization process has such a pervasive influence on the ways in which boys and girls gain a sense of their relative identities and formulate and process ideas, and since these factors influence the way in which they each organize their worlds in a structural domain, then it would seem to follow that studies that attempt to assess spatial usage and comparable aspects of performance, without considering the interactive aspects of subject matter and form, would be reviewing only a part of a much larger phenomenon.

This is a period of rapid change in terms of social values and attitudes about what is and is not sex role appropriate. Undoubtedly as the sexes redefine and reorganize their thinking about a host of fundamental issues, they will alter the forms by which they express many of their ideas. Children's drawings of war, monsters, people, and flowers reflect their prevailing conceptualizations of what is personally relevant. But the mechanisms utilized to convey these ideas are subject to alteration and are not limited by any rigid sex bound predisposition.

NOTES

1. Rhoda Kellogg, *Analyzing Children's Art* (Palo Alto: National Press, 1969, 1970).
2. Anne Anastasi and John P. Foley, Jr., "An Analysis of Spontaneous Drawing by Children in Different Cultures," *Journal of Applied Psychology* 20 (1936): 689–726; P. B. Ballard, "What London Children Like to Draw," *Journal of Experimental Pedagogy* 1, no. 3 (1912); Kellogg, *Analyzing Children's Art*; H. T. Lukens, "A Study of Children's Drawings in the Early Years," *Pedagogical Seminary* IV (1896–97): 79–110; Betty Lark Horovitz, Hilda Lewis, and Mark Luca, *Understanding Children's Art for Better Teaching* (Columbus, Ohio: Charles E. Merrill, 1967).
3. L. Kohlberg, "A Cognitive-Developmental Analysis of Children's Sex-role Concepts and Attitudes," in Eleanor Maccoby and Carol Jacklin,

The Development of Sex Differences (Palo Alto: Stanford University Press, 1966).

4. Robert R. Sears, Eleanor E. Maccoby, and Harry Levin, *Patterns of Child Rearing* (Evanston: Row, Peterson, 1957).

5. Sylvia Fein, *Heidi's Horse* (Pleasant Hill: Exelrod, 1975).

6. Sylvia G. Feinburg, "Children Play at War; One Child's War," *Learning*, 3, no. 5 (1975): 10–16.

7. For greater elaboration and details of methodology, see Sylvia G. Feinburg, "Conceptual Content and Spatial Characteristics in Boys' and Girls' Drawings of Fighting and Helping," *Studies in Art Education* 18, no. 2, pp. 63–72.

8. Kellogg, *Analyzing Children's Art;* Lark-Horovitz, Lewis, and Luca, *Understanding Children's Art for Better Teaching.*

9. Maccoby and Jacklin, *The Psychology of Sex Differences.*

10. Margaret Naumburg, *Dynamically Oriented Art Therapy: Its Principles and Practice* (New York: Grune and Stratton, 1966).

17

Female Art Characteristics:
Do They Really Exist?

MARGARET MARY MAJEWSKI

The women's movement, as we know, emphasizes the potentialities and independence of each sex. Men and women are beginning to question whether or not they are as different in their abilities as they have been taught to believe. The movement insists that our ideas about male and female abilities are due to culture, politics, and economics rather than biology. Thus, a new era for intensive research has begun.

The recent research explosion in male–female differences covers a wide range of fields and seems to be conducted primarily by women. Women artists have joined their sisters from other fields. We have begun to research and analyze art in order to identify male/female differences in such things as symbols, subject matter, and form. This was the purpose of the research I conducted for my doctoral dissertation.[1]

Several artists, writers, and critics, such as Lucy Lippard, Judy Chicago, and Miriam Schapiro, have examined this issue. An underlying premise in their writings is that people have been conditioned to think that women are inferior, passive, and emotional and that men are superior, active and, due to their sex, leaders and doers. In the context of these stereotyped ideas, Judy Chicago and Miriam Schapiro, as feminists, deliberately use symbols of sexuality in their art work. In an article written by both of these artists entitled "Female Imagery," they stated that women artists feel themselves "subject" in the world and treated as "objects." They believe that contemporary women's art should seek to define the uniqueness of female sexuality. These female artists are proclaiming that women's sexuality is equal to men's sexuality just as their art is equal to men's art. They frankly stress the "central core" or cavity of women as basic to their iconography and symbology.[2] Feminist art critics have pointed to the repeated oval and/or circular images found in the works of many women artists. They claim these are inherent in the woman's body and that this distinguishes women's art from the art of men. Nevelson's boxes, Chicago's *Desert Fan*, O'Keefe's flower houses, Schapiro's *OX*, and Remington's *Egg* are examples they cite. Lippard believes that femaleness shapes both the form and content of the art of many women.[3] On the other hand, according to both Schapiro and Chicago, men's sexuality differs so fundamentally from women's that men can not perceive what it is to be a woman. This perception differs so greatly, these women say, that men are not capable of understanding and appreciating, in depth, the female imagery of women's art.

Lawrence Alloway, the prominent art critic, in the chapter "Women's Art in the 70s," supports the view that many male as well as female artists use concave and centered compartment forms.[4] Further, Alloway questions whether or not decorativeness is more likely to show up in the art of women. When one thinks of all the works of art created by male artists, for example, in the decorative style of Art Nouveau, Alloway seems right.

Lippard wrote in 1971 that she had no clear-cut idea of what characteristics were definitely female; she went on to point out that those that seemed to be pervasively present in the work of female artists were: earthiness, organic images, curved lines, and centralized focus.[5] Two years after her original list, she came out with a second list of traits:

> a uniform density, an overall texture, often sensuously tactile and often repetitive to the point of obsession; the preponderance of circular forms and central focus; a ubiquitous linear "bag" or parabolic form that turns in on itself; layers or strata of indefinable looseness or flexibility of handling; a new fondness for the pinks and pastels and the ephemeral cloud colors that use to be taboo.[6]

In 1975 she added:

> A central focus (often "empty," often circular or oval), parabolic

baglike forms, obsessive line and detail, veiled strata, tactile or sensuous surfaces and forms, associative fragmentation, autographical emphasis.[7]

Lippard's lists are culture bound because she generalizes female art characteristics from a relatively elite group of people. So few women have broken into the male dominated art world that it must be remembered that when she and other critics speak of women artists, they are speaking of a very small and select group of women.

There is a lack of hard evidence that can empirically substantiate any list of male or female art characteristics. However, to the degree that the behavior in children is indicative of behavior in adults, the results of research I have recently completed may give some insights on this issue.

While doing research for my doctoral dissertation at Illinois State University, I asked a number of elementary school boys and girls (ages 6–12) to do a series of drawings under fairly controlled conditions.[8] The drawings were collected and rated by a team of researchers who knew a great deal about children's art, but who did not know the sex of the children who did these particular drawings. The following results seem to support some of Lippard's, Chicago's, and Schapiro's ideas regarding female art.

One of the most significant findings of my study revealed that lines drawn by girls were in fact more circular, that is, more flowing, organic, and curvilinear than lines drawn by boys. The boys lines were straighter, more angular, and geometric. My research supports Lippard's, Chicago's, and Schapiro's idea that curvilinear forms, circles, and ovals are associated with femininity.

Another result of the study indicated that girls included more human figures in their drawings than the boys did. Interestingly enough, the figures drawn by the girls showed more sex differences in body and clothing than the figures drawn by the boys. This may be related to the fact that girls mature physically earlier and therefore, may become aware of sexual differences earlier than boys. The sex of figures drawn by the boys was less recognizable than the sex of the figures drawn by the girls.

Another difference found in my study, although not directly related to Lippard's list of female adult characteristics, was that girls depicted more happy faces on people, animals, and inanimate objects than the boys did.

Finally, my study revealed that girls' drawings, whether of indoor or outdoor scenes, included more details than those of boys. Lippard, in her 1975 list, mentioned abundant detail as being characteristic of female art.

Since the results of my study apply to American girls and boys, I recognize that my results are as culture bound as the feminist art critics' lists. At present, my study is being replicated by Marlene Cox, who has collected drawings from male and female Inuit Eskimos in Baker Lake and Rankin Inlet.[9] When her study is completed, we will know whether or not the differences I found among American boys and girls are also prevalent in another culture. In the meantime, the reader should understand that neither the art critics nor I can make definitive statements regarding "universal" female art characteristics. We do not know if such characteristics really do exist.

NOTES

1. Sister (Dr.) Margaret Mary Majewski, "The Relationship Between the Drawing Characteristics of Children and Their Sex" (Ph.D diss., Illinois State University, 1978).
2. Miriam Schapiro and Judy Chicago, "Female Imagery," *Womanspace Journal* 1, no. 3 (June 1973): 11–14.
3. Lucy Lippard, "The Pains and Treasures of Rebirth: Women's Body," *Art in America* (May/June 1976): 75–81.
4. Lawrence Alloway, "Women's Art in the 70s," chapter 5 in this anthology.
5. Lucy Lippard, *Twenty-Six Contemporary Women Artists* (Ridgefield, Conn.: Aldrich Museum of Contemporary Artists, 1971), Introduction.
6. Alloway, "Women's Art in the 70s."
7. Ibid.
8. Majewski, "The Relationship Between the Drawing Characteristics of Children and Their Sex."
9. Marlene Cox, doctoral student in the Department of Art, Illinois State University, Normal, Il. 61761.

18

Society and Identity:
A Personal Perspective

JUNE KING McFEE

This chapter reflects on the flow of past events that impinged on my professional career. It was written with the hope that it would provide useful insights to younger women in the field in terms of their own progress as well as a case study for people who are concerned with the imbalances of role expectation and motivations between the sexes. I have had to do a lot of sorting in my own mind to try and select experiences that would be illustrative of problems that would be useful to others.

What has appeared is a time line of social contexts that changed as society changed and my own responses to that context as pressures within myself and my own search for identity as a woman, as an artist, and later as an art educator came into conflict with society's role expectations. I am not talking about myself so much as a woman in the interplay of psycho-social-cultural forces.

Before beginning I must state two assumptions. One, that each of us is unique, each finding our way through different aspects of the subcultures we experience though there are similarities in our experiences that are related. This is what makes a case study useful. There are things we can all learn from anyone's reflections on experience. Two, I am not at all sure that when there was resistance to what I was doing, it was because of the ideas that seemed important to me or because I was a woman or some combination of the two. I assume I could have gotten away with iconoclastic ideas more as a man than as a woman.

Based on an address to the National Art Education Association's Women's Caucus Founding Convention in Miami, Florida on April 8, 1975.

When we analyze our own experience and emerging self-concept, we need to be aware of the values and beliefs systems of the cultures we came from, the attitudes of the men and women in our families, and the dynamics produced by their likenesses and differences. The roles they play do influence children. I had some very nontypical females in my family who influenced my early sense of what a woman could be. Eighty-four years ago my widowed, paternal grandmother, driving herself and her young son in a horse-drawn wagon, was one of 20,000 people who raced into the Cherokee Strip of Oklahoma to claim land. She settled in a new town, built a sod hut, and set herself up as a dressmaker, one of the few roles open to her. She worked until she was over 70. She was a powerful, independent, determined woman all her life. Also an aunt, as I remember, in the '20s sold creosote piling for building shipping facilities, wore knickerbockers, and drove a sports car at what appeared to me to be reckless speeds.

But these women were different from those I met at school. In 1926 I remember vividly being grabbed by the shoulder by an irate teacher who told me I was not to play baseball with the boys but come up to the girls playground and stay there. The frustration and hostility to society this one act produced was very strong; it is then I became jealous of the freedom boys had, disliked what girls said and did, and developed a certain amount of self-hatred because I was female.

My mother was from the South and very much a displaced person in the then still pioneer culture of the Pacific Northwest. She very much wanted me to grow up to be a "lady," to learn social graces she found missing in that area. But she had another side—she was a gifted musician and composer with fiery Irish disposition—a veritable Martha Mitchell. Her way to resolve doing something in this world and do it in a ladylike way was in the arts. Since she had absolute pitch, I soon quit the violin and decided to be an artist—at age 12. Mark Tobey and Morris Graves were the artists around which the art world of the Northwest grew. I studied with a member of this close group (Guy Anderson), who, during the worst of the Depression, was very happy to give lessons to a scrawny, shy little girl whose mother was pushing her to be "something."

But inside the shyness other ideas were interesting me. I was obsessed with aviation—to learn to fly was my greatest goal. In the late '20s and early '30s women aviators were coming into their own. Amelia Earhart was my ideal. I studied airplane engines, drew plans, and read all I could get my hands on about these marvelous women who were fearless, skillful, and held up as important pioneers by society generally. During that period women were making tremendous progress. They were going into medicine, psychology, anthropology and, of course, education. Ruth Benedict was one of 22 women who got Ph.Ds in anthropology between 1910–1940—out of a total of 51 at Columbia, 43 percent were women! Films of the period pictured women as intelligent, competing with men in games of wit. Rosalind Russell, for example, was often cast as the girl reporter who outsmarted the men around her. Romance always triumphed, but it was more a marriage of equals, an appreciation of personality as well as sex.

It was, in many ways, a great time to be an adolescent girl, but I remember learning early that if you wanted to be popular and get taken to dances, you had to keep your interests to yourself. You didn't talk about airplane engines, women flyers, or art to boys. Being popular was something my mother cared a great deal about, and I was pushed into a social life that produced mixed feelings. To gain identity, to be someone, one had to play roles. You weren't really a person whose inside and outside self was the same. Also, now I see the trap mothers were, and still are, in to some degree. Mothers push their daughters to be popular and have dates so they can have a better pool from which to get a husband. This was the one dominant goal, not only for getting ahead, but for survival. Mothers of sons pushed them to succeed not only to prove they were good mothers, as this was their means to enhance their own identity, but to gain status through their sons' accomplishments. This is what the counter-culture threw in the face of parents. Kids were willing to gamble with their lives and their future to break this pattern. But now, six, eight, ten years later, they are back in school trying to work their way back into a system that is itself groaning with adjustments.

During the '30s I distinctly remember resenting strongly I'd been born a woman. I remember how much I admired my father and, for a brief period in high school wanted to be, like him, a lawyer. It was a great shock when he squelched that completely. No daughter of his would go into law. He'd send me to college but *not* to study law. He also told me it was a waste of time to take solid geometry or calculus, both of which I wanted to take in high school. What amazes me now is that I accepted his word as final.

This conflict of roles, between what was possible for women to be and what most of that subculture of society I was exposed to considered appropriate roles for women, were indeed in conflict. None of the women among my family's friends worked. My mother assumed I would never work. Be an artist—yes—but never enter the working world. This was in conflict with the women in the family who did work. It was the push of upward mobility, which in that era meant the women in an upper-middle-class family didn't work for money. Women were symbols of status, not beings with independent ambitions. Talents were to be used for worthy causes where one could contribute her efforts in things that added status, but one got status mainly from what the man in the family did.

During my college years I studied art in Chicago with Alexander Archipenko. He was a man who had great respect for women and their intellect. His wife was a brilliant woman. His sculptures of women always had tremendous dignity—a search for the essence of being. He gave me much encouragement and confidence. Never there nor at the University of Washington art department where I graduated did I find any experience of discouragement as a woman in art. Opportunities to exhibit in competitive shows and the W.P.A. support for the arts at that time provided many avenues for seeing one's work among other artists. There were quite a few women exhibitors.

That era of the '20s and '30s came to an end in 1941 when World War II started. Women were encouraged for that short period to do many things they had not done before in noncombat service—flying transport planes, manning alert stations, building ships and planes. My own brief time in the service taught me how isolated my life had been from much of society. It was in an Army hospital that I came to grips with the shallowness of much of what I had been taught. After the illness, I was discharged and finally entered the working world, following my husband in Air Force training from camp to camp, doing whatever work I could find. It was almost the most important part of my education. I learned much about class stratification and what it was like to be a working girl behind the counter. I met and learned to appreciate a much wider variety of people. For the first time I saw a woman who had been beaten to a pulp by her husband but who wouldn't prosecute him because he was her husband.

Then the war was over and the return of women to traditional roles began in the late '40s and early '50s. Big families became the vogue, with the postwar baby boom. The acquisition of material goods after the rationing of the war years began to accelerate. A great fear of being different or not acceptable spread through the McCarthy era. My husband and I settled down to raise a family, and I attempted to keep painting, but I couldn't fit the role of housewife and aspiring socialite, which was expected of me. Soon I started an art department in the local community college and commuted to a state college to get a master's degree. I clearly remember a close family friend, who was also chairman of the board of the college, cautioning me, "You aren't going to be a career woman, with a husband and a baby, are you?" I assured him I was. My students at the community college had a show in the main hotel, but we found them covered with butcher paper as the modern art was offensive to patrons. A battle over whether modern art should be taught in the college ensued, and my contract was not renewed to teach.

Fortunately, my husband was as dissatisfied with business as I was with living in the constraints of a conservative town of 50,000 people. As one of our old friends from the town said, we were the first straight people in town to start a counter-culture movement. So in 1954 we sold our home and his business and started over again.

I entered the School of Education at Stanford, and he picked up his undergraduate work. Competition for grades was acute. I clearly remember remarks like, "Why are you working so hard, you'll never use it." "I don't approve of your being in this program." At graduation the man sitting next to me said that his superior would not approve of me. A professor agreed it was alright for a woman to be studying music and art but not social foundations or philosophy. My advisor in art education tried to discourage me the first day, saying they really didn't have a program, why didn't I go back home. But there were people, both men and women, who were encouraging. However, if it hadn't been for one woman, Dr. Pauline Sears, who helped me accept myself as a woman as well as sharpen my intellectual skills, I would never have gotten my degree. She was a model of a professional person of national stature, who had raised two children and was the wife of another well-known psychologist.

Upon graduation, the art department hired me to teach elementary education courses and supervise secondary school teachers—a task many men at that time did not like to do. I was hired as an instructor with my doctorate for $4,800. But there were people in the doctoral program who needed help, so I developed graduate course work as an overload. During the next five years, with new people coming in, the Stanford Perceptual Studies in Art Education developed. I am very proud of these five years and the people who graduated. Most of them are very well known in art education today.

My leaving Stanford as I did would never have happened today. At that time there were very few women staff members, and they were underpromoted and underpaid. There was a policy of not hiring their own graduates, male or female. But the College of Education unanimously voted to have me transferred to that college and for promotion to associate professor. But my immediate superior in the art department disagreed vehemently with what I was doing in art education and was in a position to veto my promotion. In this case conflicts over ideas were an important factor. But I do believe that if I had been a man, two things would have happened: one, the conflicting evidence would have been considered more by the university, and two, I would have fought back, as I certainly would today. My students did all they could, but it was before the days of activist protest.

At that point my husband was finishing his Ph.D. in anthropology and was appointed to the staff at the University of Arizona. I was called by the dean of the College of Education the same weekend and offered a position. We arrived in the fall with my appointment not completed, and it never was. The president of the university refused to sign it for nepotism policies—a policy that mainly affected women. There were fifteen Ph.D.s and one M.D. in Tucson at that time who were unemployed because their husbands were on the staff.

During the three years in Arizona I was able to keep up professionally as a visiting lecturer working around the country, teaching part-time at Arizona State University, and establishing the doctoral program there. We tried to establish a research institute but could not obtain private foundation or government funding. Who ever heard of a research institute made up of females? At the end of this period was the Penn State Seminar, which was a landmark in art education. Preparing for that was a saving grace for me professionally and in terms of my own sense of purpose.[1]

In early 1965 the president of the University of Oregon was Arthur Flemming, formerly head of H.E.W. He was a man who was ahead of his time. He wanted more women on the faculty. When money became available to establish a university-based Community Arts Studies Institute, I was hired to develop it. I was also promised I could start a doctoral program in art education. There was considerable resistance to my coming.

A delegation came and asked me to give back the grant for the Institute, promised me I would never get the doctoral program off the ground, and that the university should never have hired me. I also overheard at a cocktail party that I was just a housewife the university had hired because it wanted the money from the grant.

But that was also 1965, and things were beginning to shift in the national scene. Resistance to a doctoral program faded into more apparent issues, and we have been building it ever since with the percentage of women in the program increasing every year.

All of you are very familiar with these last ten years. Opportunities for women have changed, but deep seated attitudes learned through centuries of cultural conditioning are slow to change. We have gained in legal rights, but much remains to be done. We are changing our self-concepts, but we are pioneering new domains and still finding our way. The uncertainties of the economy and resource projections ahead must not let us repeat the backward trend of the '50s and early '60s.

If you will bear with me, I would like to analyze what I see now as more subtly pervasive influences on women that may take longer to change.

One is that you are accepted as "one of the boys" in some academic contexts, not as an intellectual woman or person. You are a woman out of role—you get the "you think like a man" syndrome as if it were a compliment. No matter what your intellectual contribution, you are a lesser person if you don't measure up in some degree to the cultural stereotype. The danger is to believe this. It is hard not to when its truth is suggested to you so pervasively and consistently.

But the women's movement in many of its ramifications has been a rejection of this dualism. We are learning to respect each other as people, as professionals and as scholars and artists; support each other and do not believe the stereotypes about ourselves. What younger women and the women's movement generally have done in these last ten years has given me a new freedom and sense of support I have not had before.

Now I would like to review briefly some psychological research about sex differences and then draw some generalizations about social effects from my own experience. The stereotype is that there are many kinds of valued men, unique and different, but there is only one ideal woman, and all others are categorized as variations away from that norm. Those women who vary from the norm too much if they excel are thought of as manlike and always a lesser man.

This is changing slowly, but I believe it is part of the resistance to the Equal Rights Amendment. There is a fear of having many more dynamic individuals in society, that control of society would be lost, that change would come too fast.

I. K. and D. M. Broverman and their associates reported in a penetrating study in the *Journal of Consulting and Clinical Psychology* the effects of the depth of cultural conditioning. They asked 79 men and women clinical psychologists, psychiatrists, and social workers to write three descriptions of the ideal healthy person, the ideal healthy male, and the ideal healthy female—then an unhealthy person, unhealthy male, and then an unhealthy female. What they found was that the *unhealthy* person = an *unhealthy* male = a *healthy* female. The difference between the healthy female and the healthy person was that she was, "less competitive, less aggressive, less objective, more submissive, more dependent, more easily influenced, . . . more emotional, more conceited about her appearance, and more aversive to mathematics and science."[2] These were all professional people, supposedly less influenced by stereotyping, all conditioned by cultural values to stereotype people who are only these ways in the degree they accept cultural norms. What is frightening is that these people try to help people reach the cultural stereotype of mental health and not what may be appropriate for them as individuals. I well remember the guilt I felt when a school psychologist told me I was much too ambitious for a woman.

This study was done in 1970. I posit that greater change has taken place from 1970–1975 than at any period prior to this. The biggest force for change is women's own changed self-concepts and some increased opportunity to try their potentials in a broader range of activities. A woman no longer needs to feel she is abnormal in some degree because she has drives to be highly creative, independent, intellectual, or to take leadership. This is the heavy weight we are losing. Let's consider more data.

All stereotypes are based on somewhat false assumptions. The assumption that men are more independent and intelligent than women is one of them. When individual differences are considered, half the women are more intelligent than half the men when variations due to social conditioning are eliminated. Crutchfield, finding the average scores for women on conformity measures to be higher than men in 1955, posits that a present retest would provide a change, but even in 1955, a large percent of women were less conforming than a large percent of men—so where do many women fit in that stereotype.[3]

Marjore Honzik of the University of California compared the same males' and females' I.Q. scores at age 18 and 40 in 1973 and another group at age 17 and 48. She found I.Q. scores had not gone down over time and in some areas, such as verbal skills, were increasing. Interestingly enough, girls at ages 17 and 18 had a mean below boys, but in their 40s had a similar mean equal to men. But Honzik reported that many of the 40-year-old women reported that they expected to do much more poorly than when they were in school—when their actual I.Q. mean had gone up. Their expectations were not in line with their ability to perform.[4]

I.Q., as you know, is not thought of now as a unitary trait but appears to be a cluster of separate traits that develop at different rates and continue much longer than ever suspected with some cases of gain beyond 80. There is considerable evidence that teen-age and even 30-year-old women's I.Q. scores are lower than at age 40, which suggests either change in actual I.Q. or the influence or social expectations on women at the earlier ages that depress performance. But it is at these ages that life goals, treatment, and encouragement by schools and parents are conditioned by test results.

From my own experience and from what I have studied, we see that our experience is on-going. We continuously are in a systematic interaction between our own growth and development as we are learning from our family, adult models, peers, and the larger society and the changes in ourselves and society. Our behavior at any given time is influenced by all these factors as they are changing. As women we can say we have a better climate for developing our potential now than ever before. We are developing a peer group society to whom we can give strength and an in-group society from whom we can gain strength to be independent, intelligent, creative women, as men have had for centuries.

Our greatest need is to see ourselves and all people as people with far more potentials for development in far more different ways than our stereotypes would allow. The gentle, compassionate, sensitive, creative, intelligent male has suffered as much from stereotyping as many of us have. We need to find more ways to achieve mental health. We need broader definitions of mental health. To be full persons, we don't need to have the male goal as our goal—but as people, find what is our most natural way to define our individuality. What this means, of course, is a redefining of the nature of what society can be. It is the fear of this in ourselves and in society at large that keeps us back. But of all the single factors that could make world systems work more efficiently in this limited resource space capsule we live on is to change the status of women worldwide. The birth rate decreases as the status of women increases. Drastic reduction in the birthrate worldwide would affect the projections on resource limitation in every dimension. Coupled with more intellectually and creatively productive women, we could double our potential to solve our environmental and social problems. This may seem an unattainable dream, but more of us are dreaming, and out of such dreams come ideas and with ideas the power to develop them.

NOTES

1. Edward Mattil, *A Seminar in Art Education for Research and Curriculum Development* (University Park: Pennsylvania State University, 1966). This is a report of the conference.
2. Inge K. Broverman, Donald M. Broverman, et al., "Sex-Role Stereotypes and Clinical Judgments of Mental Health," *Journal of Consulting and Clinical Psychology* 34 (1970): 1–7.

3. Richard S. Crutchfield, "Conformity and Character," *American Psychologist* 10 (1955): 191–198.
4. Marjore P. Honzik, "Predicting I.Q. Over the First Four Decades of the Life Span," paper presented at the Society for Research in Child Development, 1973.

III
Feminist Restructuring
of Art Education

19

Professionalism and the Woman Artist

DOROTHY GILLESPIE

Women's very special talent for promoting the well-being and success of *other* people is to a large extent responsible for the success of
the women's art movement. Previously we had seen the same genius
displayed in promoting husbands, children, and employers. Yet this
woman who has been able to manage almost everything else in her
life is lost when it comes to the professional management of her own
art.

Why does that good judgement, which can be used so successfully
to support others, often turn into bad judgement when used by a
woman for herself and the presentation of her art? Why is she likely
to be haphazard about her art and not about her home? Let us examine the strange facts and find out why the woman artist frequently
cannot turn her knowledge and energy into positive actions when it
involves her own art life.

Alice Baber and I started a class, "Functioning in the Art World,"
at the New School for Social Research in the fall semester of 1975.
Our intention was to expose students, both male and female, to
various areas of the art world. We did this by arranging on-site visits
to museums where directors, curators, or public affairs officers discussed with the class the running of the institution; by interviewing
panels of distinguished artists; by visiting the back rooms of galleries
where the directors explained exactly how artists are selected for
exhibitions; and by visiting printers, art movers, artists' studios, offices of art publications, and art centers. The importance of working
together in groups was emphasized by having the students in our
class work together to arrange panels as well as to curate, promote,

and hang exhibitions of the work of the artists in the class. We also had them develop a modest publication containing articles and reviews of shows. Emphasis was placed on the value of good photographs and slides, the information that should go along with an artist's work, and the necessity for up-to-date biographies. In addition, the practical uses of a good mailing list, a good press release, and good posters, flyers, and catalogs were outlined.

The reactions were exciting, as we tried to bring students abreast of the "scene" by having lawyers speak on artists' rights, copyright laws, the government, and tax laws. As the class has been exposed to the selling, the exhibiting, the preserving, and the documenting agents in the art world, they have become aware of the need for professionalism on their part. The group endeavors have enlightened them as to what is expected of them in areas of the art world other than the creative work itself. As teachers, we can help all students benefit by uncovering for them the mysterious aspects of other areas of the art world and by showing them how to interact with those areas. This naturally includes the business areas.

Now let's go back to my earlier question: Why is that wonderful judgement used to help others missing when a women's own art is involved? Are her priorities so mixed up because of her upbringing, which stressed pride in doing things for others but not for herself?

The first thing that all artists must do is approach their art life in a professional manner. But what is *acting in a professional way?* Is it being aggressive? No. It is primarily a matter of being informed about what is expected of an artist. *After* a woman artist has left the canvas or clay or marble or wood or metal or whatever her art is made of, her judgement sometimes becomes amateurish. In some instances, it is as if a badly framed piece of work, an unusable slide, an outdated biography, or a lack of black and white photos is worn like a badge of honor by the woman artist. And so often, where not much money is available for a project and a lot of hard work is expected of all the artists involved, a woman not acting in a professional way may very well be excluded when the next group project is begun.

Since professionalism encompasses utilization of energy, understanding priorities, saving time, the fullest functioning of the individual involved, and the attitude of the artist to her art and the art world, the following suggestions are necessarily limited, but they are critical to professionalism and can all be put to good use.

It is not easy to keep up with the demands a truly professional approach makes, and the woman artist should not be reluctant to seek outside help.

It should be understood that the artist is the one most interested in her own work. It makes sense that she should be vitally concerned with the photographing, the care, the presentation, and the documentation of that work. Can she still be expecting someone else to do these things for her? If the woman artist does expect this, she is going to be deeply disappointed. Ideally she can plan that *eventually* someone else will take over those roles, leaving her to the task of making art. Certainly utilizing all our abilities to the fullest is rewarding in itself. And usually the artist is very competent when she has become aware of the following procedures:

1. Always have good slides and photographs of current art work on hand. Learning to photograph your own art is advantageous, since it frees you from appointment making or days spent with a photographer.

2. Face some facts, and if you are not doing a good job of photographing your art or if you really prefer not to, have a professional photographer do it. Whoever is doing the photography should use two cameras, one with black and white film and the other with color slide film. This will save money and time. Let's face it, its just no fun for artists to move art work.

3. Have a few of the black and white glossy photographs duplicated by a photoreproduction house. One hundred prints with copy negative should cost about $20. When taking slides, be sure that at least four of each piece of work are taken, since this is less expensive than having slides duplicated later. Of course, the artist will eventually need to duplicate some of her best slides. Never send out originals because they will probably not be returned. Have color prints made of a few best slides. These, too, can be reproduced in quantity; check photography magazines for sources and prices.

4. Be sure to put your name and address (with zip code) along with title, size, medium, and date of the piece of work on all photo-

graphs and slides. A rubber stamp is a blessing for the name and address, in terms of both time saved and of legibility. Three stamps would be useful: a tiny one for the slides, a medium-size one for the photographs, and a large one for the wrappings on art works. These can be used for years, and the frustrations and time saved are more than worth the money. Putting your telephone number with area code should be considered. Address labels tend to come off in time, but if put on very carefully, they are more acceptable than unreadable handwriting. If writing on photographs is necessary, use a felt tip pen, since a ball point usually makes marks that damage the photograph.

5. Have some good resumes typed and printed. The resume presents, to those needing information about the artist, background and data that are usually unobtainable anywhere else. The resume is essential for accompanying slides, art work, articles, and photographs as well as lectures, workshops, and the like. The more clearly the information is presented under headings, and the easier it is to read, the more attention it will receive. There are many accepted ways of compiling a resume, but it should be under headings, in any order that seems logical. Whichever of the following apply should be included at the time of printing:

Studies	Group Exhibitions
One-Woman Exhibitions	Permanent Collections
Private Collections	Bibliography
Publications	Awards
Commissions	Grants
Related Activities	Teaching Experience

Some of these may be entitled "Selective Listing" or "Partial List."

6. It is sometimes useful to have a short paragraph written out, containing biographical information and art history. This need be only three or four sentences. Since a biographical resume is one of the few things that the artist has complete control over in her life, any special information that she wants included should be a part of this documentation.

7. Include a reproduction on the resume; you could have a reproduction of a current piece of work on one side and the printed information on the other. When this is done on coated stock

(glossy paper) with good printing, it seems to have the authority of publication. Remember that your resume may be placed on a wall in the exhibiting area of an exhibition, it may be duplicated and sent to the press, and it certainly will be read by the press person assigned to the exhibition or project. Sometimes resumes are kept as a part of the archives of institutions.

8. Assemble an up-to-date mailing list. Keep a file box of these as well as having typed lists. These are musts. Among other purposes, these lists serve as promotion of events in which you are participating as well as correspondence. Xeroxed copies should be available for exhibitors (see also remarks about mailing lists in #18 about exhibitions). Sources for a comprehensive, effective mailing list include: guest books of persons attending shows in which your work is exhibited, purchasers and dealers of your work, and women's art organizations around the country.

9. For the artist trying to keep ahead of things, it is a good idea to keep a few typed statements on hand, expressing her personal view about art and about what she is trying to achieve. These might be 25, 50 and 100 words, since these seem to be the most often requested. By putting a signature underneath, any doubt about it being the artist's authentic statement is eliminated. Such statements are needed by the media, catalogers and archivists.

10. When photographs, statements, and resumes are requested, it is the wise woman artist who sends them immediately. Artists would also be wise to attend any meetings set up to discuss posters, catalogs, and press releases in conjunction with the showing of the artist's work.

11. Rule number one for an artist who wishes to exhibit is: have a body of work *ready to go*—in good condition and suitably framed—at all times.

12. When work is going to be exhibited, supply several photographs of the same piece of work to the exhibiting organization. Many times the art publications will pick up a black and white photograph at the exhibition. In New York, having black and white photos available for the press is an essential part of having an exhibition. *And* the artist should not ask that the photographs, slides, or resumes be returned. In fact, the fully functioning artists will hope that they will not be sent back, i.e., that those slides and photos will be seen over and over again. They cer-

tainly are not doing much good for the artist if they are stored in a studio.

13. When delivering art work to an exhibiting area, artists should observe the times stipulated in the directions both for delivery and for pick-up. There are very good reasons for those directions, so the artist would be wise to follow them exactly. Remember, there is nothing more aggravating for people working in a gallery, museum, or temporary exhibition space, than having work remain on the premises after the designated pick-up time.

14. Putting your name in an obvious place or places on the outside wrapping is important. This is not an ego trip; it permits the work to be returned in the same wrappings. Any directions placed on the outside will be obeyed, and naturally all work should be wrapped for its protection. All pertinent information about a work must be attached to the work itself, including the artist's name, address, and telephone number, the title, size, medium, and date of the work. Try to print or type this information. (It is not a bad idea to mention on this label that photographs are available).

15. When delivering the art work, photographs may be offered to the persons accepting the work. Remember, do not ask that the photographs be returned.

16. If exhibiting artists are involved with the hanging of a show, a very important thing to remember is that a badly hung show becomes a bad show and does not benefit even the art that occupies the best space. The artist should try to work with others who are responsible for the hanging to make a good presentation of all the work available.

17. The labels placed on the wall next to the art work in the exhibition should be consistent as to the information they contain and the placement next to the art.

18. Usually the exhibiting institution will ask the artist for a mailing list. Find out the number of names that will be accepted and present that number by the appointed time. Making sure that this list is up-to-date and that all addresses have zip codes will prevent useless returned invitations. If the project is a group endeavor, the artists should try to avoid duplicating names; it is embarrassing to have friends tell an exhibiting artist that they received four invitations to an opening.

19. Have installation photographs taken and duplicated. These serve for future presentation as well as the important documentation of the exhibition.
20. The documentation of exhibitions and projects cannot be over emphasized. Catalogs and posters along with the installation photographs may be sent to all interested institutions.

The working area is a problem to most women artists, especially younger ones. The attitude toward her work space, it seems, is directly related to the degree of dedication to her art. The space that the woman artist allots herself, in relation to the other rooms in her life, is revealing to those visiting her studio. Usually when a woman artist complains about the lack of space to work in, she is really saying that other areas and rooms in her life are more important. If her commitment to her art life is strong, the artist will arrange the *right* work area for herself. We all realize that women artists have financial problems, but so do men artists. Betty Parsons' advice to young artists is that they must find way of supporting their art for long periods of time.

The way the woman artist feels about herself and her art is probably more important than any of the above suggestions. After all, an artist can create without a resume, photographs, rubber stamps, and a separate studio. These suggestions, however, are useful in sustaining those feelings about herself as an artist that will enable her to function as fully as possible in this society, which is, at last, admitting that there is discrimination against women.

This is a rewarding time to be a woman artist. Neither the middle-aged nor the young woman artist can afford the luxury of just doing her art. There is much work ahead to show the world that women artists are just as good as men artists. There is an energy generated by working on ideas and projects with other artists that is very exciting. Role models are desperately needed for the young artists. Moreover, a true respect for the very special role that artists play in civilizations should be stressed so that it becomes an integral part of the woman artists.

When she finally accepts some of these practical truths, the woman artist becomes more generous in her associations in the local art scene. She finds that "making it" is not the ultimate goal, but, rather, that functioning completely as an artist has undreamed-of rewards;

she also discovers that functioning completely can certainly be achieved by a woman artist who strives for it. It will take hard work, but all artists know how to work hard. If a person feels she has the choice of being an artist or not, then "don't." The creative process is a demanding one, but the art experience is surely worth it. Let me share with you one of the statements that I keep on hand:

> The dedication of a life to producing works which have no practical purpose, which may or may not be preserved, which may or may not be sold, which may or may not be exhibited, and which may or may not be worth the cost of materials, is a curious phenomenon that has existed in all civilizations. The creative artist is truly the great adventurer of all times.

20

Use is Beauty

BETTY CHAMBERLAIN

Art is communication; it loses validity when it is not reaching an audience. The ivory tower attitude of just wanting to "do one's thing" while isolated in a studio defeats the function of the creative arts. Yet the ivory tower is still too readily the accepted attitude in many art schools. It is easier to do no more than teach how to mix pigments or mold plaster than to add some measure of practicality to the ingredients of good teaching.

Art students who are going to be sprung on the outside world need worldly preparation. To gain an audience in a competitive field inevitably requires some know-how, some recognition of the ways and means and pitfalls. Deficiencies in these areas are widespread in other disciplines also, according to reports of educators, and have come to the notice even of Congressional legislators. Representative Toby Moffett of Connecticut, himself formerly a teacher, declared recently: "I think schools have failed to educate for the problems of our societies," and he urged educators to teach students so that there will no longer be "people who leave school without tools for the real world."

A young art teacher related to me his experience on taking over a senior class in a well-recognized art institution. He started by asking the students how many others they thought would also be graduating in the fine arts from schools this year. The student consensus was about 3,000 to 4,000. "You had better start with 20,000 as a minimum," he countered.

"What percentage of such graduates do you believe make a living at their art after three or four years?" The class thought about two-thirds to three-quarters. The teacher suggested that—outside of commercial art, which was not their subject of study—there might be

223

a few hundred of all ages in the country who made their living by their art alone.

Doubtless many more teachers are needed who try to get their students to be aware of what they are going to face. But this one, discouraged by the unrealistic attitudes instilled by other teachers and the unsympathetic school administration, gave up teaching after a couple of years of isolated struggle and frustration.

Similar problems of educational shortcomings are prevalent in art history and appreciation courses. Here are students who might reasonably be expected to become future art buyers, since their interests and inclinations have led them into these courses. But for the most part the students are crammed with historical facts, dates, and projected slides to be memorized for exams, and the appreciation aspect gets lost. It is much simpler to teach chronology by the book than to develop an ability to form one's own judgment and enjoyment not predicated on preconceived ideas. (Efforts to achieve the latter goals are perhaps more prevalent in music courses, where "comparative performances"—such as six renditions of the same piano concerto—are presented to students to develop their own judgment. It is probably easier to compare and judge interpretive art than creative art.)

In 1975 the late Nelson Rockefeller, in a talk at the Museum of Modern Art's dedication of the Alfred H. Barr, Jr., and René d'Harnoncourt Galleries, related an incident that took place one evening in 1945, when he and three other trustees went around the Museum galleries with Alfred Barr. One of these trustees was the late Henry R. Luce, who, said Rockefeller:

> under the questioning of some of his younger editors, had a concern as to whether really "modern art" so-called was or could be a subversive influence in this country. It's hard to think of it that way now, but this was in 1945. In the galleries, Alfred conducted one of the most fascinating, perceptive, interesting, philosophical discussions, which he and Harry carried on while the rest of us observed.
>
> At the end of that evening, Harry was totally reassured as to the vitality of a free society and that, rather than being subversive, modern art in all its forms was the only true area in which freedom still existed uninhibited; that it was the greatest force for the future of America that we could have.

Admittedly there are not many art teachers of Alfred Barr's caliber, with his ability to make you see works with a fresh, personal eye and then come to your own individual judgments without bias or prejudice. If more such appreciation were taught and developed, the artist's marketplace would surely expand.

There are some recent optimistic indications in the development of personal judgment, curiously enough as an evident result of the depression-recession. A number of gallery dealers have told me that, despite or because of the economy, more people are buying art on a very different premise from the earlier period of paying huge prices for big name works to store in a vault, like putting away stocks and bonds in a safe deposit box. These often young collectors are buying after first carefully studying the work to see if they judge it good, paying little or no attention to name or prior reputation, and taking it home to live with for a week before deciding. Perhaps they had genuine art appreciation courses; perhaps they simply develop their own sense of judgment. The dealers are happy to observe such a trend.

It is the schools that can set the climate, not just for artists and art buyers, but for greater understanding and acceptance in general, whether it be by government officials, the press, or people in many other walks of life. Once the ball starts to roll, it gathers momentum. Holland is a case in point: for some years its government has subsidized artists' rents, has offered tax deductions to those who purchase work by living artists, and in various other ways has manifested its belief in the importance of art to its civilization. It may be surmised that this attitude is related to Sotheby-Parke-Bernet's report that, in 1975, of all of its eight international auction markets outside its home bases in England and the United States, Amsterdam chalked up the highest sales—more than $9 million.

TOOLS OF THE TRADE

In the area of the simple, practical tools of the trade, I am forced to believe that many art schools and/or their libraries must be woefully unequipped with obvious reference material of a useful and up-to-date nature. So many artists with "good" art educations phone or write the Art Information Center every day for easily available information about today's potentials, which should have been brought to their attention and use in the classroom.

I was fortunate in having studied modern history under the late Sidney Bradshaw Fay, who spent the whole first session teaching us how to read the newspapers as today's chronicles of history-to-be. I wonder if there are such sessions in art courses, sessions on how to keep abreast of useful information applicable right now. Do school librarians get the regular reports of the American Council for the Arts, *American Artist, Art in America,* the newsletters of the National Art Workers' Community and of Artists' Equity, and the Action Kits issued periodically by Artists' Equity in Washington, D.C., on such subjects as ethical guidelines for juried shows, business practices for artists, marketing art through dealers, clear documentation of art to protect from misrepresentation, and health hazards in the arts and their control? And, more important, do teachers refer their students to them?

Are students informed about the practical information available in standard reference volumes, such as sources of fellowships and scholarships and listings of open exhibitions in *Fine Arts Market Place* and *American Art Directory,* and monthly in *American Artist's* "Bulletin Board"? Does anyone mention the nonprofit Opportunity Resources for the Arts, a placement center for nonteaching jobs in the arts on a nationwide basis, or say that individuals may request registration forms by addressing the center at 165 West 46th St., New York, N.Y. 10036? Do they mention that most museums have personnel departments where one can apply, and some will pass on names and backgrounds of applicants they can't absorb to art dealers who are seeking assistants in their galleries?

From my experiences, I would guess that the answer to these questions in all too many instances is no. Periodically I talk to groups or classes of seniors and postgraduate students in the visual arts, and even among these students, who usually have had sufficient interest to attend after school hours, their eager questions—which may go on for an hour and a half—show a pitiful lack of such information.

A typical example—A young man due to graduate from one of the country's best known art schools, in New York City, came to see me at the Art Information Center with a report about his "training." His teacher had indeed given him some constructive technical aid and suggestions about his work but eventually simply said to him: "Now I think you had better go and get yourself a New York gallery." The young man was completely at sea; he had no idea where or how to start, what to look for or what to look out for, what might be his possibilities for income, how to try to develop an art background and reputation. No slightest suggestions of any such information or where to find it had ever been made to him in this top art school. It was the advice of an older artist friend that landed him on our Center's doorstep like a lost foundling.

Probably the most comprehensive survey yet made of the practical problems of the individual creative artist and possibilities for solutions was conducted by the American Council for the Arts (ACA) in July 1975 at its annual meeting, which was held in Cleveland. The many panels and discussion groups inevitably involved a large amount of verbiage: artists aired their personal beefs while pedagogues talked about "the viability of the total art experience" and "the comprehension of the specific dynamics of experience." (Can anyone translate for me?)

It could be helpful if schools and teachers would run down the list of subjects dealt with at the ACA meeting and check off with a sharp pencil those on which they might fill in their students with useful ideas. It is worth considering how many concerns face professional artists besides the techniques of their disciplines and skills and where they can turn for aid when they run into problems. The discussion subjects of the many ACA panels in their fairly comprehensive coverage may serve at least as partial guidelines:

Grants to artists: Methods of selection, legal structure of government programs, grants to successful and to unrecognized artists, private foundations, the New York Foundation Center.

State Arts Councils: What they do for artists, for recognition, information, referral, sources of funding, community art functions, social problems of artists as a minority group.

Commissions for artists: In public places, by corporations, to decentralize the arts, as larger marketplace, audiences, installation, direct client-artist relationships without juries or dealer commissions.

One percent for art in public structures: Legislation, political aspects, contracts, enforcement.

Art colonies: MacDowell, Yaddo, Wolf Trap Farm Park, potentials for increase.

Artists-in-residence: What is required of them, how are the residencies offered, what is the pay, who owns the work executed, what kind of space supplied: teaching or work space?

Housing and studio programs: Funding, qualifications required, private and organizational support.

Art rentals and sales: By public agencies, corporations, museums, libraries.

Legal services: Volunteer Lawyers for the Arts, publications to aid artists in special legal problems, aid in presenting art legislation proposals.

Artist organizations: How formed, Boston Visual Artists' Union, Foundation for the Community of Artists, Artists' Equity.

Management and information services: Use of agent representation to corporate market and for lectures and demonstration, State Councils' information services, community resource centers, Art Information Center.

Foundations: The range of their services.

Tax situation: If artists are employed, unemployment insurance coverage, learning to protect one's fiscal interests.

Residual rights on resale of work: Through legislation or individual contracts.

Censorship: Actions and appeals, National Ad Hoc Coalition against Censorship, Advocates for the Arts, American Civil Liberties Union, Media Coalition, grass roots support vs. legal action.

Copyright: Provisions of the new law; protection for artists against rip-offs.

Taxes: For artists' grants, for heirs, for artists' donations to museums; reforms needed.

Self-employed resources: For health, social security, unemployment, old-age coverage; National Consumers' Center for Legal Services; Group Health Association.

Contracts: Samples, guides.

Credit: Difficulties, credit unions, collateral.

Some harsh comments were made in the course of these conference sessions about the laxity of art schools in the area of practical information. Artists were encouraged toward a different way of thinking about their own position: "The artist will and must be a decision-maker, not only that his work will reach an audience, but also how it will do so."

Herein lies a challenging potential for art schools.

21

Learning to be Assertive:
First Steps Toward the Liberation of Women

BETTE ACUFF

Most women, children, and ethnic minorities in the United States have been taught that assertive behavior is the province of the white male adult. Conformity to established rules and hierarchies of power, nonassertiveness, and the inhibition of complete expression in interpersonal situations have been rewarded (and thus encouraged) by the family, education, business, and religious worlds in our society.

The advent of the women's movement expresses women's awareness that there *are* alternatives for them. They sense they have a right to attitudes and behaviors different from the traditionally passive, compliant roles they have assumed in the past. Although many women have experienced inward stirrings that they are entitled to more personal satisfactions, professional advancement, and greater self-realization, they are still trapped in old ways of behaving. This entrapment is a result of early sex role conditioning and the continued reinforcement society gives the female for acting compliantly. Efforts at achieving a stronger sense of self, with accompanying acts of self-assertion, are met with reluctance and hostility by husbands, employers, legislators, and even other women. Such hostility may engender guilt or anxiety in the woman who is trying to become assertive. Emotional support while she learns new behaviors is an important factor in success; hence the need for a reference group, which can reinforce her in persisting in spite of opposition from her family or society.

There has been an increase during the past decade in women's groups that aim to help participants discover new roles and attitudes toward self and to develop behaviors expressive of themselves as free, powerful persons. Assertiveness Training (AT) is one approach steadily gaining popularity among women. AT asserts that: "Each person has the right to be and to express him/herself, and to feel good (not guilty) about doing so, as long as s/he does not hurt others in the process."[1]

"The assertive responder seeks a solution that equalizes the balance of power and permits all concerned to maintain their basic human rights. Thus an imbalance of power, caused by a failure to respect the rights of *all* people and perpetuated by the use of indirect methods, creates a very vulnerable position for both the nonassertive and the aggressive responders, while the more functional assertive responder respects all human rights, uses direct methods, and seeks a balance of power."[2] AT, then, is concerned with the dignity of the human being and the establishment of a fair balance of power in interpersonal situations so that the rights of all involved in such transactions are protected and direct communication enhanced.[3]

Assertive training has been part of therapeutic settings for longer than the past decade. Albert Ellis, for example, has used the technique of disputing irrational beliefs or fears as a means of developing assertiveness in clients.[4] Other behavior therapies stress graduated desensitization exercises as one means of overcoming anxieties associated with interpersonal situations. AT grows out of social learning theory[5] and relies heavily on modeling, role playing, and social reinforcement by the self, group members, and leader. AT approaches are highly specific, and its aim is to build a new repertoire of behavioral responses for specific situations by continued practice of the behavior to be learned.[6]

THE ASSERTIVE WOMAN

The assertive woman is not overwhelmed by situations; she is relaxed enough to take the time necessary to assess information coming in and *to focus on what her rights are in the situation*. She *is able to state her rights* and her assessment of the situation directly, honestly, and spontaneously. She *is able to stand her ground* instead of avoiding, retaliating hostilely, or engaging in other "put downs" or indirect manipulations of others (e.g., complaining, playing the martyr, wheedling). She *is able to accept her own feelings* and *to express them directly* in "I statements" (that is, she takes responsibility for her own feelings). While she acknowledges her feelings, she also *acknowledges the feelings of others*. In spite of bullying or "put downs" by others, she persists by focusing on the expression of *her* thoughts, feelings, and desires.

BLOCKS TO ASSERTIVENESS

For many women, achievement of the level of functioning just described is very difficult. Stanlee Phelps and Nancy Austin have conducted a number of AT workshops for women and have recently published a handbook for women who may be interested in forming their own AT groups.[7] Phelps and Austin have found that fears and attitudes most frequently expressed by women are related to the following:

1. The attitude that assertiveness is unfeminine. Women have been trained by their families to be dependent; the assessments of others are the source of their self-images. Many women consider that behaving assertively and independently are the exclusive prerogatives of men; for themselves they consider such behavior totally out of the question. This attitude must be replaced by one that regards assertiveness as a *human* quality, an option for both men and women.
2. Inability to see what one's rights are in a situation. That women should consider the needs and rights of others before their own is related to their early socialization. Therefore, many women are not in touch with what their personal rights are, nor do they know where they should go to get information about their rights. This attitude must be replaced by one that respects equally the rights of self and others. This inability to see what one's rights are is coupled with some of the following attitudes.
3. The "compassion trap." This notion (exclusive with women, according to Phelps and Austin) implies that *women exist solely to serve others*. Women who hold this view of themselves believe they must provide tenderness and compassion to all at all times, they must be "supermom" to all who demand succor from them.

This attitude must be replaced by the understanding that getting out of the compassion trap doesn't mean being insensitive to the feelings of others, but means valuing one's own feelings and being responsive to them with the same care one gives to others.

4. Fear of one's own power. Women have been denied the opportunity to exercise power; they have been told it isn't "natural" or feminine for them to want it. Traditionally the exercise of power has been associated with masculinity, while women have been expected *to react* to situations, rather than *to act* to change them. The need for approval prevents many women from working to develop a sense of power. Having power also means taking responsibility for one's actions, and that can be frightening. It takes much work and practice to overcome these early conditionings.

5. Fear of criticism or rejection. This fear is the result of the confusion of approval with love. There is a fear that loss of approval means loss of love. The most common form of rejection is when someone says "no" to one's idea, request, or action. When a woman is dependent, she reacts like a child; she is vulnerable to fits of resentment or rebellion when told no. The assertive woman wants to avoid being rejected as a person, but is aware that it is natural and unavoidable to have her ideas rejected from time to time. Because she gets her reward primarily from asserting herself and not just in getting what she wants all the time, she is able to accept nos.

6. Fear of releasing or expressing anger. This fear results from confusing the expression of anger with the ideas that anger must necessarily overwhelm one or that anger is "bad." Women are trained to hold back negative feelings and to "be nice." No one has modeled for them the skills involved in the open expression of anger. Instead, their models have been other women whose behaviors consist mostly of "game playing," in which anger is subverted into expressions of fatigue or irritation, complaining, or other indirect expressions. In indirect expressions, the angry feelings are denied, while the actor attempts to make the other person feel guilty ("Go ahead, don't mind me . . .") or is overly sweet, condescending, and patronizing. Finally, the nonassertive woman frequently turns anger in on herself, thus becoming depressed or ill. These fears must be replaced with the understand-

ing that the direct expression of anger is healthy and right and
may be used to change previously intolerable situations.

7. Inability to say "no."   Women are taught, as part of their conditioning to be "feminine," to be submissive and indecisive, to let
   others decide for them. A common stereotype is the woman
   who really means "no" when she says "yes." Many women
   equate saying "no" with being selfish and not considering the
   needs of others. To change behavior, it is necessary for such
   women to learn that they have the right to say no and the right to
   consider their own needs as well as those of others.

The major difficulty women have when they begin to learn assertion is to distinguish between assertive and aggressive behavior.
Assertive and aggressive behavior differ principally in that aggressiveness involves hurting or stepping on others in the course of
expressing oneself. When women behave assertively for the first
time, they confuse their *feelings* of anxiety or anger with the *form*
of the expression and may judge their own behavior to be aggressive—when, in fact, is it assertive—because of the strong emotions they feel as they act. Sensitization to discriminate between the
two types of behavior is the first step in the AT process.

ASSERTIVE TRAINING WORKSHOPS FOR WOMEN

In workshops organized for women, participants learn the differences between politeness, nonassertiveness, assertiveness, and aggression; they develop a belief system concerning the rights of self
and others; they develop cognitive and behavior skills to deal with
dysfunctional emotions (i.e., excessive anger, guilt, and anxiety); and
they develop assertive skills through active practice methods. In the
workshop setting, AT is regarded as a skill-building technique, not as
a therapeutic method or mode.

The first step in building new behaviors is that of becoming aware
of the situations that one could handle more assertively. One technique frequently used by group leaders is that of constructing an
Assertive Behavior Hierarchy. The hierarchy is constructed using a
questionnaire by which participants identify those situations in which
they tend to behave more or less assertively. One questionnaire,

developed by Sharon Bower, suggests that participants check off items organized under headings referring to four parameters of interpersonal situations: who, when, what topics, and size of group.[8] Once an individual has identified those situations in which she is behaving in nonassertive or aggressive ways, she orders them from those perceived as most to least comfortable. This ordering of situations constitutes the behavior hierarchy for that woman, she can use the hierarchy to structure her work toward mastery of successive situations.

For example, a woman may find it relatively easy to act appropriately assertive when accepting a compliment from a friend or husband. She may behave inconsistently when giving instructions or commands to a small group of teen-agers, at times behaving in a properly assertive manner, at others behaving aggressively (in an attempt to compensate for her feelings of powerlessness). She may consistently behave in a nonassertive manner when proposing an idea or solution in a large group, especially if she perceives others in the group as authority figures. She designs a working plan for herself, first developing consistently assertive behavior for situations in which she works with teenagers. Only after she has achieved success with the first set of tasks she has set for herself, will she proceed to develop assertiveness in the more difficult and uncomfortable situations in which she is to propose solutions in groups where authority figures are present. In progressing through her working plan; she will avail herself of the suggestions and support of other participants in the AT group.

Certain essential components of the assertive response may be applied in any situation. Sometimes it is necessary for women to practice these components before practicing assertion in particular situations. Thus, the leader may lead the participants through a number of exercises that teach how to use direct eye contact while speaking; how to use appropriate body posture, gestures, facial expression, and voice pitch, rate, volume, and quality so as to convey a direct assertive message. (The group is usually broken into dyads for such exercises so that partners can give one another feedback about performance.) In addition, relaxation and breathing techniques are introduced to achieve a relaxed stance or mental attitude as a prerequisite for speaking and behaving appropriately.

Models may be drawn from the group or from a number of training films and video materials. One such film is *Assertive Training for Women*, created by Patricia Jakubowsky-Spector, of Washington University.[9]

SOME PROBLEMS DURING THE TRANSITIONAL PERIOD

1. Assertive statements.   Participants frequently have initial diffi-culties framing their statements in a manner that is assertive and not aggressive. In some, the tendency when moving from nonas-sertive to assertive behavior is to become aggressive, thus releas-ing pent-up anger in hostile, accusatory statements. Participants are taught to frame their expression in "I messages." The "I message" contains three components: (1) a nonblameful descrip-tion of another's behavior, (2) the tangible effects of this be-havior on the speaker now or in the future, and (3) the speaker's feelings about this behavior. For example, if a woman were for-mulating an assertive statement to use when someone cut in front of her in a movie line, she could say, "When people cut in front of me (nonblameful description as opposed to "When *you* cut"), I get worried (feeling) that the theater might sell out before I get my ticket, and I've gone to a lot of trouble getting a babysitter" (tangible effects).[10]
2. Potential adverse reactions.   Inappropriate attitudes toward themselves frequently are a source of difficulty for women as they move through the transitional period. They may label their assertive behavior negatively ("What a bitch I am!") rather than positvely ("I'm really being assertive. . . . I love it !"). Such nega-tive labelling tends to undermine attemps at acquiring new be-havior. Another difficulty is persisting in spite of temporary negative consequences (e.g., hostility, backbiting, aggression, and revenge sought by others as the actor behaves assertively). Participants are warned that emotional turbulence accompanies any major change in their behavior or life and that they are not to put themselves down if they aren't appropriately assertive in every situation. During the transitional period, it is important

that participants get support from friends or from the group as they encounter difficulties.

3. Choosing not to assert oneself.   Choice is the key word in the assertion process. Women are cautioned to keep in mind that though they may know how to assert themselves, there may be occasions in which they choose not to do so (e.g., in the case of overly sensitive individuals; when another individual is obviously having a very difficult time; when another person who has taken advantage of the woman's rights suddenly sees that s/he has done so and remedies the situation appropriately).

AT FOR WOMEN IN ARTS AND EDUCATION

Blocks to assertiveness identified by Phelps and Austin (e.g., fear of appearing unfeminine, fear of one's power, fear of criticism or rejection) are strongly reinforced by societal biases operating in the professional lives of women artists.

Until very recently, women art students have observed few models of successful female artists. The majority of studio and art history classes are taught by males, who present male artists as exemplars of success. Gallery owners and museum curators have consistently discriminated against women artists, refusing to admit them to shows or to purchase their work for collections.[11] Learning assertiveness for the woman artist, then, not only involves overcoming traditional feminine role conditioning in her personal life, but also involves counteracting a professional climate rife with sexist attitudes and practices (see chapters by June Wayne and Cindy Nemser in this book).

As the number of women who combine the roles of artist and teacher increases, their relationships with other women artist-teachers can provide support for their efforts to establish themselves professionally. Examples of such support groups are AIR in New York City and Womanhouse in Los Angeles. These women can also provide support for the next generation of artist-teachers as they present themselves as role models for their women students. Successful women artist-teachers demonstrate that it *is* possible for women to assert their rights to express themselves artistically and to expect to gain recognition for their efforts.

AT can be used by women artist-teachers in their classes to assist women students in developing a sense of direction when plotting careers and in acting assertively to realize career goals. For example, although a woman student may have worked through various areas of nonassertiveness in interpersonal relations (home, family, friends), she can have failed to assert herself professionally as an artist. Her teachers may have assured her that her work is excellent and original. She may have exhibited in several local shows; she may have sold a few of her works. She knows that some galleries are beginning to show women's work but nonetheless fears her work may be rejected. She is also aware that her work will never be shown or sold, unless she takes the risk of exposing her work publicly. Using AT methods, she can explore ways to handle the situation to advance professionally. She may be encouraged to explore her feelings (fears) about the step she is going to take and to play out in fantasy the worst and the best consequences of her actions. In reviewing her feelings about these fantasies, she may clarify the difference between actual and exaggerated or unreal consequences of the presentation of her work. Discrimination between real and fantasied possibilities enables her to place herself in a better position with respect to her fears. A teacher may provide a model herself or may invite successful women artists to discuss their work and the problems they have overcome in establishing themselves. Members of the group may suggest and/or model alternatives for the student; they may provide feedback as she role plays an assertive response to the situation. Perhaps she needs to sustain eye contact or to speak in a more forthright manner, rather than acting apologetically or coming on aggressively to compensate for her uncomfortable feelings. Members of the group may actually role play the rejection of her work, to enable her to place the possibility of an initial rejection in its proper perspective.

The artist-teacher may also use AT with women students who intend to become art teachers rather than professional artists. The artist-teacher has a responsibility to help prospective teachers practice assertive ways of dealing with students, with principals or other supervisors, and with parents.

Art teachers need to be especially skillful and assertive in enlightening parents about the values of the art experience for their children, since parents are either ignorant of the values of such experiences or regard art as a pleasant but unimportant adjunct to the school's "more important" business of preparing their children to compete and succeed (i.e., make more money) in society.

Frequently the principal or other teachers make unreasonable demands on art teachers to provide (on short notice) posters or other visual materials for school functions. These demands on the art teacher are regarded as perfectly reasonable requests by others, since they have no conception of the amount of time required to produce a well-designed poster or sign. The art teacher must assertively inform others in her school of the time and thought required to provide such services and suggest either that she and her students be compensated accordingly, that requests for such services be submitted sufficiently in advance to allow for proper designing and production, or that the reasonable number of such requests shall be determined by the art teacher and *not* by those requesting the service.

AT can be successfully applied in these and a number of other situations to enable women artist-teachers to function more effectively in their chosen roles—to expand their capacities, and hence, their lives.[12]

NOTES

1. Robert Alberti and Michael Emmons, *Your Perfect Right: A Guide to Assertive Behavior* (San Luis Obispo, Calif.: Impact, 1975), p. 6.
2. Collen Kelly, "Assertion Theory," in *The 1976 Handbook for Group Facilitators,* eds., J. W. Pfeiffer and J. E. Jones (La Jolla, Calif.: University Associates, 1976), p. 153.
3. Sharon Anthony Bower, *Learning Assertive Behavior with PALS* (Palo Alto: Stanford University Press, 1974), p. 6.
4. Albert Ellis, *A New Guide to Rational Living* (Englewood Cliffs, N.J.: Prentice-Hall, 1975).
5. Albert Bandura, *Principles of Behavior Modification* (New York: Holt, Rinehart and Winston, 1969); and "Behavioral Modification through Modeling Procedures," in *Research in Behavior Modification,* eds., L. Krasner and L. P. Ullman (New York: Holt, Rinehart and Winston, 1965), pp. 310–340.

6. Joseph Wolpe, "The Instigation of Assertive Behaviors," *Journal of Behavior Therapy and Experimental Psychiatry* 1, no. 2 (1970): 145–151.

7. Stanlee Phelps and Nancy Austin, *The Assertive Woman* (San Luis Obispo, Calif.: Impact, 1975).

8. Sharon Anthony Bower and Gordon H. Bower, *Asserting Yourself: A Practical Guide for Positive Change* (Reading, Mass.: Addison Wesley, 1976), pp. 14–16.

9. Patricia Jakubowsky-Spector, *Assertive Training for Women*, Parts I and II (Washington, D.C., American Personnel and Guidance Association, 1975), rental: $25.00.

10. Myles Cooley, "A Model for Assertive Statements," *Assert Newsletter* 1, no. 6 (1976): 2.

11. Eleanor Dickinson and Roberta Loach, "Does Sex Discrimination Exist in the Visual Arts?" *Visual Dialog* 1, no. 2 (December 1975): 8–10.

12. Additional readings on assertive behavior: Patricia Jakubowski-Spector, *An Introduction to Assertive Training Procedures for Women* (Washington, D.C.: American Personnel and Guidance Association Press, 1973); Patricia Jacubowski-Spector, "Facilitating the Growth of Women Through Assertive Training," *The Counselling Psychologist* 4, no. 1 (1973): 75–88; S. M. Osborne and G. G. Harris, *Assertive Training for Women* (New York: Charles C. Thomas, 1975); Michael Smith, *When I Say No, I feel Guilty* (New York: Bantam, 1975); *Assert: The Newsletter of Assertive Behavior* (Impact Publishers, P.O. Box 1094, San Luis Obispo, Calif. 94306), $6.00 per year.

22

Jurying:
Innovations by Women in the Arts

JEAN ZALESKI

All artists—women and men—have suffered from the traditional and antiquated jury system still used in selecting works for inclusion in group exhibitions. Whether the sponsoring agent asks artists to submit slides or actual work, the usual result is many hundreds (or more) of entries being received. From this large number, relatively few—50 to 100—may be selected for the exhibition by the jurors (most often male artists). The time jurors have to view each work initially sometimes is as little as 30 seconds. Given the best of circumstances, i.e., jurors who desire to be completely fair and unbiased, the time allotment makes it impossible for them to make good judgments. In that short period of time, jurors' reactions generally are to choose work for which they already have an affinity, work that is familiar to them. They may have more time to review the final selections, but by that time many excellent new or subtle works have already been rejected.

That is what happens under the best of circumstances. Everyone has her or his favorite story of the worst of circumstances. For example, two jurors, after an exhausting morning and a heavy lunch (plus a few cocktails), decide that they can't bear to look at certain colors. So from then on, one rejects every red painting and the other every blue one! Stories that seem to be bad jests are often true accounts.

Another problem with the traditional jurying method is that although, for the sake of fairness, the artists' names are usually obliterated in some way for the first selection, the jurors will regularly call out, "Oh, that's so and so's painting, put it in." All the friends get into the show. All the artists working in familiar styles get into the show. This leaves little room for anyone else.

Since most of the well-known artists (like the jurors) are men, the

result is a subtle discrimination against women artists. When the time
comes for the selection of prizes, all the names are in view. The same
choosing of friends and familiar work continues. This results in more
discrimination against women artists. Although both men and
women will agree that this type of jurying is unfair, it is inevitable
that women will be at a greater disadvantage from this method where
male jurors consistently select the work of their male artist friends
for inclusion and for prizes.

The inequities of the existing jurying system were among the first
subjects discussed by Women in the Arts. This group was founded in
April 1971, by a few women painters and writers who wished to fight
discrimination against women artists. On April 12, 1972, WIA celebrated its first birthday by staging a demonstration in front of the
Museum of Modern Art in New York City. Letters, which were
released to the press, were sent to the top six museums in New York
City:

> Women in the Arts, an organization of more than 300 members, today
> proposes a revolutionary concept of museum exhibitions. Past program-
> ming has been impoverished by discriminatory practices against women.
> ... We propose the exhibition WOMEN CHOOSE WOMEN ...
> selected by the membership of Women in the Arts to include the largest
> number of known and unknown talents.

The New York Cultural Center accepted the challenge and agreed to
host such an exhibition.

JURYING METHOD FOR WOMEN CHOOSE WOMEN

A new way of jurying was developed for this exhibition. WIA
printed ballot forms for each member. Each member proposed the
ten women artists whose work she most respected and admired.
Proposals were not limited to WIA members. Several hundred
names were received. Three WIA members—Pat Pasloff, Ce Roser
and Silvia Sleigh—were chosen to make the final selection with the
museum's exhibition coordinator, Laura Adler, art critics Linda
Nochlin and Elizabeth C. Baker, and the director of the Cultural
Center, Mario Amaya. Thus artists, the host museum, and art critics

had a voice in the final selection. Paintings and sculpture that covered a great variety of styles and media were chosen.

Women Choose Women was on display from January 12 through February 18, 1973. It broke all previous attendance records at the Cultural Center. The press reviews were excellent. April Kingsley, in the March 1973, issue of *Artforum* said: "Women Choose Women at the New York Cultural Center is a pioneering enterprise with repercussions for the entire art-institutional structure. . . . We have often heard in the past few years, since women artists have been forming politically active groups, that hundreds of talented women artists are working without recognition. This is our first opportunity to see what a large body of their work is like, and its quality more than justifies the rhetoric we have heard."

This exhibition opened the way for more shows of its type and for a somewhat more serious consideration of women's art work in general. In that sense, it benefited all women artists. However, one can't deny the fact that it benefited most those women whose work was in the show. Hard feelings were abundant among those WIA members whose work was not included. Some left the organization. Many of these were very good artists.

THE EXHIBITION WORKS ON PAPER–WOMEN ARTISTS

As a result of many meetings with the Brooklyn Museum, a promise for an exhibition had been made. Then there was a change in the directorship of the Museum. After three years of negotiation for this exhibition, WIA finally decided to picket the museum in protest. Press releases were sent out. The organization then received a telegram from the museum saying it wanted to meet with WIA. An exhibition was subsequently set for September 24–November 9, 1975.

It was decided that for this exhibition all WIA members would be included and a different method of selection of work would be used. Each artist member was asked to submit a number of her works to two other women in the art field—other artists, critics, and collectors. These "jurors" then selected one work from the pieces submitted to them, and this work was shown in the exhibition. Their names appeared on the title card of the work along with the name of the artist. Due to the space limitation of the museum, the exhibited work was limited to a 16 × 20 inch size or smaller. Plastic, Dax-type frames were required, but all varieties of works on paper were acceptable, including paintings, drawings, graphics, sculpture, collage and multimedia pieces. It was a great achievement to have every member who so desired included in this exhibition. The crowd was so large on opening day that many had to walk away and return another time. David L. Shirey, in his article in the *New York Times* dated October 26, 1975, wrote that this show "marks an important event in the history of art by women and in the evolution of attitudes by museums toward this art."

TRAVELING EXHIBITION: ARTISTS' CHOICE

Works on Paper–Women Artists created a great deal of interest in Women in the Arts in many places around the country. WIA began to receive requests from many universities for a traveling exhibition of members' work. Early in 1976, such an exhibition was organized and called Artists Choice. The selection system used for the Brooklyn Museum exhibition had worked so well that WIA members voted to use it again. Again, every member who chose to be in the show was represented by a work selected by either another artist, a critic, a gallery owner, or a collector.

A traveling exhibition of this size—134 works—requires a great deal of organization. Participating institutions are responsible for shipping and insurance costs. The small size of the work—maximum 16 × 20 inches—and the use of lightweight frames helps keep shipping costs relatively low. This exhibition has a handsome catalog accompanying it. Grant help for the catalog had been sought and received.

LOFT EXHIBITIONS

This report of WIA's innovative jurying methods would not be complete without a word about the loft exhibitions in WIA's gallery. WIA wants to give every woman artist a chance to exhibit her work. Originally, a hat was passed around at monthly meetings, and every member who wished to exhibit in the loft gallery put her name into the hat. Absent members were allowed to send in their names. Four or five names were pulled out for each exhibition.

The resuling shows were on the whole surprisingly good, even if at times uneven. They gave artists who did not yet have gallery representation a chance to hang their work next to artists with established reputations. It was a "safe" place to see one's work alongside more advanced work. It was an excellent experience for younger artists. A walk in the surrounding SoHo gallery area made it clear that these shows were as good, if not better, than the ones in the commercial galleries.

However, it was felt that the quality of the exhibitions could be improved even further. This might result in increased gallery attendance. Furthermore, it would increase the chances of obtaining funding for the WIA gallery.

In January 1978, the membership established new systems of selection for the gallery. Any member who wishes may attend and act as a voting juror when slides or original work are reviewed for four-person-shows. The 28 artists receiving the highest number of votes form their own groups of four for those exhibitions. The same jurying system will be used for 10 percent exhibitions, large group shows in which each artist selected may hang one piece. One show a year will be a nonjuried open wall exhibition in which any member may hang one piece.

The gallery is a cooperative venture. The exhibiting artists work together to design and mail announcements, do public relations work, plan the opening reception, and sit during the show.

These are some new selection methods that have been developed. They are not the perfect answers; they are not suitable for every exhibition. WIA receives many requests for smaller exhibitions of larger work. Some curators insist on selecting their own exhibitions. Giving every member an equal chance is an unshakeable policy of WIA. Many think-tank sessions have been held. It is clear that no one method can ever be right for all exhibitions. WIA will individually tailor the selection policy for each show.

Efforts must still be expended to correct the inequities of the systems used in the selection of work for museum exhibitions and acquisitions. The typical present museum exhibition selection and acquisition system is a direct product of the art establishment complex, which includes major museums, major galleries, major critics, and major collectors and excludes others. WIA is dealing with this problem by collecting statistics as well as continuing dialogue and correspondence with the New York museums. WIA is also trying to educate the public so that they will understand and, hopefully, support what WIA is doing. Radio, TV shows, and direct contact methods are being used by the organization.

It is hoped that both female and male artists will share a more sensible system of selecting work for exhibitions, one that will not only be fairer to the individual artist, but will profit humankind in general by bringing to the public a broader representation of fine art being currently produced. We cannot depend on the established institutions to accomplish this. Not only must artists stay aware of how the various art institutions are selecting work for their particular programs, but artists must make their opinions and their needs heard. In addition, it is important that artists' groups look to their own exhibitions for innovative and equitable selection methods.

23

The Education of Women as Artists:
Project Womanhouse

MIRIAM SCHAPIRO

The Feminist Art Program at the California Institute of the Arts was joyous and exhausting work. Judy Chicago and I embarked on a team teaching experiment and found our collaboration in such an intensive teaching situation inspiring and liberating. Ideas and energy cascaded from one teacher to another, and the feeling that one did not have to carry the entire responsibility for the program freed us.

METHODS OF TEACHING: GROUP OPERATION

Twenty-one young women artists elected to join this exclusively female class. We did not teach by fixed authoritarian rules. Traditionally the flow of power has moved from teacher to student unilaterally. Our ways were more circular, more womblike; our primary concern was with providing a nourishing environment for growth.

Classes began by sitting in a circle; a topic for discussion was selected. We moved around the room, each person assumed responsibility for addressing herself to the topic on her highest level of self-perception. In the classical women's liberation technique, the personal became the political. Privately held feelings imagined to be personally held "hang-ups" turned out to be everyone's feelings, and it became possible to act together in their solution, if there was a solution. Our use of this technique served a different purpose. As artists we search for subject. It is often wearying to struggle alone for

247

the courage to bring to the surface material that would be fit for artistic form. In our group we made rules based on mutual aesthetic consent to encourage and support the most profound artistic needs of the group.

Sometimes the struggle for subject matter assumed a different cast. We were able to find material to make art from, but we sensed that the material was inappropriate. There are some interesting unwritten laws about what is considered appropriate subject matter for art making. The content of our first class project, Womanhouse, reversed these laws. What formerly was considered trivial was heightened to the level of serious art making: dolls, pillows, toys, underwear, children's toys, wash basins, toasters, frying pans, refrigerator door handles, shower caps, quilts, and satin bedspreads.

CONCEPTION OF WOMANHOUSE

Womanhouse began as a topic for discussion in one of our class meetings. We asked ourselves what it would be like to work out one of our closest associative memories—the home. Our home, which we as a culture of women have been identified with for centuries, has always been the area where we nourished and were nourished. It has been the base of operations out of which we fought and struggled with ourselves to please others. What would happen, we asked, if we created a home in which we pleased no one but ourselves? What if each woman were to develop her own dreams and fantasies in one room of that home? The idea seemed like a good one.

Some of the women found a house in downtown Los Angeles—a wreck of a house, an old abandoned mansion large enough to accommmodate all of us, but sick with disuse. It was very far from school, which meant that some students who lived in the dorms on campus had to travel each day with companions from the class who had cars and whose responsibility it was to fetch and carry them every day. Many of the women had jobs as librarians and waitresses and had to commute the enormous distance from the school to the house and back again, sometimes twice a day. There was no adequate plumbing in the house. We made certain to have our lunch in a nearby restaurant so that we could use its facilities. There was no heat; we worked in winter swaddled in sweaters. After a while the sinks filled up, and we had no water except from a tap outside where we rinsed out our brushes.

Despite such inconveniences in this age of affluent school situations—and I cite them only in the pedagogical context—Womanhouse was conceived and executed with sustained energy and commitment. If the idea for a class was mind-blowing, the inspiration for work was enough to reveal solutions to difficult work problems.

CREATION OF WOMANHOUSE

The first job in Womanhouse was to replace 23 broken windows. The art of glazing was unknown to both Judy and myself. Working out of our circular methods, it was discovered that the father of one of the girls owned a hardware store and was willing to teach the women to install windows. So while a crew went out to buy paint to paint the entire house, another crew traveled 40 miles to the hardware store to get the special instruction they needed. A plus out of this experience came when the father donated the glass. Lumber was ordered to build new walls where they were needed for practical and/or aesthetic reasons. Some of the women learned wallpapering techniques for refurbishing one of the upstairs rooms. Still others scraped and refinished floors; and ultimately a crew painted the outside of the house. After locks and a telephone were installed and an electrician provided some elementary information on wiring, we settled down to the real work of transformation.

Out of our consciousness-raising techniques came the motif for the kitchen. As we expressed our real underlying feelings about the room, it became obvious that the kitchen was a battleground where women fought with their mothers for their appropriate state of comfort and love. It was an arena where ostensibly the horn of plenty overflowed, but where in actuality the mother was acting out her bitterness over being imprisoned in a situation from which she could not bring herself to escape and from which society would not encourage such an escape. Three women collaborated on the kitchen. They painted everything a store-bought pink—refrigerator, stove, canned goods, toaster, sink, walls, floor, ceiling. Drawers were papered with collages of far away places. On the ceiling and walls were attached fried eggs, which transformed themselves into breasts as

they traveled down the walls. Five molds were made from clay showing this transformation, and they were created in a spongy material
and painted realistically. The reality of the woman's condition that
was epitomized by this kitchen, coupled with a consistently high
level of quality art making, made the experience of walking into our
nurturing center breathtaking.

Another room on the first floor was our dining room, brilliant in
color with a sensuous wall mural of fruit and flowers, a stenciled rug
on the floor, much bread dough sculpture representing ham, turkey,
fruit, vegetables, a three-layer chocolate cake, and butter, oversized
vinyl wine glasses holding a bit of burgundy cloth representing
Cabernet Sauvignon, and finally a marvelous recreation of a chan-
delier created out of vinyl and wired for electricity.

Also on the first floor was a small black room with a weblike
enclosure made of crocheted rope, its oval apertures and overtones
of womblike space suggesting a primitive hut. Outside its door was a
laundry room with hanging laminated stockings and a tub filled with
suds.

Womanhouse's three bathrooms reflected the different aspects of
female life. One was painted stark white. A shell held boxes of
Kotex, deodorants, and hygiene apparatus. A white plastic wastebas-
ket was filled to overflowing with soiled Kotex. On the floor next to
the basket lay one Tampax, painted red—one out of the 10,000
a woman uses in her fertile lifetime. The second bathroom was an
homage to our societal obsession with cosmetics. The entire room
was red: a red fur covered toilet and bathtub, a single red bulb in the
ceiling, red hair curlers, red combs, red brushes, and 100 red
lipsticks. The last bathroom revealed our nightmares. A woman
made of sand, totally vulnerable, lay in the tub. Her medicine chest
was open to expose several cosmetic bottles, again filled with sand. It
was a reverse of the notion that a woman covers her body with lotion.
Her body is imprisoned by her cosmetics. A menacing, black bird
hung from the ceiling threatening the woman's naked body.

One of the larger upstairs rooms of Womanhouse recreated for us
the bedroom in Collette's "Cheri." One entered this room to find a
performance in progress. A woman dressed in pink silk and antique
lace sat at a dressing table repeatedly "making up," then removing
her makeup, and then making up again. There was an opulent Persian rug on the floor, a mahogany canopied bed with satin pillows,

old porcelain water pitchers, and antique dresses hanging in musky, perfume-scented corners.

Three of the rooms in the house were "painted," created by three women who wished to possess their spaces through their personalities as painters. The first was oval in shape, with oversized leaves painted side by side, moving around the room, extending in height from floor to ceiling, and across the floor. These leaves changed in color from green to red, newness to decay, reflecting a subjective mood change in the artist as she worked in real time. The second, a small closet, is painted in *trompe l'oeil* style—a self-portrait of the artist as she stood within a mysterious night time interior-exterior moonscape. She raised her hand. Finally, one of the women created for us an environmental abstract expressionist interior. The bed, the chest, the chair, the vase of flowers, the ceiling, floor, windows, and walls were all covered with paint gesturally marked as if the artist's hand was compelled to touch it all.

A smaller room on the first floor was less environmental, more museumlike. Here a wall was built with an aperture cut out to reveal what could be a Punch and Judy show, only instead we saw six open rooms of a woman artist's doll house. The tiny house, with its miniature kitchen, studio, bedroom, and so on, was touched by wit and irony; it was the creation of two older women who allowed themselves to regress in the age of magical belief.

A younger woman created for us a secret room within an ordinarily messy room—a typical student's room. The environment became the confrontation between reality and fantasy, and its effect was shocking. The inner space, constructed in canvas, is circular, extending from floor to ceiling. A soft pink inscape was painted on the interior walls. The ceiling was draped like a tent, and the floor was padded. There was a large, luxurious satin hassock to sit on, and the lighting was both delicate and sensuous.

Across the hall, an oversized nursery had a rocking horse six feet high, stars on the ceiling, a rainbow mural, and a tremendous crib and dresser. Its size and proportion invited us to be children once again.

Between the upstairs rooms, two closets were reconverted: one into an "obsessive" shoe closet, with hundreds of multi-colored, ribboned, sequined shoes; the other into a pastel linen closet with a department store mannequin emerging from its shelves.

Down the hall a white bride mannequin stood at the top of the staircase, bedecked with ribbons, flowers, veils, and a smile. Her train extended to the foot of the stairs slowly discoloring to a muted grey. We saw her—dirty, grey, used—crash headlong into the bottom wall, the entire front half of her body invisible.

The vestibule of Womanhouse emerged in biological, weblike skeins of rope and foam capillaries, treating the sensation of hazardous motion.

And, finally, Womanhouse's garden contained a work created by a sculptor who made for us a series of hard plastic animals—a dinosaur, a spider, and others—surrounded by masses of handmade tropical leaves. The young artist's conception dealt with aspects of her own biography. Her early life in Florida brought her into contact with fearful alligators and snakes; and thus her sense of controlling her early animal terror motivated her garden pieces.

In an effort to reach out to the community of women artists so that our students could connect with the real world of art making, we invited three women artists from Los Angeles to participate in the house. One woman hung beautiful quilts on the upstairs landing: one woman provided vacuum formed curtains for the kitchen windows (which had formerly only been exhibited in snow-white exhibition spaces). They fitted in perfectly. The last woman hung a pillow quilt in the doll house room, displayed her lingerie pillows there, and hung a stuffed dress whose abdomen was protruding so that it became the pregnant personage. These women loved showing their works in Womanhouse. For them it was natural.

EVALUATION

For Judy Chicago and myself, our experiences as feminists had provided us with a context for a meaningful teaching experiment. We reevaluated our own experiences as young art students and made the transition into teaching young women art students. We permitted them to be themselves on all levels; to express their womanly art as they saw fit. We did not legislate what might be fit subject matter for them. We waited to see what it turned out to be, urging them on at every step of the way to do what ever it was they did best. And the breakdown of role playing that occurred inspired the women to assume greater responsibility. Urging young women artists to make

extraordinary demands on themselves is hazardous. Societal expectations for young women are not demanding. They are expected to
fulfill their biological roles as wives and mothers and not much more.
We dealt with our young women students as artists. It required work
for them and for us; we were reminded again and again that it is
indeed the responsibility of all older, "established" women artists to
serve as role models to their young women students, models as
productive, integrated artists as well as women.

Our students too set goals for themselves, and they came through.
It wasn't always easy. They had to cope first of all with being part of a
group; but they retained their individuality and provided warmth,
comfort, and support for each other. They tasted the professional life
by creating a large, complex work of art. They put it on exhibition
and found themselves exposed and in a position of having to cope
with feedback from the public. This was more difficult. The situation
plunged them into reality and away from their "safe," childlike, art
student fantasies of how they wished their world, their art, and their
lives to appear to other people. They made the first step from student to professional. At times they cried; but in the end they tran-
scended their illusions and learned the art of coping with "the way
things really are."

When the house went on exhibition, extensive media exposure
brought all segments of the public to the opening. Ordinarily the
public comes to an exhibit self-consciously wondering what to think
about the art. Without a program they are lost. At Womanhouse,
women, particularly, walked into what was essentially their home
ground, knowing instinctively how to react. They cried when they
saw the cosmetic performance piece. They gasped at the kitchen.
They shook their heads wisely when they looked at the bridal piece.
The shoe closet was familiar, the menstruation bathroom belonged
to them, the stockings were theirs; and the aesthetic distance provided by the controlled environment at Womanhouse allowed them
to respond with fullness to the honor, joy, and beauty of the house
which, in the end, was really theirs.

24

Feminist Education:
A Vision of Community and Women's Culture

ARLENE RAVEN

Each October since 1973, women from all over the United States and Europe come to the Woman's Building in Los Angeles to study at the Feminist Studio Workshop, an alternative learning institution. The ages, backgrounds, and levels of intellectual or artistic development of these women vary, as do their fantasies and expectations of what they will experience in our intensive two-year program.

The ideas and methods of feminist education that I will discuss evolved at the Feminist Studio Workshop and were developed with Judy Chicago, Sheila de Bretteville, Suzanne Lacy, Ruth Iskin, Deena Metzger, and Helen Roth. It seems appropriate that our theories and methods evolved from our collective work because we believe that the essential purpose of feminist education is to create a community.[1]

Over the past several years, my colleagues and I have modified and expanded our original visions of women's culture and the feminist learning process. While we first focused almost exclusively on each woman's growth and work, we now recognize the vital importance of collectivity as a precondition for truly effective individual creative work. The consciousness-raising format has been the center and backbone of our process. The aspiration of feminist education is, above all, to expedite creative work that will make significant assaults on traditional cultural assumptions.

Thinking of a learning situation as a community is not, of course, indigenous to feminist education. The idea, largely as rhetoric, was in widespread use from colleges to communes during the 1960s. It was a manifestation of the general spirit of that time. Ethnic power and women's movements had demanded a reexamination of institutional structures in regard to the distribution of social, political, and economic power. Community in schools, governments, or other groups implied flexibility or egalitarianism. Structures and relationships could be based on humanitarian principles with human-centered as well as production-centered or capital-centered goals.

There were reasons for the failure of the great majority of these optimistic experiments: not recognizing the enormous continual personal changes that implementing new structures would require; not understanding how fragile such communities were because they were at such odds with their surroundings, and not realizing how thoroughly they could be devalued and annihilated from without and within. As veterans of these kinds of experiences, we recognized the overwhelming difficulty of building a feminist community. All the techniques, structures, and concepts that form our process of feminist education, therefore, are directed toward the development of personal strength. We need this kind of growth to be able to function in our day-to-day relationships and our work which is a vision we know to be antithetical to the characteristic modes of operating in the world.

The idea of a feminist community challenges our previous pattern of isolation from one another. Relationships in the feminist community, moreover, are based on shared goals and values as well as a commitment to work. In the past, women's relationships have not been based on a chosen life work outside of mothering. Connections have instead been made through blood ties (family relationships and organizations like the PTA, which extend from them) and leisure activities (bridge, bowling, volunteer work). Women's friendships have been prescribed by their fathers and husbands (the status of their fathers and husbands within the society).

The demand for mutual support and responsible mutual criticism in the feminist community is clearly in opposition to the apparent competition among women in public. Although our major lesson in the area of criticism consisted of: "If you can't say anything nice, don't say anything," we could engage in the most blatant criticism, trivializing ourselves and other women, in cattiness and idle gossip.

All women come to the feminist community in the situation of oppression. In the early stages of the women's movement oppression was commonly attributed to *them*, i.e., men, society, role conditioning, or early gender-related training. While not denying all these as real sources of oppression, we have concentrated on the oppression women bring to their relationships with themselves and other women. We have dealt with self-hatred, which prevents achievement of personal and professional goals. Support is learned, just as oppression is learned. The work of the community depends on each member's making the transition from oppression to support. This means altering day-to-day behavior as well as analyzing the conditions that have brought about personal and cultural devaluation of the feminine. We consider the lack of development of which I am speaking to be a social and political problem indigenous to women and minorities requiring changes in social structures. When support prevails, there is a surge of energy in the group. As a great deal of interest develops among members in one another and in each other's work, there is an increase of individual as well as collective power.

The Feminist Studio Workshop raises for ongoing discussion four issues that reveal women's apprehension of power: authority, sexuality, money, and work. Authority, for example, has been a central issue in the women's movement. In an effort to avoid duplicating inflexible authoritarian power structures, women's organizations attempted to create leaderless structures, only to discover that leadership is a necessary factor in any group. We find that women have difficulty acknowledging the authority of other women as well as assuming authority themselves on the basis of their own skills or knowledge. In the FSW we focus on each woman becoming her own authority. This may mean acquiring expertise in a certain field, developing the feeling of competence in general, or becoming aware of the privileges and responsibilities of leadership. The support of women's competence by other women is a necessary condition before women can contribute meaningfully in the public arena today.

The topics of authority, sexuality, money, and work are not only subjects for frequent dialogue and debate but are a central focus in practice at the Workshop where the expansion of women's powers is a major goal. Consciousness-raising is the core of the structure we use. It allows for closeness, promotes political awareness, and serves to bring up raw material for art and other creative activities. Women come to consciousness-raising believing that their lives—particularly the points of pain, dissatisfaction, or inadequacy—are entirely individual. In fact, the life experiences of women in the social sphere are often similar to those of other women. The recognition of this by members of a consciousness-raising group is on the one hand painful because that is the nature of women's real situation in our society. On the other hand, it is also comforting because that situation is a group or class problem as well as an individual one. Through consciousness-raising, we can rid ourselves of the isolating fantasies of Cinderella, which we carry inside as our secret selves; these dream images contribute to women's infantilism.

In addition to consciousness-raising, activities are organized around project, criticism, community, and apprentice groups, as well as open discussion. Each is designed to make a specific contribution to the feminist educational process. We seek to create a women's culture based on the lives, experience, and visions of women.

The Feminist Studio Workshop was first conceived as an alternative art school for women. We continue to encourage women to participate actively in the art professions. We focus on the possibility of refashioning professional life, to expand the time for one's own creative work. However, our primary commitment is to the feminist community as a source of energy and support for all of our activities.

The Woman's Building in which we are located, is a public center for women's culture. In it women have the opportunity to create a concrete alternative to male supremist institutions, which do not support them or their work. Our constituency is the art audience and the general public. We have broadened our understanding of art to include historical research, printing, community organizing, administration, and "the gentle art of mutual aid."

There has been some amount of debate among artists and critics about the existence of a women's art, a feminist art, or a female art. Our primary goal is the exploration of women's individual and collective experience. We feel that the nature of woman's art is the content of her experience transformed in the process of making art; it reflects her environment—past or present. The form of each woman's art will vary just as her connection to institutions and relationships in her life varies. We see all women's forays into the public sphere as an extension of our community and our community as an extension of their efforts. In our feminist context, the function of art is to raise consciousness, invite dialogue and transform culture.

This definition of the function of art reflects our acknowledgment of the social nature of art. We are also committed to building an audience for women's work. In the past art that directed itself specifically to an audience with an overt social orientation has generally been called protest art or political illustration. Such art has never had the status of the various "isms," which have been surrounded by the aura of the "mystery of creation" and the "artist's creative process."

However, the forms that have developed in our feminist context, contrary to the tenets of earlier political protest art, have had a personal connection to the thoughts and lives of each woman. The forms that that have emerged—journal writing, performance, as well as in traditional media—have taken on special meaning when this personal connection was multiplied by more and more women sharing the same or similar experiences. Major art forms may emerge or develop out of this. Whether the social structure of the present art world will permit them to be recognized as major, however, is still an open question.

The existence of a feminist community—even in concept—is in profound conflict with the general society in which it occurs. While the colleges and art institutions that have on occasion invited and hosted our feminist programs have appeared to be congenial settings for those efforts, the programs have instead acted as foreign bodies on the organism of the university and, as any foreign body in an organism, have resulted in infection, fever, and ultimate rejection. The fundamental conflict is not primarily one between men and women; the difference is between the world views of people who participate in a feminist community and the traditional world views of the society in which they work and live. The ability of a feminist community to disrupt does not lie in its apparent separatism but in its strong critique of our culture's values and its position as a concrete alternative. The existence of a public forum for women's culture is essential to the dialogue that women must now have and is feminist education in its most fruitful form. Women's creative work can reveal a feminist vision of the future that moves us toward a more humane, egalitarian world.

NOTES

1. Our work at the Feminist Studio Workshop was preceded by Judy Chicago's women's class at Fresno State College, the Feminist Art Program, Womanhouse (Judy Chicago, Miriam Schapiro, Arlene Raven), the Women's Design Program (Sheila de Bretteville), and women's literature and writing classes (Deena Metzger), all at the California Institute of the Arts.

25

Sisterhood and Radical Feminist Art Education in a Catholic Women's College

JUDITH STOUGHTON

Sisterhood is a powerful and traditional reality. Whether we think of female tribal elders guarding, increasing, and communicating ancient wisdom and rite or of religious sisterhoods preserving and augmenting their heritages through the centuries, or of the radical contemporary feminist sisterhood probing and confronting tradition while working eagerly to create a just and humane society for all, we are in touch with a life-giving creative power and spirit.

Feminist art education at The College of St. Catherine in St. Paul, Minnesota, brought together the riches of the traditional and new feminist sisterhoods. The Sisters of St. Joseph of Carondolet who own and direct this college are an American group with some 3,500 members in Japan, Peru, and states from Hawaii to New York. Their history is filled with accounts of strong-willed women who moved out onto the cutting edge of the unknown to create and sustain radical answers to problems not yet solved by the larger society.

In Le Puy-en-Velay, France, the first six sisters, who came together in 1650, worked to alleviate social problems in their region so effectively that the sisterhood spread rapidly to other parts of southern France. The courage of their convictions brought death by guillotine to several sisters during the French Revolution. Others went underground and emerged again in Lyons and various parts of France with leaders strong enough to have a progeny today of 35,000 sisters of St. Joseph around the world. The Lyons group sent eight pioneer women to St. Louis in the 1830s to teach the deaf and other uncared for people. By river boat, covered wagon, and horseback the St. Louis sisters responded to needs throughout the nation, coming to St. Paul in 1851. Here they opened Minnesota's first private school and first high school for the education of girls and young women, St. Joseph's Academy. The sisters were soon also at work nursing cholera victims in a log cabin hospital, subsequently replaced by St. Joseph's Hospital, Minnesota's oldest hospital, serving patients from 1853 to the present day.

In 1905 they opened the first private college for women in Minnesota. Sister faculty were sent to study in the museums of Europe and the universities of Munich, Paris, Florence, Oxford, Madrid, Chicago, Columbia, and Minnesota at a time when few women were enrolled and Catholic opinion deemed these places "dangerous to the faith." By 1938 the academic reputation of this women's college was such that it was granted the first chapter of Phi Beta Kappa given to a Catholic university or college.

As colleges multiplied, many closed or merged with men's schools. Some sisterhoods relinquished ownership of their schools; however, St. Catherine's kept its identity as a women's liberal arts college, owned and directed by the sisterhood. It belongs to a five-college consortium whereby women and men students can elect classes on five campuses, but the resident population and student government remain a women's world at St. Catherine's. This long and steadfast record of quality liberal arts education for women prepared the ground into which a feminist art education program was planted.

In keeping with its historical penchant for a faculty of diverse preparation and gifts, St. Catherine's hired Robert Clark Nelson to direct its new art galleries and expanded art department in 1972. Coming from a professional designer's business and painter's world, as well as previous coed college teaching, Robert Nelson looked with a fresh eye at the unique strengths of this women's college.[1] Women's shows were invited into the galleries; exhibition tours, discussions, readings, and films were offered to the college community and the public; women artists of the area were invited to an open screening of their work. Kathryn C. Johnson was curator for an important Women's Work Show, and subsequently one entire year of gallery space was given to women alone. Carole Fisher joined the faculty in 1973 to help develop a feminist art program. She was curator for Judy Chicago's show, Metamorphosis, in 1975. As department chairperson, Nelson eagerly supported visiting women artists and a new course that the faculty approved, Women in Art. A month-long Feminist Art Workshop in January 1975, was so successful that an experimental Women's Art Core Program was planned, approved, and funded by grants for the academic 1975–1976 year.

From here on I speak out of personal experience as art historian in that program and two other concurrent feminist art history courses offered in the regular nonexperimental class schedule. I write also out of my long experience of belonging to a women's community. When the new wave of the women's movement came along, I sensed a coming together and centering of my political, professional, and spiritual concerns for bringing about a a just society. Our sisterhood had long been involved with women's education, and we were glad to see more women seriously entering the professions; however, I was not facing the radical new perspectives indicated by the feminist movement for educators of women in the arts.

The women from the Feminist Studio Workshop in Los Angeles changed all that. In January 1975, Judy Chicago came to our college with her exhibition, feminist art workshop sessions, and public lectures. Arlene Raven and Ruth Iskin shared their expertise in the same 1975 interim class and in public sessions. The input of these three women was critical in planning our year-long Women's Art Core program for 1975–76. Over the years, dialogue with many women artists and scholars visiting St. Catherine's prepared for the new program, which was in turn nourished by the presence of more creative women in the arts. The list is long including: Alice Babar, Mary Abbott, Nancy Piene, Dore Ashton, Jean Sutherland Boggs, Jean Gillies, Betsy Damon, Marisol Escobar, Harmony Hammond, Sheila de Bretteville, Elaine de Kooning, Lucy Lippard, and Rosalyn Drexler. During several weeks of the 1976 term Miriam Schapiro shared slides, stories, critiques, and friendship.

The new program was team-taught by three faculty members. Sister Ann Jennings coordinated the entire five-course program. Carole Fisher, who had joined the faculty to help develop the feminist art program, was responsible for studio work, and I taught the art history. Carole and Ann brought their planning and teaching experience from the 1975 interim. We three teachers went out to the Women's Building in Los Angeles for a series of classes at the Feminist Studio Workshop in the spring of 1975. Ann spent the summer there, and I spent a preparatory summer doing feminist art history research, while Carole continued her personal exploration in the studio, working toward her St. Catherine's Gallery two-woman show with Betsy Damon.

When the experimental program for 25 women began in the fall of 1975, a Monday through Friday two-class time block from 8:30 to 12:00 and large top floor studio space were assigned to it. From within the experiment unbroken time and space were great boons.

Art history was taught as a two-course survey of art with focus on female artists, patrons, and images, thus bringing to light new information and fresh insights that altered standard interpretations of art history. Weekly half-day sessions provided time for extended dialogue, inquiry, and enjoyment. Because of the varied backgrounds ranging from college freshmen to one woman with her M.A. in art history, students were asked to keep at hand any standard survey of art history so that they could fill in background material according to their needs. An example of the focus was the approach to ancient Near Eastern art through studying the particular cuneiform tablets that bear liturgical hymns of the priestess, Enheduanna. Fortunately this woman described herself in her own poetry praising Inanna, so it was possible to reconstruct some of the temple life around her activities as poet, theologian, and priestess. With the emphasis on this gifted woman, Sargon took his place in Akkadian history as her father, and the study of temple architecture and Mesopotamian myth was off to a good start.

Later in studying Golden Age Greece, one research project on Parthenon sculpture centered on a study of the image of Athena, the political use that was made of her image, and the previous forms it had taken all the way back to her cult in Libya. Motivation to fill in this kind of information was exceptionally high, and long hours were spent in digging out information needed to clarify the history of art from a feminist perspective.

How was this different from a regular survey of art history? The feminist focus expanded content and made fresh research demands on students and faculty. Instead of learning the content of a text and lectures and proving their knowledge on an examination of that content, students were tracking down footnotes and getting back into the sources used by textbook writers. They were engaged in challenging the completeness and interpretation of the historical record as well as the current record of living artists. Along with gallery shows and visiting artists, contemporary women artists, historians, and critics were studied by all available means.

A second way in which the feminist approach was different was the responsibility accepted by students for sharing accurate research and personal reflection based on data. At the end of the year an art history marathon night went on from 5:00 P.M. until midnight because there was still so much to share. In this kind of class the teacher abandons the old securities of a series of predetermined lectures. The limits of topics are no longer neatly defined because students are continually raising questions and suggesting new insights. Certainly some faculty and guest lectures are part of the input, but a more important faculty role is that of a continuing researcher in feminist art history; there is constant need for fruitful clues that can lead beyond present textbooks. The disciplined scholarship of faculty is also needed to restrain students from making declarations of fact out of suppositions they want to be true.

Another difference is that the class becomes a community of women who care about one another's progress. They expect, need, and support one another's achievement. Although there were individual instances of boredom, hostility, and laziness, the general level of learning and enthusiasm for art history was incredibly high. Many students remained together in a collective, whose members can be called on for lectures in feminist art history. Thus the pattern of responsibility for continued research and sharing goes on.

Because core students were also involved in consciousness-raising, studio work, and critiques, these aspects all interacted fruitfully with art history. Students were encouraged to get at personal content and express it in the most suitable medium. A study of Chinese art bore fruit in a delicate and moving series of serigraphs. Greek vase painting and architectural detail appeared transformed by personal vision in drawings and photographs, while both spontaneous ritual and planned performance grew out of the experience of holistic learning. Mind, body, imagination, and spirit were all active, growing, and productive.

This kind of cognitive and affective growth was not as evident in the other feminist art history courses I taught in the regular curriculum. The community bond and unbroken dialogue among core students gave them the best learning experience without any doubt.

Nonetheless, similar content and methodology in the other classes, although pursued in a more limited way, brought the history of art to life for students in a way not experienced before. I am aware of several students from these classes who are continuing their research and giving feminist art history lectures. In both kinds of courses students did become sisters and colleagues, and happily, the professor or Sister became simply a small letter sister.

Has feminist art education affected other classes at all? Yes, I am aware of involving students much more in planning courses according to their needs and desires, with shared responsibility for input and care for the achievement of all, rather than grade-conscious competition. Renewed emphasis on content as well as form and on group work as well as individual work seems to be as helpful to men students as to women.

Women's studies in all fields help complete the historical record and are well accepted in a women's liberal arts college, but this is only one component of feminist education. Without a radical alteration of schedule, environment, and grading, an expanded content and changed methodology are limited in their effectiveness. They can only prod students and faculty toward becoming a sharing, nonauthoritarian, caring community of creative people. Fully effective feminist art education either breaks the old institutional mold or it must take place in alternative educational environments.

Some schools are able to sustain really experimental programs alongside traditional ones with varying degrees of tension; however, the high visibility, the energy, and the imagery of a successful feminist art education program may be too much for the present readiness of many institutions.

How does our experience of feminist art education within a Catholic women's college relate to the present state of the sisterhood responsible for the college? These women have all been involved very recently in community evaluation and rapid adaptation of lifestyle to contemporary life. Many individual sisters have moved out of institutional work, while remaining members of the sisterhood, to seek radical answers to problems our society has not yet solved. Individual sisters hold widely divergent views, while still remaining together on essential commitments.

Sisters from the traditional sisterhood who choose to work in feminist art education may also need to leave institutional work to be effective. This is not because of the nature of the sisterhood but because of the institution whose liberal arts faculty as a whole, lay and religious, male and female, is receptive now only to the women's studies stage of development.

In the larger society many persons have no interest in feminism. In traditional sisterhoods many women have no such interest. On the other hand, women from both groups are already bringing together their own particular strengths, talents, and life-styles into a life-giving creative and powerful sisterhood. The Women's Art Core Program at St. Catherine's proved to be a catalyst effecting such cooperative growth.

NOTES

1. Robert Clark Nelson, Chairperson of St. Catherine's Art Department, in a letter to the administration and faculty wrote: "What should be our part in educating women in the arts? Not that our department is not already educating women for the arts but it seems to me we are educating women only incidentally. Our procedures could be applied to anyone, any group, any sex. I feel we have to do something more. It is our place and our responsibility to develop programs, procedures, and become a part of the new rising tide in the arts. In the 1950s the major movement in the visual arts was Abstract Expressionism. In the '60s it was color field and Minimal art. In the '70s it is women's art. I believe this is a decade of women on many fronts, and the movement by women in the visual arts is the single most original, powerful innovation today."

26

Architecture:
Towards a Feminist Critique

ELLEN PERRY BERKELEY

Architecture has always been very much a "gentleman's profession." In 1948, an architectural journal found that only 108 practicing architects were women.[1] Twenty-five years later, when the American Institute of Architects appointed a task force to study the status of women in the profession, the task force found that only 1.2 percent of the 42,043 registered architects were women.[2]

Because the numbers have been so small, the "built" environment has indeed been "man-made." Only very recently have the image and actuality begun to change—and only very slightly. But young girls can at least think of themselves as architects now, through efforts such as these:

- A slim book for the beginning reader (aged four to ten) called *What Can She Be? An Architect*. The book never hints that being a woman and an architect is unusual; it simply shows a real person in her daily activities as both.[3]
- An educational package for teenagers produced by a New York group, the Alliance of Women in Architecture. The package has a lively videotape (showing professional women and men), a pamphlet on architectural education, and a slide show on the work of women architects.[4]
- A brief animation on TV's *Sesame Street*, in which a little girl draws lines that magically connect to become drawings of buildings. "Maybe, some day, if I wanted to, I could be somebody who makes buildings, or bridges, or even whole cities."

But the old messages linger. Girls may now play at carpentry, but the sexist sell of TV toy commercials still shows boys mainly in an adventurous arena and girls mainly in the shelter of home.[5] The messages are still different for girls and boys.

IMPLICATIONS OF "ENVIRONMENTAL COMPETENCE"

An extremely provocative analysis of these mixed messages is found in a paper on "The Development of Environmental Competence in Girls and Boys" (by Susan Saegert and Roger Hart, of the Department of Environmental Psychology of the City University of New York).[6]

Girls and boys are clearly allowed different freedoms in their spatial range, Saegert and Hart write. Boys are expected to explore more and to get into more trouble—"boys will be boys" as the saying goes. Girls are expected to become "companions" to their mothers, helping with the domestic chores while boys run the errands. More startling: "Boys modify the landscape more frequently and more effectively," say Saegert and Hart. When girls do build houses and forts (less often than boys), girls modify the spaces more often in their imaginations—bushes become walls, branches become shelves, rocks become seats. Rarely do girls make fixed walls or roofs, preferring to put considerable effort toward "the detailed elaboration of the interior" with drapes, bottles, pots, and pans.[7]

Erik Erikson noted similar differences in his studies—boys created elaborate buildings with protruding towers; girls made "simple walls which merely enclose interiors, with an emphasis by ornamentation on the vestibular access to the interior." But Saegert and Hart doubt that the explanation lies "only or even" where Erikson placed it. In Erikson's words "the analogy between the sex differences in play configurations and the primary physiological sex differences, that is, in the male the emphasis on the external, the erectable, the intrusive, and the mobile—in the female, on the internal, on the vestibular, on the static, on what is contained and endangered in the interior."[8]

Instead, Saegert and Hart argue, suitable activities for the two sexes are strongly influenced by the attitudes, rules, and expectations of adults and peers:

> Erikson should have noticed that girls are encouraged from early on to decorate and to play out social events in interiors—notably in dolls' houses—while boys are encouraged to build them.[9]

Saegert and Hart conclude that because girls are restrained by parents, teachers, and peers (in their exploration and manipulation of the environment), they are denied "a possible area of competence and adventure." Lack of experience and lack of confidence tend to diminish the spatial ability of girls—an ability of general value (in mathematical reasoning and general problem solving) and of critical importance in certain occupations such as architecture. The development of spatial ability is complex—it is partly inherited—but Saegert and Hart point out that no sex differences in spatial ability can be noticed until the age of eight. By adolescence, however, boys are far ahead, and in adulthood the ability can be found in 50 percent of all men and 25 percent of all women.[10]

Still, women make up considerably less than 25 percent of the professions requiring this aptitude, note Saegert and Hart. An interesting four-page paper by Jon J. Durkin, called "The Potential of Women," also mentions the 50 to 25 percent differential. Durkin suggests that the aptitude of "structural visualization" is basic to "the physical sciences, medicine, all forms of real engineering, architecture, city planning, building, mechanics, etc."[11] To this list I would add design in all its three-dimensional forms: sculpture, industrial design, and the like.

Undeniably, the development of these aptitudes—structural visualization and spatial ability—is still being inhibited among girls. The final word in the paper by Saegert and Hart is compelling:

> The difference in the experience of the two sexes is analogous to (and usually includes) the difference between the knowledge about an environment gained when one is a passenger in a vehicle and when one is the driver. . . . The driver is allowed decision making, experimentation, and self-directed learning of the environment, while the passenger can only suggest and observe.[12]

THE FEMINIST CRITIQUE

Quite apart from the image that women and girls have of themselves, however, is the image that men and boys have of them. The architectural profession, overwhelmingly male, has never been hospitable to women, considering them merely adept at domestic architecture, the only sector of the profession deemed fully appropriate for women and, therefore, the only sector not fully *in* the profession.

The professional schools, too, have never been hospitable to women, hoping to "counsel away" all but the most stubborn and single-minded. Private tutoring and apprenticeship were widely accepted routes into the profession in the early days; the only difficulty was finding a teacher or sponsor who would accept a woman. But the major place for an architectural education increasingly came to be the collegiate schools of architecture, the schools within the established centers of learning. Some of the most prestigious schools accepted women fairly late; Harvard took women for the first time during World War II, and one woman recalled, 30 years later, "no one was fooled for a minute. . . . they needed us to replace the men being drafted."[13]

Instead of dwelling on the factors keeping women out of the architectural profession, however, let us look at the possibilities suggested by the presence of more women in the architectural profession. Simply having more women architects would be a hollow victory. I believe that the real problem for a thoughtful woman is not whether she *is* accepted into the profession as it is now, but whether she *wants* to be accepted into this profession as it is now.

Many women (and men too) believe that the profession is not doing its best for the users of buildings (hospital patients, office workers, residents, and so on), and some of these women are bringing a feminist perspective to this critique. One architecture student, in her graduate thesis, proposed an entirely new "environment for birth," in which childbirth is considered a natural event and not an illness. Another graduate student evaluated several well-known housing projects built for married students, but evaluated them from the viewpoint of the young mothers in the projects. She concluded that the daily life of these women was not carefully considered in the design of the projects, and as a result the women's lives were filled with inconveniences and loneliness.

The feminist critique is not merely a critique without action. One architectural office, composed entirely of women, designed a low-budget project for a restaurant being run by women; to save money on the construction, the architects designed interiors that could easily be built by the clients. Then, knowing that women often lack basic carpentry skills, the architects instructed the clients in the skills needed.

Some women—faculty members in the architecture schools—have developed entire courses on issues important to women. One course, at Columbia University, has studied the impact on women of urban planning in America. It concluded that the assumptions made by planners about women have often been out-of-date and rigid, confining women to home and society roles that women do not want and, in fact, do not any longer fill.

Such courses and projects in the architecture schools are still rare, perhaps because they require the approval of administrators who are mostly men. It is for this reason that the so-called alternative institutions for women have been created by women in many fields.

WSPA: THE WOMEN'S SCHOOL OF PLANNING AND ARCHITECTURE

I was one of the seven women who started the Women's School of Planning and Architecture, the first such school to be completely founded, financed, and run by women. (We call it WSPA, pronounced WIS-PA.) We held the first session of WSPA during August 1975, the second during August 1976, and the third during August 1978. Each time we rented facilities of an existing university: one in Maine, one in California, and one in Rhode Island. Each time we had more than 50 women living together and learning together for an intensive two-week session.[14]

The reasons for the creation of WSPA are summed up in the poster announcing the 1976 session: "Our purpose remains two-fold—to create a personally supportive environment for the free exchange of ideas and knowledge, and to encourage both personal

and professional growth through a fuller integration of our values
and identities as women with our values and identities as designers."
An account of what we did will further explain our purposes in
starting WSPA:

- We wanted to avoid the hierarchical system found in most traditional schools. We hoped that every participant could be a
  teacher in her own way, and to a rewarding extent she was. In
  addition, some participants from the first session became coordinators (our term for organizers and teachers) for the later sessions.
- We wanted to bring together women involved in various ways in
  the design of the built environment. We had landscape architects, planners, architects, weavers, carpenters, interior designers, environmental psychologists, and others. We learned a
  great deal about our work, our world, ourselves, and we left with
  new strength in our combined ideas and abilities.
- We wanted to give every woman a sense of her own validity; we
  wanted to honor the special interests and skills of every woman.
  In a profession composed primarily of men, women are often
  made to feel different and unworthy; we wanted our women to
  feel different, if they chose to, but no less worthy.
- We wanted to have women of all ages and all levels of experience. The age range, in fact, was 18 to 58. The mix was extremely stimulating and important to everyone: to students looking for role models, to teachers rethinking traditional methods,
  and to practitioners seeking contact with new people and new
  ideas.
- We wanted to provide (and experience) a new kind of living-
  and-learning situation. And we did—talking, laughing, crying,
  learning, working, playing together for almost 24 hours a day for
  two jam-packed weeks.
- We wanted—not least—to offer courses and approaches not
  found in the conventional schools. Thus, in the first session, we
  evaluated the built environment from a feminist view. We
  explored our ideas and values with a new openness. We discussed the several professional offices in which cooperation, and
  not hierarchy, was the goal. We studied planning by interviewing
  local women (mostly nonprofessionals) who were changing their

own communities. We learned carpentry. And so on. Our second session expanded on some of these subjects and added others: politics and ideology in planning; architectural tapestry; energy-conscious design. Our third session centered on a single theme, "Workplaces and Dwellings: Implications for Women," and drew on the experiences of women working in the public and private sectors of development in this country and elsewhere. During each session, the schedule left room for spontaneous discussion on diverse subjects and on projects brought to WSPA by participants.

WSPA has meant different things to different people. For some it has been an impetus for major change in professional direction. For others, it has been an eye-opener in the possibilities of a supportive community. For those of us involved as coordinators, it has been an often agonizing attempt to create a new model (and a continually evolving model at that)—a new model of education, of community, of organization, of professional responsibility. WSPA has been an attempt by one group of women to pursue goals we consider important, and to pursue them in ways we consider honorable.[15]

TOWARDS A NEW PROFESSIONALISM

The real questioning by some women architects, it seems to me, is towards a new definition of professionalism—what one does, why, how, and for whom. And the new feminism has often seemed stronger than the old professionalism.

Some design professionals, for instance, have been urging women who lack a design background to honor their hopes and dreams about the environment.[16] Others have been working with clients in a more open way (and working with each other in a more open way, which is equally important). Others are trying to make the larger public aware of women's needs so that the built environment of the future will not restrict, demean, and frustrate women as it has in the past.[17]

Still others are looking toward a time when men and women will share in the responsibilities of home and family, while sharing in the challenges of productive and creative work outside the home.[18] Until more feminists become architects—or until more architects become feminists—the society will be stuck with such absurdities as these:

- In a major new office building, only the men's rest rooms are outfitted with lights to encourage reading. (Is it assumed that reading by women would be "wasting company time"?)
- A man can take his little daughter neither to a public men's room nor to the ladies'. (Is it assumed that baby-tending is not a daddy's job?)
- Tiny closed-off kitchens are unpleasant to work in and disruptive of social relationships. (Is it assumed that opening a kitchen to public view is unacceptable, but that making the lady-of-the-house into a scullery maid is "refined"?)

I have emphasized function over form here to emphasize the fact that architecture is more than a visual art; indeed, some of the worst of the "form-making" in twentieth century architecture has denied all human needs, female and male, and architects of both sexes are rebelling against such arbitrariness of design. Whether women architects will find their own imagery, however, and whether this imagery will be exclusive to women is another question. Not many women architects have the desire or the security (emotional and financial) to think about this question, although the phallic skyscraper comes in for some light-hearted ridicule and heavy-handed abuse. My own view about skyscrapers is that they can be humane or inhumane, according to many qualities of form and function. And my own view about special imagery is that it must be approached with caution. An imagery may not be natural to an entire group of designers and may not be universal to an entire group of users. Ultimately, my plea is for an architecture that meets people's needs—individual needs, including aesthetic needs. I am wary of having any special imagery foisted on people just because an architect (of whatever sex) thinks it will be good for them.

WOMEN AND CHANGE

I am not a prophet, but I can't resist thinking that for the architectural profession to survive in any real sense—doing well at the important tasks—the profession (and the education for it) must respond in precisely the directions suggested by various women.

What are these directions? For one thing, a new link with the great mass of nonprofessionals, accepting them as people with their own values, not as tasteless slobs to be manipulated for a fee (if they *have* the fee). From this follows all else—a new working relationship with clients, a new sensitivity to users, a new demystification of architectural ideas and skills and jargon.

Some men surely want this—and don't just say so because it is still fashionable to want to be relevant. Conversely, some women surely want "in" to the profession as it is, want membership in an elite profession and do not want that profession to change. Yet it will change and partly because of women. The architectural profession will lose some of its elite status as the percentage of women rises. And the profession will thus be open even further to women. Men know well what they have been doing, keeping women out of their clubs and professions, out of their world.

What women make of their presence in the architectural profession is a great unknown.[19] I defend, eagerly, any woman's right to do any kind of architectural work (including the work that the stereotype finds her "best suited" for, namely, domestic architecture), especially if she does so in a way that responds to women's changing needs and life-styles—and men's, too. Housing is the basic shelter of a society, no less important than all its monuments. New kinds of housing can encourage new social relationships or can more gracefully support the existing relationships.

Women have been making environments longer than women have been studying to be architects. We can wait eagerly to see what may happen when the environment is no longer "man-made."

NOTES

1. "A Thousand Women in Architecture," *Architectural Record* 103 (March 1948): 105–113; 103 (June 1948): 108–115.
2. *Report of the Task Force on Women in Architecture*, American Institute of Architects, 1975. For further information on the AIA's task force and affirmative action plan, write to the AIA, 1735 New York Avenue NW, Washington, D.C. 20006.

3. Gloria and Esther Goldreich, with photographs by Robert Ipcar, *What Can She Be? An Architect* (New York: Lathrop, Lee and Shepard, 1974).

4. For information on the availability of this package, write to the Alliance of Women in Architecture, P.O. Box 5136, FDR Station, New York, N.Y. 10022.

5. "The Sexist Sell," *Toy Review* 1, no. 3 (December 1972): 62.

6. Susan Saegert and Roger Hart, "The Development of Environmental Competence in Girls and Boys" in *Play: Anthropological Perspectives*, ed. Michael A. Salter (1977 Proceedings of the Association for the Anthropological Study of Play). (West Point, NY: Leisure Press, 1978), pp. 157–75.

7. Ibid.

8. *Discussions on Child Development VIII* (Proceedings of the Third Meeting of the WHO Study Group on the Psychobiological Development of the Child, eds. J. M. Tanner and Barbel Inhelder). (London: Tavistock Publications, 1955), p. 112.

9. Saegert and Hart, "The Development of Environmental Competence in Girls and Boys."

10. Ibid.

11. Jon J. Durkin, *The Potential of Women* (Boston: Human Engineering Laboratory, 1971).

12. Saegert and Hart, "The Development of Sex Differences.

13. Letter from Margaret (Peg) K. Hunter to *Architecture Plus*, July 31, 1974. For a full discussion of the extraordinary Cambridge School of Architecture and Landscape Architecture, which educated almost 500 women (and no men) between the years 1915 and 1942, see Doris Cole, *From Tipi to Skyscraper: A History of Women in Architecture* (Boston: i press, 1973). Her chapter on the Cambridge School was also published in *Architecture Plus* 1, no. 11 (December 1973): 30–35; 78–79.

14. The founding coordinators of WSPA were: Katrin Adam, Ellen Perry Berkeley, Noel Phyllis Birkby, Bobbie Sue Hood, Marie Kennedy, Joan Forrester Sprague, and Leslie Kanes Weisman.

15. For information on past or future activities, write to WSPA at Box 311, Shaftsbury, Vt. 05262.

16. Noel Phyllis Birkby and Leslie Kanes Weisman, "A Woman-Built Environment: Constructive Fantasies," *Quest: A Feminist Quarterly* 2, no. 1 (Summer 1975).

17. Clare Cooper, *Easter Hill Village: Some Social Implications of Design* (New York: Free Press, 1975). This is an excellent analysis of what

Cooper calls "the dichotomy of male-dominated provision vs. female-dominated consumption of a home environment."

18. Ellen Perry Berkeley, "The Swedish Servicehus" *Architecture Plus* 1, no. 4 (May 1973): 56–59. The service house can be defined as multi-family housing with certain services readily available for purchase or already included in the rent: food from a central kitchen, day care, and assistance on all kinds of daily chores and emergency needs. See also Dolores Hayden, "Collectivizing the Domestic Workplace," *Lotus* 12 (1976) reprinted as "Redesigning the Domestic Workplace," *Chrysalis* 1 (1977).

19. *Women in American Architecture: A Historic and Contemporary Perspective*, ed. Susana Torre (New York: Whitney Library of Design, 1977) provides the most comprehensive look at women in architecture yet published. This volume accompanied the exhibition at the Brooklyn Museum organized by the Architectural League of New York through its Archive of Women in Architecture. For information on the use of the Archive and the loan of the exhibition, write to the Archive at 41 East 65 Street, New York, N.Y. 10021.

IV
Feminist Mandates For
Institutional Change

27

Returning to School:
Nontraditional Women in the Visual Arts

HELEN COLLIER
and
JESSIE LOVANO-KERR

Women who return to college after an absence of five or more years may already, it seems, be a major component of our student population rather than the oddity they once were, and it is clearly time that the universities reexamined the appropriateness of the services they offer these students. Bureau of the Census data for 1974 show that enrollments in that year included a higher proportion of older students than at any time since the early 1950s: one in three undergraduates was over 25, and one in ten over 35. And a very significant proportion of those older students consisted of women: 42 percent of those under 35 and 53 percent of those over 35.[1]

The trend to increased enrollments of older women has been evident for some years. The number of women over 30 enrolled in higher education courses throughout the country doubled between 1963 and 1973.[2] And the trend continues. For example, in 1977 the University of Wisconsin at Green Bay reported not only that more women were enrolled than men—for the first time in its history—but that the significant growth in the female student population was among the group over age 25.[3] The phenomenon of increased enrollments among older women is a recent development, but one of such substance and apparent permanence that it has profound implications for colleges and universities, for the women themselves, and (as this chapter emphasizes) for visual arts programs.

By 1975 women clearly dominated enrollments in the visual arts. In that year they received more than three-quarters of the bachelors degrees in art education, two-thirds of those in art studio, and four-fifths in art history/art appreciation, and of all recipients of master's degrees in the visual arts area, 53 percent were women.[4] The ages of these students are unfortunately unrecorded, but it is probable that returning women students over 25 were well-represented. A search of professional literature shows no sign that visual arts programs are attending to the special needs of the mature, returning women students, though changes in the curricular structure and the counseling programs for visual arts students are clearly appropriate. The purpose of this chapter is to suggest where those changes need to be made.

From experience with the influx of veterans after World War II and the Korean War, we know that an infusion of adult values possessed by older students affects a number of processes and structures in higher education. As the number of women returning to colleges and universities increases, their impact on what is taught and how it is taught may be even greater, especially because their economic situation and needs tend to be complex. The conjunction of two forces should make professional educators aware of the need to modify their institutions: (1) the impact of enrollment by older students, compensating for the predicted decline in younger student enrollment caused by lower birth rates beginning in the mid-1960s; and (2) the growing awareness of older women students concerning their own needs.[5] To make its future easier, higher education needs to ask: What are these needs? How do they affect the institution? What factors other than age distinguish returning women students from traditional women students? What can be done to improve the quality of experience and education for returning women students in the visual arts?

CHARACTERISTICS OF THE NONTRADITIONAL WOMAN STUDENT

To clarify possible changes in programs, curricula, and services, we need to define the characteristics of nontraditional or mature women students as a group.

Demographic Information

Nontraditional women students range in age from the mid-20s through the 50s. Many are married. Many have children. Many have been married and are now separated, divorced, or widowed, and a smaller proportion have remained unmarried. A high proportion have worked or are working, generally in a fairly low-income career. Typically they have begun a formal education beyond high school, but they tend to have been away from school for at least ten years. The population profile of a special women's program (WING) at Queen's College of the City of New York seems representative: an average age of 38 (range 23–53); married with children; some previous formal education beyond high school.[6]

The Generational Effect

Because of generational experiences, each age group tends to have a homogeneity that is helpful to their educators, but teachers cannot expect the same homogeneity in a group whose members were born any time between 1920 and 1950. As Lillian Troll has convincingly demonstrated, to begin to understand adult students we must first account for the effects of different life experiences among the various age groups, what she calls "the generational effect.[7] The following summary of Troll's findings suggests some of the differences between returning women students born variously in the 1920s, 1930s, and 1940's.

1. Women born in the 1920s were young children during the Depression, and they tend, therefore, to have witnessed or experienced economic want. They were deeply involved in World War II. They produced the postwar baby-boom, and they were the generation described by Betty Friedan's *The Feminine Mystique*. Compared with their successors in the 1970s, their lives—at the crucial decision points during adolescence and early adulthood—were highly restricted by a succession of strong cultural influences beyond their control.
2. Women born in the 1930s were children during World War II, with their menfolk often absent in the Armed forces or, after the war, enrolled in college. They became teen-agers in the post war

period of increasing affluence. Compared with women of the previous decade, they married early, had children earlier, and produced large families. When they reached their 30s, they began to be affected by the women's movement and other changing opportunities and expectations in the social, political, and economic environment.

3. Women born in the 1940s, as either war babies or part of the baby boom, grew up taking for granted a "modern" life their predecessors had not experienced: the age of the automobile, television, atomic bombs, space travel, routine exposure to the internationalization of communications, availability of labor-saving devices, and so forth. Apparently freer from cultural determinants than their predecessors, this group grew more diverse sooner. In the 1960s some married young and bore children early, while others "dropped out" with the support of the growing youth culture. The growth in national attention to the needs of women began to affect them while they were still young but not until a majority had already made crucial choices as to life-style—choices the 1970s have seen many of them unmake.

Without elaborating on the nature of the women students born in the 1950s and 60s, the generation to which higher education is currently directing its primary attention, it can still be seen that older women have values, attitudes, motivations, and life-styles constructed out of very different cultural experiences from more youthful students.

Developmental Aspects

In addition to the influences of their culture on their past development, older women are also affected by present cultural influences, especially those related to their age and socio-economic situation. Bernice Neugarten suggests in her various writings that whereas the early stages of human development are dominated by biological events, the adult stage is governed much more by social events, and certainly there is a complex relationship between chronological age and the experiences and circumstances of life.[8] Some of those social and economic influences especially affecting older women are: (1) the growth of children, which frees a woman's time and energy and lightens her commitment to homemaking; (2) divorce, separation, or death, which result in sharp economic and social changes; (3) internal shifts in the life span perspective brought about by increasing age and typified by the recognition that time is not endless and that goals cannot be postponed much longer; (4) widening opportunities in the labor market, accompanied by changing social and economic aspirations both by and for women; and (5) a marked shift from previous strong affiliation needs to new and equally strong achievement needs.

This last influence may be the most important. Women tend to have been raised by the "vicarious achievement ethic" as identified by Jean Lipman-Blumen, finding a large part of their identity by affiliation with others, notably husband and children.[9] The shift to achievement needs, as discussed by Troll,[10] is exemplified by an adult woman moving steadily into a period of outward expansion during her 30s, 40s, and 50s. At this time women become more concerned with the outer world, and they experience a greater need to make some achievement in it, thus neatly matching the reverse tendency that tends to occur simultaneously in men. Changes of this magnitude, occurring often unrecognized in both men and women, tend to create friction and conflict in marriage, and they encompass such a major shift in role expectations that they may well be one of the worst problems confronted by nontraditional women students.

Thus, basic factors of adult development are likely to create in many mature women a desire and/or a need to return to school, which remains our society's major avenue either for completing career training set aside years before, or for starting a new career, or for acquiring additional skills to move upward in an existing career.

Personality

Personality differences between adult and traditional women students have long been apparent to educators, and the adult students' higher level of achievement and stronger career motivation are now being confirmed by research. One study, for example, showed Wellesley College's older women students higher both in achievement attained through independence and autonomy and in the degree to which they respond to the inner needs, motives, and experiences of others—an attribute thought to have been developed by the nurtur-

ing role socially assigned to older women.[11] In another study, older
married women students had higher levels of achievement motivation and lower "fear of success" scores than did unmarried traditional
women students.[12] As teachers often recognize, personality differences of this nature often dramatically affect students' approaches to
a curriculum.

Vocational Development

There is evidence that women's vocational interests are organized
very differently from men's and tend to crystallize later.[13] Ginzberg
found that the career planning of women contains a great deal of
uncertainty; it is regulated by such factors as financial status, choice
of a marriage partner, and freedom in marriage.[14] Freedom seems to
be determined by the attitude of husbands toward educated and
career women and by the number of living or planned children. The
interrupted career is often chosen by women, rarely by men. Wom-
en's choices are, therefore, often made on the basis of whether a
career is such that one can move out of it and back to it at will.

Many older women returning to college are in the process of
freeing themselves from influences and patterns that determined
their earlier choices. Only in their 30s, 40s, or 50s do they crystallize
a career choice. Vocational theories developed for males do not fit
them, nor do vocational theories developed for young people,
whether male or female. For the first time in their lives, they may be
making a serious commitment of the kind males usually make at a
much earlier age and younger women either make while young or,
like their predecessors, postpone.

The Multiple Roles

Mature women live in a web of responsibilities: as wife, mother,
daughter to aging parents, community participant, worker, or friend.
In addition to the student role, older women students thus fulfill
multiple roles that younger women students have not yet assumed
and that vie for their time and energy. They have commitments both
they and society expect them to fulfill. The world outside the educational institution gives them approval for fulfilling these customary
roles, but not (as yet) for the student role. Often, therefore, they

function as students without support in their home, work, and social life—indeed, often with overt or implied disapproval. At the same time, the educational institution does not fully recognize their needs, aspirations, and difficulties. The result is that as individuals and as a group they remain isolated and unsupported wherever they function, with a resultant intensification of the multiple roles, which often results in conflict and, for the student role, defeat.

Age Bias

Our culture tends to perceive men as growing wiser, more distinguished, and more competent with age, but it sees older women as less needed and attractive.[15] There is thus a double bias against gender and age, against which returning women students must contend. They often report feeling that teachers do not "take them seriously." Such attitudes affect their own self-concepts, and lowered self-esteem further distorts the responses of the educational institution. Achievement expectations both of and for older women may well be lower than for men ("Why would you want to go back to school?") or inappropriate for a successful career ("I have to do something to fill in my time.") In particular, we find some evidence that youthful educators do not expect older people to be planning for a career at all, an activity they see as the prerogative of the young.

IMPLICATIONS FOR CHANGE

The implications for needed change in programming, academic advising, and counseling in the visual arts for the returning women students are reflected in the previous discussion. Basic considerations of this group differ from the traditional student and are fundamental in determining change. Returning women students:

1. are older and generally more highly motivated; their values and attitudes toward education differ from those of the traditional student.
2. are more career oriented, more highly committed to a profession and the pursuit of a profession since conflicts regarding

career or marriage, faced by younger women students, have been resolved or are being openly confronted.

3. may be less mobile because their multiple roles may limit job possibilities to a specific geographic location and may require more innovative, nontraditional visual arts career options.

4. usually have very limited time or very specific times when classes, advising, and counseling can be scheduled, because of multiple roles.

5. have special financial aid needs related to part-time status and their multiple roles.

6. have social and communal needs that differ in kind from those of the traditional student, since the educational institutions have support systems and resources geared to the younger student, particularly the younger male.

7. need to be evaluated for admission by methods that differ from current procedures, which are designed for the traditional student.

8. may require special assistance in reestablishing basic academic and study skills.

9. are experiencing stresses and frustrations related to school that differ in kind and intensity from those of traditional students and require recognition by staff and faculty of these special problems they are facing.

10. because of the limited educational and general career opportunites they have had, little awareness has developed of viable heights to which they can and should aspire in a profession.

RECOMMENDATIONS

The following recommendations, based on the needs of returning women students, are proposed for possible changes in visual arts programming, academic advising and counseling.

For Visual Arts Departments

1. Career options in the visual arts should be researched to determine alternatives to the traditional role of teaching at the

elementary, secondary, or college level as a primary or secondary profession. Alternatives might include:

    a. Nontraditional teaching areas such as: learning and recreational centers for the older person; continuing education classes and other nondegree programs; museum education programs; art therapy; exceptional children in hospitals and special schools; children's classes after school hours; parks and recreation programs; and camp programs.

    b. Nontraditional art careers for women such as: architecture, industrial design, scenery design, or art director/arts administrator.

    c. Graphic independent careers such as: craft alliances or outlets, artist or gallery cooperatives, or free lance designing of fabrics, stationery, book illustrations, greeting cards and other decorative or utilitarian objects.

2. Program changes should include the necessary preparatory courses for new career options and availability of refresher courses to up-date the skills necessary for reentry into a field long vacated.

3. Each visual arts department should be cognizant of the job opportunities in the arts in the immediate vicinity and advise students accordingly so that decision making for the non-mobile student can be based on reality.

4. Psychological and social support groups consisting of returning women students should be organized within departments.

For Universities

1. Flexible scheduling of courses and advising hours should be adopted. These changes might include evenings and Saturdays if need is demonstrated.

2. Adequate and inexpensive university supported and initiated child care facilities should be established to serve all women in the institution.

3. More opportunities should be available for self-instruction and advance placement.

4. Provisions should be made for faculty orientation to the special characteristics, needs, and problems of returning women students.

5. Financial aid should be made available for the part-time student.

CONCLUSIONS

Demographic and social changes are occurring within our society that will affect our educational, political, and economic institutions. For example, we are approaching zero population growth while the average age is increasing yearly. Not only is our population becoming older, but people are living longer lives and working more years—many are opting for second careers and mid-life careers. Adult and continuing educational programs are increasing and expanding. Research on adult human development is revealing the unknown physical and intellectual potential of older adults. Research on the development of women has been instrumental in the passage of a number of state and federal laws on women's rights and in raising the consciousness of both women and men about the status of women in our society. As a result, women are in transition—exploring alternative life-styles and their own identities. Many of these women return to school in mid-life to reexamine undeveloped potentials interrupted by early life decisions and to pursue newly discovered motivations and aspirations. They need special assistance for reentry into a situation long synonymous with youth in which processes, procedures, and services are still primarily geared to serve the traditional student.

If institutions are to respond to the predicted fast-growing enrollment population, i.e., mature women, changes in institutional processes, structures, and services must begin to take place. Concurrent with these larger institutional changes, visual arts departments, in order for their programs to be relevant to their own student population, which is overwhelmingly women and, increasingly, mature women, must examine their programs and processes and begin to make immediate changes. The recommendations suggested in this chapter would be a start in implementing this needed change.

NOTES

1. "School Enrollment: Social and Economic Characteristics of Students," *Current Population Reports* Series P-20, no. 286 (Government Printing Office, November, 1975), pp. 1–2.

2. Esther M. Westervelt, "A Tide in the Affairs of Women: the Psychological Impact of Feminism on Educated Women," *Counseling Psychologist 3 (1973): 5.*

3. *The Women's Newsletter* (University of Wisconsin at Green Bay) (March 11, 1977): 1.

4. "Degrees Awarded in Various Fields, 1975," *Chronicle of Higher Education* 13, no. 13 (November 29, 1976): 8.

5. Adelene Levine, "Between the Stages of Life: Adult Women on a College Scene, *Educational Horizons* 54, no. 4 (Summer, 1976): 154–162.

6. Judith B. Brandenburg, "The Needs of Women Returning to School," *The Personnel and Guidance Journal* 53, no. 1 (September, 1974): 11–18.

7. Lillian E. Troll, *Early and Middle Adulthood* (Monterey, Calif.:Brooks/Cole, 1975), pp. 11–13.

8. Bernice L. Neugarten, ed., *Middle age and Aging* (Chicago, University of Chicago Press, 1968).

9. Jean Lipman-Blumen and Harold J. Leavitt, "Vicarious and Direct Achievement Patterns in Adulthood," in *Counseling Adults*, eds. Nancy K. Schlossberg and Alan D. Entine, (Monterey, Calif.: Brooks/Cole, 1977), pp. 60–76.

10. Troll, *Early and Middle Adulthood.*

11. Betty Lou N. Marple, "Adult Women Students Compared with Younger Students on Selected Personality Variables," *Journal of the National Association for Women Deans, Administrators, and Counselors* 40, no. 1 (Fall, 1976): 11–15.

12. C. Tomlinson-Keasey, "Role Variables: Their Influence on Female Motivational Constructs," *Journal of Counseling Psychology* 21 (May, 1974): 232–237.

13. Lenore W. Harmon, "Career Counseling for Women," in *Psychotherapy for Women: Treatment Toward Equality,* eds., Dianne A. Carter and Edna I. Rawlings (Springfield, Ill: Charles Thomas, 1975); David P. Campbell, *SVIB-S CII Manual* (Stanford: Stanford University Press, 1974).

14. Eli Ginzberg and Associates, *Life Styles of Educated Women* (New York: Columbia University Press, 1966).

15. Lillian E. Troll and Carol A. Nowak, "How Old Are You?—The Question of Age Bias in the Counseling of Adults," in *Counseling Adults,* eds., Nancy K. Schlossberg and Alan D. Entine (Monterey, Calif: Brooks/Cole, 1977), pp. 98–107.

28

The Status of Women in Art

JUDITH K. BRODSKY

The Women's Caucus for Art is a national organization of women artists, art historians, museum curators, critics, and educators. Established in 1972, it is independently incorporated but maintains close ties to the College Art Association.

The Coalition of Women's Art Organizations was initiated in 1977. Its purpose is to achieve full equality for women in art by uniting the efforts of the many groups who are already working towards this goal locally and nationally across the United States. There are over 200 such groups—women's art collectives, women's cooperative galleries, publications devoted only to women in art, and art schools only for women.

We laud the idea of a White House Conference on the Arts, and we recommend that the particular problems of women in art be one of the specific subjects to which the conference addresses itself.

We feel that the federal government with its preeminent position in the arts, a position that has resulted from the activities of the National Endowments during the last ten years, can do much through its programs and initiative to provide effective leadership in improving the status of the large number of women in art in the United States.

The arts are not a field in which there are few qualified women. Women represent about 50 percent of the pool of professional artists.[1] Yet women artists do not have the visibility of men. Studies reveal that prestige galleries devote only 15 percent of their one-person shows to women artists.[2] One-person exhibitions by women

---

This testimony was delivered before a congressional hearing on a proposed White House Conference on the Arts, December 17, 1977, at the Juilliard School, New York City. It has been shortened, and the statistics have been updated for inclusion in this volume.

made up only 10 percent of the shows given to living artists by the three major New York museums during 1976 and 1977.[3] From 1928 to 1972, of 995 one-person exhibitions at the Museum of Modern Art, only five were by women.[4] Furthermore, most major exhibitions at outstanding museums contain very little work by women. American Master Drawings and Watercolors, an exhibition organized by the American Federation of the Arts to celebrate the Bicentennial year and supported by a grant from the National Endowment for the Arts, included work by 177 men and nine women. This exhibition was seen at the Whitney Museum, New York, the Fine Arts Museums of San Francisco, and the Minneapolis Institute of the Arts.

Can it be that the majority of women artists are not as good as their male counterparts? Proof that this is not the case exists in juried shows where work by women makes up anywhere from a third to a half of the pieces chosen.[5]

Women who teach studio and art history fare no better. In 1972–1973, 40 percent of all studio degrees at the master's level were awarded to women, but in a survey of 164 art departments, women comprised only 22 percent of the studio faculty.[6] From 1972–1974, women made up 49 percent of the recipients of the Ph.D. degree in art history but held only 22 percent of the positions in art history departments granting the doctoral degree, and only 14 percent of the tenured positions.[7] It is interesting to note that while faculties are male dominated, at least two-thirds of all art students in America are female.[8]

Very few women are at policy making levels in the arts. For example, from 1965–1975, only 23 percent of the members of the National Council on the Arts have been women, and virtually no major museum in the country has a woman as its director.[9]

These statistics give some idea of the scope of the problem. What are the possibilities for solution?

First, what can be done through existing programs?

1. More individual grants to women. While the average percentage of all fellowships awarded by the National Endowment for the Arts to women has improved—in 1976 and 1977, it was 33 percent—only 10 percent of General Services Administration commissions for art in public places have gone to women. With

the high degree of institutional discrimination against women already described, individual grants become a way of providing funds directly where they are needed.[10]

2. Increased appointment of women to government grant-awarding boards, commissions, and panels. The percentage of women on National Endowment grant advisory panels was only 25 percent in 1975. In 1976 and 1977, it improved to 30 percent. Since much discrimination seems to stem from unconscious societal attitudes, inclusion of more women on grant-giving and policy-making boards would give more balance to the judgements made by these boards and result in more equitable decision making.[11]

3. Another area in which the government can make vital impact is through the enforcement of Equal Employment Opportunity Commssion guidelines in federally funded cultural institutions such as museums, universities, and performing arts centers. As mentioned earlier, few women direct museums; even fewer chair university art departments. Yet almost all museums and universities receive federal funding.

Secondly, what new programs or legislation provide solutions to end discrimination against women in the arts?

1. Perhaps most important is the correction of the deficiency in Title VI of the Civil Rights Act of 1964, which prohibits discrimination on the grounds of race, color, and national origin in federally assisted programs but not on the grounds of sex. All grants made by the National Endowments for the Arts and Humanities fall under Title VI. While subsequent legislation has provided for a ban on sex discrimination in many other federally assisted programs as, for example, in elementary, secondary, and higher education, at no time has there been legislation or an executive order prohibiting sex discrimination in the grants made by the National Endowments. This deficiency should be corrected either through an amendment to Title VI itself or through additional legislation.

2. Women in art have created many alternative opportunities for themselves since opportunities in the established art world have been so limited. These alternative galleries, exhibitions,

magazines, and schools involve a large number of women as makers and audience for this art. The conference might consider why these groups exist and the possibility of support for them as an additional arts category with additional funding. This would be one way to funnel funds directly to the women's art community.

3. The conference should consider the establishment of a federal commission or congressional oversight committee to ensure equality for women in all federal programs for the arts. This committee would also initiate further studies in discrimination. The commission or committee would issue an annual report on the state of women in the arts.

4. Another topic for discussion might be how federal, state, and local funding sources can mandate a priority of significant funding for community arts projects that promote greater visibility and participation of women in the arts.

5. The conference should also address itself to the problem of art educational institutions in which the esthetics and the history of women artists are ignored. Since most art students are women, exposure only to male esthetics and male art history perpetuates their feelings of being second class citizens.

In conclusion, women in art have always been sustainers of the art world but have received little recognition or reward as doers within that world. Mothers, not fathers, bring their children to museums, but those children see only art by men. Women students fill art schools, but their teachers are men and when they graduate, they have little chance to show. Women make up over 57 percent of museum staffs as volunteers; the directors of museums, though, are mostly men.[12] It is time for women artists to be seen, for women to participate in the art world as policy makers, and for women in art to receive the recognition and reward they deserve.

NOTES

1. This figure is supported by a number of surveys, among them a survey by the College Art Association of its membership in 1976. Of the artist

members who responded, 47 percent were women. The results of this survey appeared in *The College Art Association Newsletter* 1, no. 3 (November 1976): 5.

2. Brenda Price, "An Artists' Gallery Guide," *Feminist Art Journal* (Spring 1976).

3. Survey carried out by the author based on the listings in *The New York Times* for exhibitions at The Museum of Modern Art, The Whitney, and the Guggenheim Museums.

4. Eleanor Dickinson and Roberta Loach, "Does Sex Discrimination Exist in the Visual Arts?" *Visual Dialog* 1, no. 2 (Winter 1976): 22–25.

5. Ibid.; Judith K. Brodsky, "Some Notes on Women Printmakers," *Art Journal* 35, no. 4 (Summer 1976): 374–377.

6. *Digest of Education Statistics* (Washington, D.C.: U.S. Department of Health, Education, and Welfare Education Division, 1975); Barbara Ehrlich White and Leon S. White, "Survey of the Status of Women in College Art Departments," *Art Journal* 32, no. 4 (Summer 1973).

7. *Survey of Ph.D. Programs in Art History*, pamphlet (New York: College Art Association, 1975).

8. In 1975, of 16,193 recipients of the bachelor's degree in art (studio and art history), 10,901 were women. *Statistical Abstract of the United States* (Washington, D.C.: Government Printing Office, 1975).

9. *The Creative Woman: A Report of the Committee on the Arts and Humanities of the National Commission on the Observance of International Women's Year* (Washington, D.C.: Government Printing Office, 1975), pp. 20–21 for museum information; p. 30 for Council percentages. At the request of the author, the Visual Arts Program of the National Endowment for the Arts provided figures on the number of women council members for 1976 and 1977. For those years, the percentage was 26 percent, indicating no real change.

10. The figures on fellowships were provided by the Visual Arts Program, NEA, to the author. Women in the Arts Foundation, 435 Broome Street, New York, N.Y. 10013, furnished the information on the General Services Administration.

11. *The Creative Woman*, p. 25; and figures for 1976 and 1977 from the Visual Arts Program to the author.

12. *The Creative Woman*, p. 22.

About The Contributors

Bette Acuff, Associate Professor, Department of Art and Education, Teachers College, Columbia University, became interested in assertiveness when she began graduate school at Stanford University. She is "in process" as an assertive person and as a painter.

Lawrence Alloway is Professor of Art History at SUNY at Stony Brook, New York, art critic for *The Nation*, and author of *Topics in American Art Since 1945* (New York: Norton, 1975).

Ellen Perry Berkeley is one of the founders of the Women's School of Planning and Architecture; she is a former Senior Editor of the *Architectural Forum* and *Architecture Plus*.

Judith K. Brodsky, a printmaker, is Chairperson of the Art Department, Newark College of Arts and Sciences, Rutgers, The State University of New Jersey. She was President of the Women's Caucus for Art and an organizer of the Coalition of Women's Art Organizations.

Bette Chamberlain writes the "Professional Page" for *American Artists*. She is the founder (1959) and Director of the Art Information Center, Inc., in New York City.

Helen Collier is a psychotherapist and author of *Counseling Women* (Monterey, Calif.: Brooks/Cole, 1979). **Jessie Lovano-Kerr** is Dean for Women's Affairs, Indiana University.

Sylvia Gruber Feinburg is the Director of Student Teaching in the Eliot Pearson Department of Child Study, Tufts University. She has been involved for many years with children's art, child development, and early childhood education.

Elsa Honig Fine is the author of *The Afro-American Artist: A Search for Identity* (New York: Holt, 1973), *Women and Art* (Montclair, N.J.: Allanheld & Schram, 1978), and coeditor of *Women's Studies and the Arts* (New York: Women's Caucus for Art, 1978). She is currently working on *English Women and Their Art* and a study of the self-portraits of Käthe Kollwitz.

297

Mary D. Garrard is Professor of Art History at American University, Washington, D.C. She was President of the College Art Association's Women's Caucus for whom she compiled *Slides of Works by Women Artists: A Sourcebook* in 1974.

Dorothy Gillespie, an artist, is Coordinator of the Women's Interart Center and on the faculty of the New School for Social Research in New York City.

Jean Gillies is an Associate Professor in the Art Department of Northeastern Illinois University where she has taught courses on the images of women in art and, for several years, headed the women's studies program.

Ruth Iskin, an art historian, is Director of the Woman's Building Galleries, on the faculty of Feminist Studio Workshop, and an Editor of *Chrysalis*. She was Codirector of Womanspace and Editor of the *Womanspace Journal.*

Barbara White Kazanis is an Associate Professor of Art Education at the University of South Florida who is interested in the functions of imagery.

Lucy R. Lippard is a feminist art critic whose most recently published books are *From the Center: Feminist Essays on Women's Art* (New York: E. P. Dutton, 1976) and *Eva Hesse* (New York: New York University Press, 1976).

June King McFee, Head of the Department of Art Education, University of Oregon, is the author of *Preparation for Art* (Belmont, Calif.: Wadsworth, 1961) and coauthor of *Art, Culture and Environment* (Belmont, Calif.: Wadsworth, 1977).

Rachel Maines is the Director of the Center for the History of American Needlework and teaches needlework and history of textiles at the University of Pittsburgh.

Margaret Mary Majewski teaches art courses at Edgewood College and at Madison Area Technical College, both located in Madison, Wisconsin.

Margaret Mead, the cultural anthropologist, was the author of many books from *Coming of Age in Samoa* (New York: Morrow, 1928) to *Letters from the Field* (New York: Harper & Row, 1978), the second volume of her autobiography.

Joan Mondale, an amateur potter, is Honorary Chairperson of the

Federal Council on the Arts and Humanities and author of *Politics in Art* (Minneapolis, Minn.: Lerner Publications, 1972).

Cindy Nemser was the Editor of the *Feminist Art Journal*. She is the author of *Art Talk: Conversations with Twelve Women Artists* (New York: Scribner, 1975).

Linda Nochlin, Professor of Art History at Vassar College, was the Cocurator of the exhibition and coauthor of the catalog *Women Artists: 1550 to 1950* (New York: Knopf, 1976).

Gloria Feman Orenstein is Assistant Professor of English at Douglass College where she has been Director of the Women's Studies Program. She is the author of *The Theatre of the Marvelous: Surrealism and the Contemporary Stage* (New York: New York University Press, 1975).

Gordon S. Plummer is Professor of Art Education, University of Cincinnati. He is author of *Children's Art Judgment: A Curriculum for Elementary Art Appreciation* (Dubuque, Iowa: Wm. C. Brown, 1974).

Arlene Raven is an art historian. She is a founder of the Feminist Studio Workshop, the Center for Feminist Art Historical Studies, the Women's Building, and the Women's Community, Inc.

Miriam Schapiro is a painter who exhibits regularly at the Emmerich Gallery in New York and the Mitzi Landau Gallery in Los Angeles.

Judith Stoughton, Congregation of St. Joseph, is Professor of Art and past Chairperson of the Art Department of the College of Saint Catherine, St. Paul, Minnesota. She was a Fulbright Scholar, a Mellon Fellow, and an art editor of the *New Catholic Encyclopedia*.

June Wayne is an artist who is involved in painting, printmaking, tapestries, films, video, and writing. She was the founder of the Tamarind movement on behalf of lithography and directed it until 1970.

J. J. Wilson is Professor of English and **Karen Petersen** is Curator of the Women Artists Slide Collection, both at Sonoma State College, California. They are coauthors of *Women Artists: Recognition and Reappraisal* (New York: Harper & Row, 1976).

Jean Zaleski, a painter who exhibits at the Alonzo Gallery in New York City, was Executive Coordinator of the Women in the Arts Foundation, Inc.

Index